The Urbana Free Library

To renew: call 217-367-4057
or go to "*urbanafreelibrary.org*"
and select "Renew/Request Items"

D1416008

BATTLEGROUND 1948

BATTLEGROUND 1948

Truman, Stevenson, Douglas, and the Most Surprising Election in Illinois History

ROBERT E. HARTLEY

Southern Illinois University Press
Carbondale

16 15 14 13   4 3 2 1

Library of Congress Cataloging-in-Publication Data

Hartley, Robert E.
Battleground 1948 : Truman, Stevenson,
Douglas, and the most surprising election
in Illinois history / Robert E. Hartley.
    pages   cm
Includes bibliographical references and index.
    ISBN-13: 978-0-8093-3266-3 (cloth : alk. paper)
    ISBN-10: 0-8093-3266-3 (cloth : alk. paper)
    ISBN-13: 978-0-8093-3268-7 (ebook)
    ISBN-10: 0-8093-3268-X (ebook)
    1. Presidents—United States—Election—1948.
2. Truman, Harry S., 1884–1972. 3. Stevenson, Adlai E.
(Adlai Ewing), 1900–1965. 4. Douglas, Paul, 1892–1976.
5. Elections—Illinois—History—20th century.
6. Illinois—Politics and government—1865–1950.
7. Democratic Party (Ill.)—History—20th century.
I. Title. II. Title: Truman, Stevenson, Douglas, and
the most surprising election in Illinois history.
E815.H37 2013
977.3'04—dc23   2013000551

Printed on recycled paper. ♻
The paper used in this publication meets the minimum
requirements of American National Standard for
Information Sciences—Permanence of Paper for
Printed Library Materials, ANSI z39.48-1992. ♾

To David Kenney: teacher, adviser, collaborator, friend
To the women in my life: Mary, Carolyn, Ruth, Lucy, Emma
To Thomas Schwartz for his contributions to preserving Illinois history
And for Dan Moore

CONTENTS

Gallery of illustrations follows page 96.

Preface

As most people understand, elections happen often at the local, county, state, and national levels. At times it seems there is one continuous election campaign under way with no relief in sight. Consequently, we tend to grow weary, and there is a higher level of apathy when some elections seem less important than others. With so many opportunities to vote, is any one election more important than another? And when can you tell?

All things being equal—which they never are—most elections have about the same impact. The more elections, the greater the opportunity for change, and also the greater the tendency for the status quo. The pendulum swings periodically to avoid extended periods of extremism. In our republic, the frequency of elections relieves pressures and makes for orderly, sometimes predictable outcomes. That is textbook stuff, worth keeping in mind. However, reality looks different. Occasionally the picture is changed by the times, candidates, issues, and attitudes, and mostly by public reaction, making it difficult to predict ahead of time. When the people rally and the candidates sense the importance of those reactions, unexpected outcomes can happen.

Some elections in Illinois have been more important than others, usually because of what happened in their wakes. In the course of time, there are elections that make the ground shake—for example, the first elections of statehood in 1818, or Lincoln versus Douglas in the 1858 senate race, or the presidential election of 1860. Or consider 1913, when U.S. senators first were elected by the people instead of by legislatures.

Usually, we don't know the lasting effects until the returns are in and those elected have served at least a minimal amount of time. It can take decades to digest the results.

It would be possible to dismiss the 1948 Illinois elections as just another old election story, of which there are dozens. Buried as we are in the present, and looking toward the future, the past is a blur, especially for those who have no special interest in it. But to push 1948 aside is to miss the nuances that are so much a part of politics and, in this case, make for a meaningful tale, with reverberations for decades.

This book deals with an election that by any standards was one of the most significant in the state's history, and also for the nation. It was the first general election after the victories and agonies of World War II, with a restless population free of war worries in Europe and Asia and anxious for change. When veterans returned and families began thinking again of life and liberty, they found many of the same politicians in office touting the same ideas they had heard before the war. Unable to fully understand this unrest, newspaper reporters and pundits bet that the 1948 outcomes would be lopsided in favor of Republicans, from the grass roots to Washington. Illinois Republicans looked like a sure thing to continue the political domination that had begun in 1940, and loyalists anticipated a federal administration led by Thomas E. Dewey. Conventional wisdom, wishful thinking, and newspaper guesswork failed to catch the public mood and sentiment.

Nothing turned out as predicted. Democrats at the federal and state levels nearly wiped the slates clean, retained the presidency, changed the power in both chambers of Congress, tossed Republicans out of office in wholesale numbers, and altered the course of history. The man no political party expected to be elected president, Harry S. Truman, confounded everyone and kept alive the diminishing hopes of Democrats for a continuation of the New Deal. How could election outcomes take such a sharp turn without the political intelligentsia seeing it coming?

The answer lies only partly in the actual federal and state campaigns of 1948, although they were important, with some surprises in the final weeks playing a crucial role in the outcome. Perhaps the biggest surprise of all was that Truman's appeal gained important ground in the final months while hardly anyone noticed. Illinois was an essential part of Truman's strategy to earn electoral votes. Failure to win the Prairie State might well have doomed his candidacy.

The roots of the Illinois campaign reach back into the 1930s and to the personalities and issues that blossomed in the early 1940s. As one might expect with politics at the highest levels, ambitions often overcame common sense. Many in office and in powerful party positions were blind to happenings on the ground. In Illinois, the background and experiences of main players such as Governor Dwight Green, Senator C. Wayland Brooks, and Democratic candidates Adlai E. Stevenson II and Paul Douglas played vital roles, but the story, as it unfolds in the following pages, is about more than personalities and campaign statements.

A few people, such as Chicago operative Jack Arvey, saw that change was necessary for the Democratic Party to regain power. He brought new faces to the campaign, invigorating the Chicago political machine in time to influence the outcome. At one time, Arvey hoped to replace Truman on the ballot, but when that effort failed, the Chicago machine did what it was expected to do for Democrats. As voters listened and watched candidates for state office cross the state many times to argue local and federal policies, Truman's Illinois strategy added a special flavor to the contest. The president's three high-energy whistle-stop trips and a Chicago appearance as the campaign ended unquestionably fired up partisan voters and boosted the state's role in the national outcome.

In the blush of triumph, Democratic winners believed the party would remain in power for at least a decade. However, they were badly fooled by the vagaries of Illinois politics. By 1952, Republicans were back in control at the state and federal levels. Before the 1950s ended, the pendulum was moving again, ushering in almost two decades of divided—some would call it balanced—state government. The 1948 election gave rise to Democrats and Republicans who would influence politics, and in some cases national outcomes, well into the 1970s.

The 1948 election altered the political landscape in a way no one could predict. New faces in state government sent the official remnants of depression and war into retirement, or at least into hiding. A fresh generation started to make its mark, leaving behind the New Deal (in label mostly), memories of wartime isolationism, influences of organized crime, and cronyism in many hamlets and cities. A clean sweep? A totally new day? No, but enough change that historians can agree that some of the state government's worst habits died.

Politics and campaigning in the years leading to 1948 look primitive when compared to those of the twenty-first century. Changes in communications, tactics, issues, and the flow of money paint a much different picture today. But current gimmicks should not mislead us. The need for change is constant, and, as in 1948, outcomes are dependent on citizen action more than on the words of public officials. That makes the days of Truman, Green, Arvey, Brooks, Douglas, and Stevenson meaningful. In 1948, the people drove the outcome.

Acknowledgments

Hardly anyone who played a prominent role in the Illinois elections of 1948 is around to voice opinions and offer reflections. Fortunately, some wrote and spoke about their participation before historians took over. We have the autobiography of Paul Douglas, the oral history of Robert Howard, the unpublished memoir of Senator Scott W. Lucas, and lengthy books such as the biography of Adlai E. Stevenson. The papers and recollections of Douglas, Stevenson, Dwight Green, and Paul Powell and the library devoted to Harry S. Truman provided details and continuity. All were essential to this narrative, as were books that focused on specific individuals such as Chicago mayor Edward Kelly. There are a number of fragments concerning 1948 on the record but no narrative that ties everything together or goes deep into the details of the year of decision. This book is designed to complete the record.

Generally speaking, those writing history avoid relying too heavily on newspaper accounts. In doing the job of writing the first draft of history, those in the press often make mistakes, misspell names, distort the actions of principals, and miss the nuances. Nonetheless, the importance of newspapers in covering politics and informing the public during the 1940s made a thorough analysis of print media necessary. It was essential to have more than one or two sources of news reporting in order to spot the errors and discover the missing parts. I relied on three Chicago newspapers—the *Daily News*, the *Sun-Times*, and the *Tribune*—for a variety of accounts of the same news stories and also on downstate papers such as the *Peoria Journal*, the *Springfield State Journal*, and the *East St. Louis Journal.* A thorough reading and understanding of reporters and editors of the *St. Louis Post-Dispatch* was critical, considering the paper's importance to the election outcome. The work of Taylor Pensoneau, former *Post-Dispatch* reporter and chronicler of the Shelton brothers and their gang activity, was extremely useful.

Claire Fuller Martin, a researcher based in Springfield, and Amanda Bahr, formerly at the Louisa H. Bowen University Archives and Special Collections at Southern Illinois University Edwardsville, contributed vital information. I leaned heavily on research conducted earlier for my books and history articles, which means I must again express appreciation for the talented and helpful employees at the Abraham Lincoln Presidential Library and Museum. That is where many of the images for the book were found, thanks to the labors of Mary Michals and Roberta Fairburn. Other images appear due to the generosity of the *Centralia Morning Sentinel*, the U.S. Senate Historical Office, the Herrin City Library, and Gary Hacker of the Johnson County Genealogical and Historical Society.

I have come to depend on my wife, Mary, who always gets a first and last look at my work, for her candid comments, understanding, and encouragement. I am thankful for experienced journalists and academicians who agreed to edit and to comment on the manuscript; they included D. G. Schumacher, Fletcher Farrar, and my good friend and coauthor of two books, Dr. David Kenney. Regardless of their fine work, I am responsible for the accuracy of the content. Finally, I continue to be thankful and impressed with Southern Illinois University Press's devotion to publishing books on Illinois public affairs and with the work of its editor-in-chief, Karl Kageff.

BATTLEGROUND 1948

1. The Democrats Disintegrate

REPUBLICAN REVIVAL

The election of 1948 in Illinois was more than the sum of many parts. While it is essentially a story based on details of the 1930s and 1940s, it echoes into the twenty-first century, suggesting something of greater importance to the state than a recorded election upset.

Woven throughout the two decades is a tale of raw politics manifested in development and domination by competing political machines: Democrats and Republicans. In large part, they reflected the height of regional political coalitions. They feasted on patronage and bloated government payrolls, not unlike the example today of overwhelming one-party control from grass roots to high office. The borders of regional politics have changed, especially with the diminishing impact of southern and central Illinois, resulting in a power center concentrated in the northeast portion of the state around Chicago and its suburbs. Efforts at political reform through the decades have fostered strong rhetoric but produced only occasional results, due largely to the resistance of party organizations and an ever-present desire for power. This has left state government with something of a decades-long hangover reminiscent of the 1948 election period, if not a carbon copy.

The role and influence of crime and corruption in the election outcome is a commentary on the lack of a statewide commitment to law enforcement and on a culture with roots in the lawlessness of the 1920s. It took years to reduce the smell of organized crime across the state. For example, in St. Clair County, the gangster influence remained another fifteen years in spite of a campaign by those elected in 1948 to shut down gambling. The crime committee hearings in Chicago and St. Louis by U.S. senator Estes Kefauver in the early 1950s exposed the depth of illegal and corrupt activity but did little more than inspire a few interest groups, individuals, and newspapers to seek change. Criminal activity was ingrained in Illinois politics and was not easily expunged. In spite of legislative successes, there are undisclosed campaign activities today that threaten to undermine elections and confidence in government. The culprits are not shadowy underworld characters but are presumably respectable citizens who have figured out how to scam the election process. The echo from the earlier time is "pay to play" political schemes, which have been exposed in modern Illinois.

Certain campaign themes from the 1948 era sound familiar to those living in the twenty-first century. Republican candidates claimed that Democrats running for president, the U.S. Senate, and state offices had a socialist agenda. Newspapers sympathetic to the Republican cause— primarily the *Chicago Tribune* under the leadership of Robert McCormick—pounded away on the theme, focusing on opposition to social programs and policies of the New Deal. In today's world, the accusations and denials are more likely to surface on cable television and talk radio, but they do resonate with the earlier theme.

The 1948 election also is a reminder of how uncontrollable events can influence a campaign outcome, especially when appearing in the final stages. The political impact of the Centralia coal mine disaster in 1947 on the race for governor cannot be overstated. Until the final weeks, Centralia still grabbed statewide headlines. Equally significant were revelations and accusations of political corruption and connections to organized crime that produced newspaper headlines and editorials almost daily through the campaign's final months. The potential for political surprises still causes sleepless nights for candidates, but there is no better example of their impact than the election of 1948.

The first six years of the 1940s were a disaster for Democrats in Illinois. After riding high across the state in the 1930s, the party's political world collapsed. During the 1940s, Republicans had almost total control.[1] With Franklin D. Roosevelt no longer living to arouse Democrats after early 1945, it appeared that nothing could stop the GOP through the rest of the decade.

No wonder that Republicans—and their backers such as the widely circulated *Chicago Tribune*—thought they could equal the Democratic dominance achieved with the Great Depression and the Roosevelt era. While Democrats controlled at least one chamber of the legislature and the governorship through the 1930s, those high moments were tied directly to Roosevelt and the national Democratic tide and were abetted by a crack-the-whip political machine in Chicago. Enthusiasm for Democratic leadership changed somewhat with internal party disagreements about U.S. involvement in Europe's war and FDR's decision to serve more than two terms.

In the 1940 elections, Republicans recaptured Illinois state government. Dwight H. Green was elected governor, and C. Wayland "Curly" Brooks, a dedicated opponent of FDR's policies, won a U.S. Senate seat. The party controlled both houses of the state legislature. Of the twenty-six congressional seats, Republicans won eighteen, compared to just nine in 1938. Democratic reign ended, leaving one U.S. senator and the secretary of state as remnants of the 1930s. Roosevelt provided little help, defeating Wendell Willkie in Illinois by just 102,000 votes out of nearly 2.2 million cast.[2]

Putting the blame entirely on a third Roosevelt term does not paint the complete picture, however. Quarreling Illinois Democrats made winning almost impossible. Henry Horner, elected governor in 1932 with the backing of the Chicago party machinery, won a second term in 1936 after splitting with Chicago mayor Edward Kelly and the co-captain of the machine, Patrick Nash. Quarrels among Democrats made for a fractious second term. Horner died in October 1940, and Lieutenant Governor John Stelle, a Horner foe aligned with Chicago until 1939, became governor for ninety-nine days. He threw out Horner appointees—newspapers said 250 of them—and quickly changed the face of state government. By election time in 1940, almost any Republican could have won the governorship.[3]

Even with Democrats who were able to hang on in office, internal party feuds remained. A good example was the U.S. Senate race in 1938 when Scott W. Lucas, an ally of Horner, won a bitter primary battle over organization favorite Michael Igoe and then defeated the Republican candidate while receiving only lukewarm backing from the machine.[4] Hard feelings left over from the Horner-Stelle battle and the 1938 Senate race helped sink Democratic chances in elections throughout the 1940s.

The familiar image of the Republican Party in the 1940s was the handsome face of Governor Green. Born on 9 January 1897 in Ligonier, Indiana, he served as a pilot instructor during World War I. He finished undergraduate education at Wabash College at Crawfordsville, Indiana, and earned a law degree at the University of Chicago. Green worked as a lawyer in Chicago from 1922 to 1926, then left for the Bureau of Internal Revenue in Washington. That led to a position in Chicago as assistant to U.S. attorney Edward E. Q. Johnson, concentrating on income tax evasion cases against Prohibition-era hoodlums. Green rose to public attention in 1931 as prosecutor of Chicago gangster Al Capone, who was sentenced to ten years in prison for evading his income tax.[5]

When Johnson stepped down in 1932, Green succeeded him as U.S. attorney for northern Illinois. The most sensational case during his tenure was prosecution of Samuel Insull Sr., head of a $4 billion public utility system. This gained Green enormous attention, although a jury acquitted Insull of bankruptcy, embezzlement, and mail fraud. After three years as U.S. attorney, Green returned to private law practice, but he was not forgotten. During those high profile years, Green had caught the attention of Robert McCormick, editor and publisher of the *Chicago Tribune*. With strong newspaper backing, Green ran for mayor of Chicago in 1939. He surprised everyone by defeating former mayor William Hale "Big Bill" Thompson in the primary but lost to the incumbent Kelly in the general election, receiving 43 percent of the vote. His strong showing in Democrat-dominated Chicago made Green a hero among Republicans anxious for a return to power. It was only a small step to candidacy for governor in 1940.[6]

While Republican hopes rose with a popular gubernatorial candidate, the Democrats were self-destructing. More than anything, Lieutenant Governor Stelle wanted to succeed Horner, with whom he had quarreled since the 1936 election. However, the governor, so physically sick he could hardly perform his duties, cut a deal designed to deny Stelle the prize. Horner and his archenemy Mayor Kelly buried the hatchet long enough to slate Harry Hershey of Taylorville for governor in the 1940 primary election and leave Stelle outside looking in.[7] That did not dissuade the McLeansboro Democrat. Stelle rallied supporters, mostly from downstate, to contest the machine's choice of a "Harmony Slate." In his announcement to run, Stelle referred to Kelly and Horner as "self-appointed dictators of Illinois."[8]

However, that was not Stelle's last blast. Before the primary election, he declared himself acting governor and attempted to take over administration of the state, claiming Horner too ill to carry out his sworn duties. The move brought Horner from his sick bed to the governor's office and prompted the attorney general, John Cassidy, to declare Stelle's action illegal. Stelle's grandstand play failed, as did his candidacy. Hershey won the primary, and Stelle resumed his role as lieutenant governor until Horner died in October. The war between Stelle and friends of Horner lasted until Stelle died in 1962.[9]

Green had no easy road to victory. Having spent little time outside Chicago, he ran a high-energy statewide campaign that took him to all 102 counties, covering more than 123,000 miles and delivering at least 1,000 speeches. He defeated Richard J. Lyons, a popular country orator and legislator from Lake County, in the Republican primary.[10] Once nominated, Green went on the attack against a third term for Roosevelt and aggressively accused the Kelly administration of graft and corruption.

Just before Election Day, Green blasted Democrats in Chicago and Springfield, declaring to voters, "Out of a dollar, you pay nearly a third in hidden or direct taxes. The New Deal, and the Kelly-Nash-Statehouse Machine, takes this money to feed slush funds, and vast armies of pay-rollers. You have one hope of saving your schools and the future of your children, to restore your unions to your own control, to give your wives and your children more of the comforts and luxuries which they deserve. That is by voting Republican on next Tuesday."[11] That combination of attacks in 1940 was enough to elect him governor over Democrat Hershey by 256,945 votes, 53 percent of the total.[12] Green received more votes in Illinois than President Roosevelt, who won over Wendell Willkie by just 102,000 votes. The new governor, one of the state's youngest chief executives at age forty-four, had not served a day in elective office or in Illinois state government.

Green's background and campaign statements left an impression with voters and newspaper reporters that he would be independent-minded and assertive, bringing new faces to public service and giving Republicans reason to forget the weak and corrupt governors of the 1920s. The *Chicago Daily News* liked the prospect so much it endorsed Green, although it previously had favored Democrats.

Testing the reform waters early in his administration, Green outlined a proposal for expansion and modernization of the state police. But opponents from both parties showed Green that he had to pick easier fights if he wanted to make changes. The Kelly regime argued against the changes, as did the state sheriffs' association and Republican county officials in rural areas. All stood their ground against presumed state incursions into local control of law enforcement. Confronted by the opposition, Green withdrew the proposal.[13] It made him cautious for the balance of the term.

Robert Howard, a *Tribune* reporter during the 1940s after stints with the Associated Press and the *Chicago Sun*, said of Green's approach to governing, "He let the opportunities go by. It was just another administration so far as Republicans went."[14] Howard knew Green and studied him as a campaigner and governor. He added, "Green never was brilliant and I'd never even call him intellectual, but he had a good grasp of the state situation. He was willing to work hard. . . . One of his knacks was that he could take a speech that he'd never seen, carry it in his pocket, be introduced to an audience, and then he'd place it on the rostrum in front of him and talk to the audience. As far as they knew, he wasn't reading the speech." As to Green's Republican credentials and relationships, Howard said, "He was strictly an organization man so far as politics went." On the social side, Howard noted that Green liked to party: "He loved to drink scotch, loved to have parties at the mansion for newspapermen and others. They would go far into the night."[15] In its obituary of Green years later, the *St. Louis Post-Dispatch* commented further on Green's personal behavior during his two terms as governor: "He watched his diet and swam and played golf, but smoked as many as four packages of cigarettes a day. His heavy smoking was an unconscious habit."[16]

World War II put a damper on all but essential governmental functions, permitting Green and other Republicans across the state to establish party discipline and to control costs by limiting legislative initiatives. The organization became known as the "Green Machine." While its purpose was to build a durable GOP presence and to perpetuate party people in office and appointive positions, it also fed Green's ambitions. With the governor's people taking care of administrative details, he had time to build contacts outside Illinois and throughout midwestern Republican circles. He had an eye fixed on national office.

Green's political system produced large quantities of cash from political appointees, rank-and-file employees in state government, and people and organizations doing business with the government. The process by which a political party demanded contributions to Republican coffers and Green's campaigns was called a "lug." Democrats had a similar arrangement for funds from state employees.[17]

Some of Green's time was spent working closely with officials of the *Chicago Tribune*, especially Donald Maxwell, the paper's powerful and politically active city editor. Using his contacts with Green and associates in Springfield, Maxwell arranged for press conferences on issues and subjects of special interest to the *Tribune*. During Green's first term, the paper did not have a resident correspondent in Springfield; when press conferences were scheduled, Maxwell sent a Chicago reporter to cover the event. His assignment was to ask a prearranged question that would provide the basis for an article advancing the *Tribune*'s agenda.[18]

Green was an isolationist who believed that the federal government should be small. He chose not to make that a major issue early in his term, because that could have opened him to intraparty quarrels. While supportive of many conservative domestic programs during the war, he maintained a bipartisan approach toward the war effort and for the most part kept opinions of Roosevelt's handling of the conflict to himself. He called a special session of the legislature to amend laws that would facilitate voting by men and women in the armed services. In terms of state taxes, he and the GOP legislature cut the sales tax from 3 percent to 1 percent, raised taxes on liquor, and introduced the first tax on cigarettes. When it came to social reforms, Green supported many New Deal ideas.[19] He supported prolabor legislation and spoke approvingly of unions, unlike many Republicans of the time.

Green's conservative sidekick through the Republican years of the 1940s was Curly Brooks, elected in 1940 to fill a vacancy resulting from the death of Democrat James Hamilton Lewis in 1939. After Lewis's death, Governor Horner appointed James M. Slattery to fill the vacancy until the next general election. Horner biographer Thomas Littlewood told the story of how close Stelle, the governor's enemy, was to naming Lewis's successor. Horner was returning to Illinois from a recuperative stay in Florida; an hour after Horner's train crossed the border into the state, Lewis died. By that margin, Stelle was deprived of making the appointment.[20] Slattery, who ran Horner's 1936 campaign in Cook County, was chairman of the Illinois Commerce Commission and a member of the governor's advisory "cabinet." As a candidate for the Senate, Slattery faced lukewarm support from the Chicago machine because of his ties to Horner.[21] Robert Howard remembered that the *Tribune* attacked Slattery relentlessly, referring to him as "Strong Box Slattery," implying "there was something wrong with the collection of campaign funds" in 1936.[22]

Brooks had gained prominence as a World War I hero, first as an enlisted man in the Marines and later after receiving a battlefield commission. Wounded seven times, he received the Distinguished Service Cross and the Croix de Guerre for his valor. His war record and activity in the politically influential American Legion increased his value as a candidate in later years.[23] Brooks never let anyone forget his war record and wounds received, especially during political campaigns. He finished college at the University of Chicago after the war and earned a law degree from Northwestern University in 1926. After two years as an instructor of law at Northwestern, he served for seven years as an assistant state's attorney in Cook County, helping prosecute members of crime organizations. Thanks to a convenient political alliance that developed in the early 1930s between the Democratic machine leadership and the *Tribune's* McCormick, Brooks became the favored candidate in the 1940 Senate election.

The Brooks-McCormick alliance had its roots in 1931, when a *Tribune* news employee named Jack Ingle had been murdered. The paper immediately called for justice and elevated Ingle to hero status. However, it developed that he had associated with underworld characters and had provided them with information about police activity. Embarrassed by the revelations, McCormick needed vindication. Brooks provided it by leading the prosecution and conviction of Ingle's killer.[24] As a result, McCormick adopted Brooks and sent him into the political arena in 1934 for a statewide at-large congressional seat. Brooks lost, but McCormick had another political duty ready.

After Mayor Kelly's scheme to dump Governor Horner in the 1936 primary failed, Kelly and McCormick agreed to support Brooks for governor in the general election. Never a threat to the popular Horner, Brooks lost by 385,000 votes. While the attempt to destroy Horner backfired on McCormick and Kelly, it earned Brooks a political favor from the two powerful men when the Senate seat opened in 1940. Kelly had no interest in backing Slattery, and McCormick wanted his man in Washington. Brooks struggled, winning by just 20,827 votes. In a classic Chicago machine maneuver, Kelly held back returns from 400 precincts in Chicago until late on election night when Brooks needed help.[25]

The new senator became an eager mouthpiece for the publisher's anti-Roosevelt and isolationist agenda. Among many *Tribune*-inspired votes, Brooks opposed the draft and lend-lease proposals and aligned himself with isolationist organizations. Liberal publications such as *The Nation* liked to make fun of Brooks for his appearance as well as for his politics. In one issue, the magazine referred to his "round, heavy, puckered face capped with tight curls which look as though they are held down with a patent hair concoction."[26]

Arriving in Washington in 1941, Brooks faced having to start a campaign for a full six-year term, a campaign influenced heavily by impending war, readiness of the nation, and Roosevelt's sympathy for wartime allies. In advance of the 1942 election, the biggest surprise was Mayor Kelly's announcement that he would run against Brooks. The mayor intended to campaign on a pro-Roosevelt and New Deal platform, but his plan ran full-force into the prevailing animosity between leftover Horner allies and Chicago interests.[27] Lobbying by Senator Lucas and Navy secretary Frank Knox, a Chicago Republican, prevented Roosevelt from endorsing Kelly. The mayor thus told the Cook County Democratic committee on 5 February he would not run, and the committee endorsed Raymond S. McKeough. Also in the Democratic race was Thomas J. Courtney, Cook County state's attorney, who had opposed U.S. intervention in Europe before Pearl Harbor. His supporters included Senator Lucas.

Angry party reaction to Kelly's arrogance and Courtney's position on war caused state and national Democratic officials to pull the plug on both. After Kelly withdrew, he shifted support to McKeough, Second District congressman, friend of the mayor, and stalwart member of the organization. The McKeough play prompted further speculation about an alliance between Kelly and McCormick of the *Tribune*. Presumably, for his support of a weak candidate, Kelly was to receive backing by McCormick for mayor in 1943.[28]

Given Brooks's voting record against FDR's programs and his backing by the anti–New Deal *Tribune*, the White House brought out its guns, aiming at a gaffe the senator made at the time of the Japanese attack on Pearl Harbor. On 6 December 1941, Brooks had mailed franked copies of a speech titled "This Is Not Our War" to citizens across Illinois.[29] The speech arrived in homes days after Pearl Harbor and the declaration of war by Congress. Brooks's opponent, McKeough, accused the senator of treason, and Washington sympathizers joined the hunt. Brooks retaliated by accusing Democrats of "Gestapo tactics" designed to destroy him and the *Tribune*. McCormick said the opposition to Brooks was from the "international set, composed of women and effeminate men."[30]

Brooks picked up support from Green, who disappointed his moderate supporters by calling Brooks a great patriot and statesman.[31] Republican primary candidate Warren Wright, elected state treasurer in 1940, challenged Brooks with a speech titled "Why I Am an American" after the senator's antiwar comments. The *Tribune* labeled Wright an internationalist, which in the minds of editors at the paper was a political sin. Brooks won the primary by 550,000 votes and prepared for the battle with Chicagoan McKeough in a fight between the Chicago organization and the Green Machine.

In the general election campaign, Democrats attempted to pin the label of "obstructionist" on Brooks and other Republicans in Illinois who ran as anti-Roosevelt candidates. In contrast, newspaper advertisements for Brooks featured slogans such as "A Fighting Senator" and "He Kept His Word."[32] He campaigned against waste in government and as a patriot with a hero's record in World War I. Kelly, instead of staying in his Chicago office, made appearances downstate for McKeough, offering aggressive rhetoric. At one point, he said a Brooks victory would "make Hitler happy."[33] Needless to say, McCormick was not happy with Kelly. Commenting on the Brooks-McKeough contest, obviously a battle between party machinery, independent papers such as the *Chicago Daily News* and the downstate *Quincy Herald-Whig* deplored the lineup, accusing the Republicans of isolationism and the Democrats of deliberately putting up a weak candidate.[34]

Brooks overwhelmed McKeough—labeled "small potatoes" by the *Tribune*—by 202,876 votes and racked up an advantage of 200,000 votes downstate. With job security for six more years, Brooks adopted every *Tribune* editorial page assault on the New Deal, foreign entanglements, and Roosevelt's social programs. Brooks believed he reflected the attitude of a large number of Illinois citizens who supported the war effort but disliked Roosevelt's domestic and foreign initiatives. The Republican victory was part of a national trend that gave the party its best midterm results since 1926.[35]

An interesting sidelight to the 1942 campaign involved a Chicago city councilman and university professor named Paul Douglas, whose political ambitions had grown during the 1930s. In 1938, Douglas won election as an independent alderman from the Fifth Ward in Chicago with the blessing of Mayor Kelly. Having watched Douglas question the machine's agenda and refuse to take orders from the mayor's office, however, Kelly realized that Douglas as a U.S. senator would be too risky. Kelly considered McKeough a safer bet. Without a nod of support from Kelly, Douglas ran in the Democratic primary against McKeough. Surprisingly, the underdog Douglas won 99 out of 102 counties.[36] However, he lost the big ones controlled by the Chicago machine, and McKeough won by almost 300,000 votes. Douglas learned the hard way that his ambitions for a political future had to include accommodation with the organization. Douglas put politics on hold and headed to service in the Marine Corps at age fifty-one.

With Democrats on the run, McCormick and the *Tribune* had the Republican Party and the state's highest officials in a tight grip. In the background of this drama was Mayor Kelly. Although Green had campaigned against the machine in 1940, he soon dropped his criticism of Kelly and appeared to have reached an accommodation on issues and legislation of interest to Chicago. However, cooperating with the mayor and toning down rhetoric were different matters from contesting him in an election, as Green learned in Chicago's 1943 city election. Republicans were on a roll and considered Kelly vulnerable to accusations of corruption and graft. Green chose his state finance director, George B. McKibben, a Chicago lawyer, to run against Kelly.[37] McKibben, discovering there was no shortage of issues, took the offensive against racketeers and hoodlums and promised to clean up the crooked liquor business. All that was missing was help from the *Tribune*, which refrained from criticizing the mayor. Green joined McKibben and other Republicans during the city campaign, picking up on the mobster issue. Speaking from a sound truck in front of city hall, Green accused Kelly of coddling gangsters. McKibben attempted to connect mobsters and labor unions as favorites of Kelly.[38]

Campaign issues in the early 1940s provided a look at arguments that would be heard in subsequent state elections. Republicans raised the specter of Democratic-sponsored socialism by suggesting that the Kelly-Nash machine was copying Roosevelt's New Deal playbook. Democrats responded with accusations of mismanagement of state funds by the Green administration, which included McKibben.

Kelly won reelection easily with 54.6 percent of the vote. The *Tribune* broke its silence after the election, saying Republicans lost because they did not adequately attack the New Deal.

FEEDING A POLITICAL ORGANIZATION

The growth and endurance of a political machine depends on money and influence, an appeal to party loyalty, and opportunity to serve. It is sustained by legions of friends, cronies, hangers-on, and bona fide public servants who are attracted by employment benefits and policy agendas. The Republican organization headed by Green had plenty of time to expand. Much of what occurred during Green's first term amounted to solidifying power, such as padding the government payroll with friends, regardless of whether or not the jobs were more than just payoffs. The war years provided little incentive for reform or new ideas, which could cause only stress, dissatisfaction, and controversy. With a golden smile and comforting countenance, Green exuded supreme confidence with little forward motion.

Green's personal qualities made him attractive on a national level. Demand for his time took the governor away from Illinois politics and elevated his appeal as a prospective national candidate. While he traveled nationally, business and political controls in Illinois fell mostly to those he put in charge. When crisis arose or less than honorable influences were in play, his absences made controversy more likely and costly. Green's attention outside Illinois caused few public ripples in the first term, but they would become more apparent later.

The tight connection between gangsters and politics in Illinois from the 1920s through the 1950s has been well documented. Newspapers in Chicago and St. Louis wrote endlessly of illegal activity that flourished in and near metropolitan areas. However, gambling and multiple forms of vice knew few boundaries. From the bottom of the state to the top, in hamlets and rural county seats, operatives found ways to compromise law enforcement and stifle public oversight. Payoffs and bribes were commonplace. Much of the action sprang from Prohibition, but gangs gained momentum after booze was again legal in 1933. The likes of Al Capone and the Shelton brothers gang of southern Illinois received constant newspaper notices, but they felt no pressure to change their habits.

In the 1940s, attitudes of state officials aided illegal behavior and local corruption. Governor Green allowed counties and cities to control their own law enforcement operations. State policemen were political appointees used primarily for traffic control on state roads. The attorney general did little more than counsel state's attorneys at the county level about the growth of gambling and gang activity. When confronted by newspapers with specific cases of gangster activity, state officials shrugged and said it was up to local authorities to correct the situation.

Local officials said they had everything under control. Occasionally they rounded up petty operatives or threatened to crack down on gambling, but any change was momentary. Illegal operations resumed when the heat was off. When state and local law enforcement officials looked the other way, payoff money flowed in gratitude to assure that illegal operations would not be constrained. The general citizenry, mostly untouched by gambling and vice, paid little attention to editorials or independent candidates calling for reform. They reelected officials regardless of their attitudes toward corrupt practices.

A lack of campaign finance disclosure—laws were passed decades later—gave politicians cover to accept funds from all manner of sources without fear of public awareness. As the 1944 election approached, those charged with gathering dollars for Green's reelection campaign—they were called "collectors"—took advantage of the governor's disinterest in corralling illegal and unethical operations. Years later, newspaper reporters followed the money in 1944 and found that syndicated gambling operators across downstate Illinois had contributed more than $100,000 to Green's campaign, a handsome sum in those days.[39] People involved in gambling, punchboards, and slot machines wanted assurances the governor would not interfere with their lucrative activities.

Green's collectors called on the gambling kingpins and obtained protection money from them. The largest sums came from heavily populated areas, but the donations stretched across the state, from the southernmost counties of Alexander and Pulaski to Peoria and Tazewell Counties in central Illinois. In Peoria and Tazewell, the estimate of contributions to Green's campaign was $35,000—substantial money in 1944. The principal contributor was Clyde Garrison, the local gambling czar. In St. Clair and Madison Counties, across the Mississippi River from St. Louis, $40,000 flowed to the campaign. Dan McGlynn, an East St. Louis lawyer and St. Clair County Republican leader, did the collecting. Another $20,000 came from Macon and McLean Counties (Decatur and Bloomington). The primary contributor was a Decatur liquor dealer involved in Republican politics.[40]

During the 1944 election, none of that information was known publicly. The collectors and their contributors worked out of sight. The extent of Green's knowledge and participation was not known, although he unquestionably would have denied any association with gamblers and their money. The campaign for governor was fought on the classic issues of an incumbent's record and a challenger's promises. Green's Democratic opponent was Thomas J. Courtney, a native of Chicago who had served in the state senate from 1927 to 1933 and as Cook County state's attorney since 1933.[41] He had the backing of the Chicago machine but was not well known outside the city.

For the fourth time, Roosevelt appeared on the ballot for president, although he was ill, looked haggard, and rarely hit the campaign trail. His Republican opponent, Thomas E. Dewey, was governor of New York and a distinguished crime fighter. Dewey had plenty to attack in terms of Roosevelt's record, but at election time, many voters did not want to change presidents before the war ended. One of Roosevelt's most loyal supporters in the Senate, downstate Democrat Scott Lucas, sought a second six-year term against Richard J. Lyons of Libertyville, whom Green had defeated for governor in the 1940 party primary.[42] Lucas had made peace with Mayor Kelly and in 1944 was the Chicago organization's favorite for the vice presidency, after it became clear that Roosevelt did not want Henry Wallace on the ticket. When Lucas and others could not get sufficient convention votes, the Illinois delegation supported Missouri senator Harry S. Truman.[43]

Republicans could not rest easy in spite of past victories. The Chicago Democratic machine, diminished but still dangerous, had to be reckoned with. Roosevelt, healthy or not, could expect legions of New Deal faithful to vote. But other than Lucas, Illinois Democrats had little to cheer about in terms of familiar names on the ballot. An exception would have been Edward J. Hughes, secretary of state since 1933.[44] However, the Democratic Party lineup changed with the death of Hughes in June 1944, when Governor Green appointed Republican Richard Yates Rowe, a nephew of Civil War governor Richard Yates, to fill the vacancy until the election.

State treasurer William G. Stratton, who by law could not serve consecutive terms, wanted Green's nod to run for secretary of state. Green rejected the appeal, however, and backed A. P. Benson, a state senator, who defeated Stratton in the primary. Benson faced Edward J. Barrett, a sergeant in the Marines who was hospitalized with wounds and could not campaign. When Democrats began taking over the state political picture in the 1930s, Barrett aligned with the Chicago interests, serving as state treasurer from 1931 to 1933 and as state auditor from 1933 to 1941. During those years, he developed a close association with John Stelle. Barrett and Stelle formed an alliance that combined Democratic strength in Chicago with voters in southernmost parts of the state opposed to Governor Horner.[45]

Democrats had much at risk in the 1944 elections. If Lucas and Barrett could not carry the day and none of the challengers to incumbent Republicans could win, Democrats would be completely shut out of executive offices, a rarity in Illinois political history. The picture in legislative races was not encouraging, either. Turnover of Democrats in the legislature left few with experienced backgrounds, decreasing impact in the policy processes and limiting the potential for leaders. Further losses would give super-control to Republicans.

Paul Powell, first elected to the state House of Representatives in 1934 from a district deep in southern Illinois that included his hometown of Vienna, was one of the few Democratic survivors in the 1940s. When he entered the House, Democrats controlled both chambers of the legislature and most of the state's elected officials. He made little advancement until Republicans regained control of the House in 1940. By 1944, he was one of sixty-nine Democrats in the House, while Republicans had eighty-four members. With ten years' experience, Powell had learned how to get along with diverse members of his party and with Republicans. He also had become friendly with Stelle.

Stelle could sense that Powell would someday hold a position of power in the legislature, and he wanted to make sure they had a lasting friendship. With a safe legislative seat in Johnson County, Powell in 1944 was ripe for a House leadership position. After his election victory, Powell became the minority whip with responsibility for obtaining and counting votes, no matter how few they were.

There were no upsets at the top of the ticket in the 1944 Illinois elections. FDR won Illinois's electoral votes and election to a fourth term. Scott Lucas coasted to victory for a second six-year term that would see an acceleration of his fortunes in Democratic Party leadership. Edward Barrett was elected secretary of state, continuing his slow but steady climb in positions of increased statewide responsibilities. A major upset victory for Democrats occurred when Emily Taft Douglas, spouse of Paul Douglas, defeated isolationist Stephen A. Day for the seat in Congress that was elected statewide and called "at-large."[46]

Among Democrats returning to the General Assembly, Paul Powell continued membership on the Illinois Budgetary Commission, where he exerted influence on the allocation of state funds. The party also appointed Powell as downstate political director of the state central committee. With a high profile, he had responsibility for regaining lost ground outside Chicago in the 1948 elections. Powell was poised to become the most powerful legislator in Illinois.

On the Republican side, Governor Green defeated Thomas Courtney, Arthur C. Lueder was reelected auditor of public accounts, Conrad F.

Becker won the position of state treasurer, and George F. Barrett, no relation to the Democrat Edward Barrett, captured a second term as attorney general, assuring Republicans of another four years in control of state government.

The surprises were in the numbers, not in the outcomes, and showed encouraging gains for Democrats. Roosevelt, weakened as he was and in poor health, grabbed 51.52 percent of the vote, compared to 50.98 percent in 1940. He did this while receiving 70,000 fewer statewide votes than four years earlier. Roosevelt improved his vote total in Democratic-dominated Cook County by 107,000, while Thomas E. Dewey drew that many fewer votes in Cook than Willkie had received in 1940. The machine did its work for Roosevelt.[47]

Lucas also benefited from the machine's efficiency, drawing almost as many votes as Roosevelt statewide and winning Cook County with 58.3 percent of the vote. The senator's downstate strength boosted the victory margin to 217,230 over Lyons.

The shock for Republicans appeared in vote totals for governor. Green had won his first term in 1940 by 257,000 votes. His reelection victory in 1944 was by the dramatically thin margin of 72,271, although he won ninety-one counties to eleven for Courtney. Reporter Robert Howard said later that while Courtney had Democratic machine support, there was always a question of whether Democrats had preferred to stick with Green rather than elect someone who had previous run-ins with Chicago leadership. Robert Howard told this story of election night to illustrate the closeness of the contest: "Green and Courtney both lived in the Edgewater Beach Hotel. Courtney came in, so the story is, around midnight—told the hotel staff he'd been elected governor. Green, being a night owl, came in two or three hours later. Somebody started to offer condolences, and he said no, he'd been elected governor. . . . The late returns from downstate changed the matter."[48]

It was true historically that incumbent governors often had narrower margins of victory in second elections, but Green came shockingly close to losing to a man who had spent his entire political career in Chicago and had little exposure to downstate audiences. To some degree, this reflected the strength of Roosevelt and Lucas downstate, where Green had done so well in 1940. It made Republicans nervous.

Green was rebuked by normally friendly newspaper editorial pages, which increased the pain of a close race. Editors of the *Bloomington Pantagraph*, usually loyal to Republicans, wrote, "There is no call for the

Republican party chieftains in Illinois to congratulate themselves. New and better leadership is called for."[49]

Did the payoffs to Green's campaign for protection from law enforcement make any difference in the close election outcome? The money did not change historic voting patterns. The counties targeted by collectors for money to aid Green in 1944 were Democratic strongholds, such as Macon, St. Clair, and Madison Counties. Peoria County, reliably Republican, gave Green 55 percent of the vote.

As Illinoisans moved through 1945, the news was dominated by the death of Roosevelt, the succession of Harry S. Truman to the presidency, the end of war in Europe, and victory in the Pacific after Truman authorized dropping two atomic bombs on Japanese soil. Pressures built immediately for the return of American troops and a measure of normalcy at home after years of living with the constraints of war. Postwar attitudes would have a bearing on the 1946 midterm elections as voters sought a change in the status quo that had become familiar through the Roosevelt years.

Settling in for a second term, Green flexed his muscles. He provided Mayor Kelly with support in the legislature that enabled Chicago to undertake a gigantic highway program.[50] Green and Republican legislators also moved quickly during the 1945 session to create a commission for coordinating all veterans' affairs. They appropriated $385,000 to pay bonuses to returning veterans, setting in motion a program that eventually would include all conflicts beginning with World War I. Payments were to begin in 1947. Meanwhile, confident of the future with Republicans again in place, Green took time from state affairs to travel the nation in response to praise for his leadership. If the clamor went to Green's head, he was not the first to dream of great moments.

Soon after Green's victory in 1944, Republicans interested in running for governor in 1948 began plotting. In the history of Illinois, beginning in 1818, no governor had served more than two consecutive terms, or eight years, although there was no constitutional provision or law prohibiting more than two terms. Another reason for Republican hopefuls to think Green would go away after his second term was that he had spoken against three terms for state and federal officials on several occasions.

During his campaign in 1940, Green had said at Arcola, "We want no third term dictator in Illinois or in the nation." The second reference was to Roosevelt seeking a third term. In Decatur during the 1940 campaign, Green had said, "We are in a fight to the finish to preserve the American form of government and our system of free enterprise. The 1940 campaign is the last hope for the preservation of these American principles. A third term would destroy them." On another occasion he referred to "the constant emergencies and crises[,] in each one of which the president has managed to increase his own power. And lastly has come the attempt for a third term, last and greatest of the attempts to innovate and change American democracy."[51] While two of those were aimed directly at the president, he implied there was something evil about third terms for any chief executive. The final reason to discount a third term was Green's overt campaign for the vice presidency.

One of those waiting not so patiently in the wings was George F. Barrett, elected to his second term as state attorney general in 1944. Historically, attorneys general in the state worked independently of the governor, and in some cases not comfortably. Barrett had not enjoyed an especially close relationship to Green. Although Barrett was considered part of the Green Machine, he had built an organization of his own across the state among state's attorneys and law enforcement officials. He had their support largely because he refused to interfere with their handling of local matters related to gambling and corrupt practices. His carefully stated policy was that local officials had responsibility for handling their jurisdictions and the attorney general should not be involved other than as a consultant. Barrett's favorite response to press inquiries about his responsibilities was, "I have nothing to say."[52]

By early 1946, Barrett appeared to be in campaign mode for governor. At one point, he sent a letter to all state's attorneys except those in Cook and St. Clair Counties—Democratic strongholds—urging a crackdown on gambling.[53] A few weeks after sending the letter, he claimed credit for a reduction in criminal activity, for which he offered no hard numbers. Few outside Barrett's circle saw this as the beginning of a crusade against gambling. There were too many Republicans involved. This charade appeared to overlap with criticism of Green as being allied with Mayor Kelly in Chicago, which he was to some extent. Friends of Barrett said the attorney general hoped to kick up enough trouble among Republicans downstate to break up the friendliness between Green and Kelly. He was alleged to have said that Green could get nowhere in Illinois politics without Kelly. All of that was futuristic, though, as Green had not indicated his next political move. However, it presaged a party struggle if he declared for a third term.

A DEMOCRATIC SAVIOR APPEARS

Among thousands of Illinois war veterans who returned to the state in 1945 and 1946 was Jacob M. Arvey, a resident of Chicago. When he entered military service in 1942, Arvey was the third most powerful Democrat in Chicago and therefore a major cog in the political organization headed by Mayor Kelly and his partner in the political organization, Pat Nash. By all standards of the time, Arvey was a political "boss." He gave up that role to an understudy in the Twenty-Fourth Ward of the city to serve as judge advocate for the Thirty-Third Army Division in the South Pacific. He eventually reached the rank of colonel.

During Arvey's absence from politics, the machine became an embarrassment to Democrats who watched the Republican Party rise to dominate Illinois government. At the war's end, an angry group of the city's political elite wanted Mayor Kelly removed and looked to the returning veteran Arvey to get the job done.

When Arvey entered the military, he had earned a place of respect in Chicago's political history. He was a good example of someone who had started at the bottom and climbed to the top in politics by virtue of his connections and, to a large extent, his performance. In Chicago it was not enough only to know the right people. At some point, politicians had to prove their worth at the ballot box.

Arvey was born on 3 November 1895 on LaSalle Street in Chicago to a Jewish couple from Poland. Jacob, or Jack as he was known, was the first of their children born in America.[54] Jack worked before and after school helping his father at the family milk store on Pacific Avenue. After his father died when Arvey was thirteen, the family moved into the Twenty-Fourth Ward north of Maxwell Street on the city's Near West Side, where he attended the Chicago Hebrew Institute. The family's difficult financial circumstances required him to work during the day and attend school five nights a week. From the time he was fifteen, he kept this routine until he graduated from John Marshall Law School in 1916. He passed the bar examination and went to work as clerk at a law firm for five dollars a week.

His life in politics began in 1914 when he volunteered for his law professor William J. Lindsay, who was an independent candidate for judge in the Twenty-Fourth Ward. Arvey remembered later, "I knew nothing about canvassing a precinct, but I took my job seriously, and got a great many votes for him against the machine."[55] Lindsay won the race. Jack's work for him attracted the attention of two political organizations that both wanted him to work in the 1915 mayoral election. Arvey chose the Roger Sullivan faction and campaigned for Robert M. Schweitzer for mayor.

Arvey's reputation as a campaigner helped him get a job in the office of Cook County state's attorney Maclay Hoyne, and in a short time he became an assistant state's attorney. Later, he decided to start his own law firm with partner Paul Holleb after he concluded that prosecuting criminals was not to his liking.

Arvey came to the attention of Mike Rosenberg and his brother Moe, who were political bosses in the Twenty-Fourth Ward. He became active in Mike's campaign for Democratic committeeman in that ward. In 1923, twenty-seven-year-old Arvey won the office of ward alderman with the backing of Rosenberg, the ward political leader, as a reward for services. Arvey began a long and productive history as a top politician in both the ward and the city. In the election for alderman, the story goes that he received help from his mother for perhaps the only time during his career. Arvey's opponents had started a rumor that he was not really Jewish. Mrs. Arvey, mother of eight, went to a rally to answer the question "Is Jack Jewish?" She answered in Yiddish, "What else?"[56] Arvey won with 5,558 of the ward's 9,430 votes.

In league with the Rosenbergs, Arvey and a majority of Jews in the ward backed the local Democratic ticket in 1922, but in 1924 they cast a majority of votes for Republican Calvin Coolidge for president. The next year, Mike Rosenberg died and was succeeded by his brother Moe. Arvey and Moe supported Republican William "Big Bill" Thompson for mayor in 1927 but chose in 1928 to support Democrat Al Smith for president. In time, leaders of the Twenty-Fourth Ward joined with the faction that elected Anton Cermak mayor of Chicago in 1931 and thereafter became predictable Democratic Party leaders.[57]

A key to Arvey's success as a ward operator was his relationship with people. Arvey described the importance of that connection: "Let me put it in a crude way—put people under obligation to you. Make them your friends. You don't like to hurt a friend. And that's politics—put a man under obligation."[58] Running the ward organization became a full-time job for Arvey and his lieutenants. The relationship between voters and precinct captains tightened along family lines.

Arvey claimed that Cermak built the machine that was inherited by Kelly and Nash and later by Richard J. Daley. Arvey and the Jewish Twenty-Fourth played a major role in Cermak's election as mayor of

Chicago over Thompson. The payback for Arvey was appointment as the mayor's floor leader on the city council. Known as "young and ambitious," Arvey learned how to get things done in the aldermanic world.[59] With the death of ward committeeman Moe Rosenberg in 1932, precinct captains unanimously elected Arvey as committeeman and political leader. Working the strings of the organization successfully in 1932, Cermak and Arvey were largely responsible for the election of Henry Horner as governor, the first Jew to hold that position in the state's history. In his mid-thirties, Arvey found himself at the top of the Chicago political heap, in full stride with the kingmakers.

The city political picture changed dramatically in 1933 with Cermak's assassination while sitting next to President Roosevelt in Miami, Florida. State law held that until the next election, a successor could be appointed only from the city council. County chairman Nash conferred with Arvey and concluded that having one Jew as governor and another as mayor of Chicago would not sit well with other ethnic groups in the city, especially the Irish. Nash backed Ed Kelly, who was not a council member and had never run for public office. Horner and the legislative leadership were persuaded to change the law to allow appointment of someone not on the council.[60] With that accomplished, Nash appointed Kelly, who was chief engineer at the sanitary district, as mayor, and the Kelly-Nash organization was born. Convinced they needed Arvey in a position of power, Kelly and Nash chose him as chair of the city council's finance committee, a position of immense power in the city.

City and state politics became tense shortly after Kelly was appointed mayor and then became nasty in 1935 after he was elected to a full term as mayor. Kelly and Horner came to a parting of the ways, in alleged disagreement over horse-racing policy. Arvey said that Horner refused to honor a Kelly appointment.[61] In truth, it may have been either, both, or other reasons. The rift could not be healed. Kelly and Nash decided to support an opponent of Horner in the 1936 primary. The timing was wrong for Arvey to support Horner and turn his back on the organization; he told the governor that the party came first.[62] Arvey supported Dr. Herman Bundesen, Chicago health commissioner and the mayor's choice in the primary. The Twenty-Fourth went 10 to 1 for Bundesen, but Horner won in a close contest. After Horner's easy general election victory over Republican C. Wayland "Curly" Brooks, everyone settled in for open warfare in one of the nastiest aftermaths of a gubernatorial race in state history.

For the next five years, Arvey maintained his role as committeeman for the Twenty-Fourth Ward and handmaiden of the machine. He also continued as chairman of the city council's finance committee. When World War II began, Arvey gave up all his positions in Chicago government and began a four-year term in military service.

Upon returning to Chicago in 1946, Arvey vowed not to reenter politics—at least that was what he said years later. Politicians in Chicago had other ideas for him, including Mayor Kelly, who wanted to appoint him to the board of the Chicago Park District. Arvey remembered, "I'd worked, during the time I had gone to school, as a busboy and a waiter in a restaurant of the district. It appealed to me and I took the job."[63] One thing led to another, and soon he was back as committeeman of the Twenty-Fourth Ward, thanks to a timely resignation.

In addition to being mayor of Chicago, Kelly was chairman of the Democratic Party. As such, he held much political power. Unhappy party leaders in the city, especially the Irish, approached Arvey about seeking the party chairmanship. There had been friction within the party for some time before Arvey returned from the war, in part because Democratic fortunes in the state had plummeted. But in Chicago, the primary reason for unrest among ethnic groups was the mayor's support of open housing that benefited blacks and threatened to upset the status quo in ethnic neighborhoods. The various ethnic groups had their favorites for chairman but could not gain consensus. Consequently, Arvey was the compromise choice. Many of those making the selection saw him as a stalking horse that could quickly be removed after dumping the mayor.

Kelly could accept Arvey's position because of their close relationship. The mayor assumed he would be chosen to run for reelection, although in recent elections his margin of victory had declined. If he worried over rumblings among political associates or the bombardment of news reports about corruption in city ranks, he gave no indication. He expected to run again and that Arvey would make it possible.

Before reaching that milestone, however, the party and its leadership faced the 1946 midyear elections. Only two state officers' jobs were on the ballot: treasurer and superintendent of public instruction. Otherwise, the focus was on members of Congress and county positions. Traditionally, eight congressional seats in the city and county were controlled by the Democratic organization. Beyond that, Democrats hoped for the best. Downstate voters would determine seventeen members of Congress, and statewide one seat would be decided at-large. In addition to Cook County, Democrats held the district that included the Democratic strongholds of St. Clair and Madison Counties and the statewide at-large seat held by Emily Taft Douglas, daughter of the distinguished Chicago sculptor Lorado Taft. In Congress, she was a staunch supporter of Democratic foreign policy initiatives and formation of the United Nations. During much of her time in the House, her husband, Paul, was recovering from several surgeries to correct injuries received in the war.

Opposing Mrs. Douglas was William G. Stratton, thirty-two, a veteran of statewide elections and an ally of Senator Brooks in congressional affairs. In 1940, he was elected statewide congressman-at-large and became the youngest man in the Seventy-Seventh Congress. In 1942, he ran for state treasurer and won by 250,000 votes. In 1944, Stratton challenged the authority of Green's machine and ran for secretary of state but lost in the primary. He then joined the navy and spent two years as a lieutenant junior grade.[64] Again without support of the Green Machine, he decided to run for congressman-at-large in 1946 against Mrs. Douglas. Strongly opposed to Harry S. Truman's foreign policies and a supporter of tax reductions and a smaller federal government, Stratton carried 97 of 102 counties and defeated Mrs. Douglas by 367,469 votes.[65]

Republicans demolished Democrats across Illinois, winning the races for superintendent of public instruction and treasurer and maintaining a majority of 15 to 1 in downstate congressional seats by much larger margins than in 1944. The single Democratic victor from the strongholds in St. Clair and Madison Counties, Melvin Price, won by just 2,000 votes.[66] The shock to Democrats came in Chicago and Cook County, where party candidates failed in five districts and in county positions. When the dust settled, Republicans held twenty congressional seats and Democrats six. There was no place for Mayor Kelly to hide. Demands were immediate for his replacement.

The mayor would not go quietly, no matter how much he was to blame. He told everyone that he would seek reelection in April 1947. Nevertheless, the chorus of opposition grew. Paul Douglas said he would launch an anti-machine campaign for mayor if Kelly ran again. Opposition to Kelly came quickly from the *Chicago Tribune*, which had been a longtime backer of the mayor. Another supporter, Marshall Field III, said his newspaper, the *Chicago Sun*, would oppose Kelly. Ethnic forces, already aligned against Kelly because of his housing policy, called on Arvey to stop the bleeding.[67]

Arvey needed ammunition, so officials of the party authorized a straw poll of politicians after the election; it showed that the Irish, Poles, and Bohemians were all against the mayor. Armed with the results of the poll, Arvey and two others met with Kelly after the election. The meeting ended with matters unresolved. However, after a few days, Kelly capitulated.[68]

Meanwhile, Democrats discussed who would run for mayor with the party's blessing. Arvey said Kelly and others suggested Martin Kennelly, a businessman of high standards who headed the local Red Cross operation and was active in civic affairs. Furthermore, he was nonpartisan and a relative political newcomer. What did he have going for him in terms of facing the electorate? The answer: he was not Ed Kelly, or Pat Nash, or Jack Arvey. He was the anti-machine man. On 19 December 1946, Arvey asked the Democratic Central Committee to favor Kennelly as the candidate for mayor. Committee members had no other name to suggest, and they went along. Predictably, the choice confounded almost everyone, including the Chicago newspapers. Showing party loyalty, committee members gave lip service to the selection. Behind the scenes, they called Kennelly "Fartin' Martin" and "Snow White."[69]

With 1947 and the Chicago mayoral election just ahead, Republicans were gleeful, especially Governor Green. After sweeping the 1946 elections, including positions in Cook County, Green believed Republicans had an opportunity to win the mayor's chair for the first time since the days of Big Bill Thompson in the 1920s. Who would have thought that Chicago politics would come to that?

A MACHINE IN TROUBLE

Jack Arvey's intuition about the need to provide a nonpolitical candidate for Chicago's mayor in 1947 had a downstate Illinois parallel that would play a vital role in 1948 election outcomes. A similar scenario was under way in St. Clair County, the home base of the second most powerful Democratic machine in the state, across the Mississippi River from St. Louis.

Long a bastion of Democratic votes and corrupt practices, the county was on the verge of a cleansing process of its own brought on by an electorate weary of the political status quo and cozy relationships with organized crime. There was no maestro the likes of Arvey to orchestrate the show. In St. Clair County, a World War II hero led the cleanup effort and ignited voter interest in reform candidates.

The postwar years in St. Clair County provide a case study in the insidious relationship of crime and corruption and the rise of efforts by citizens and reform politicians to change a way of doing business that stretched back into the nineteenth century. At the local level, a revolt occurred that propelled the subjects of corruption, commercial gambling, and political payoffs into the statewide election picture.

For years, a widely told story served as popular evidence to demonstrate a link between the gangster army of Chicago's Al Capone and Frank "Buster" Wortman, who took over the rackets in the East St. Louis region during and after World War II.[70] A half-sister of Wortman, Ruth Virginia Wortman, then age twenty-two, was arrested in Kennett, Missouri, in 1947 and charged with driving a stolen car across the state line. Miss Wortman, a Chicago resident, told sheriff's deputies that she had borrowed the car from Ralph Capone, brother of the Chicago crime king, to drive to Carl Shelton's funeral. Shelton had been murdered at Fairfield, Illinois, on 28 October 1947. After the funeral, she had driven to Missouri to visit friends. She explained that Carl Shelton was her godfather.

That anecdote tied together three of the state's most notorious organized gang operations—Capone's, the Shelton brothers', and Wortman's—with beginnings in the 1920s. Wortman had worked for the Shelton brothers and succeeded them as crime boss in southern Illinois. No longer rackets leaders in a large part of the state, the Sheltons had taken their operations to the Peoria area. Capone gang remnants wanted to play in downstate Illinois but never got a foothold.

In spite of the Ruth Wortman story, there is no irrefutable evidence that Wortman and agents of Capone formed a bond in the mid-1940s to expedite a takeover of legal and illegal activities in St. Clair County. Certainly, none of the principals of those groups ever admitted such conspiracies. There is, however, a mountain of circumstantial evidence and testimony regarding joint operations. Federal law enforcement agencies watched the principals closely.[71]

FBI agents who worked the east side of the St. Louis region and who had access to the best information the bureau could collect believed that Wortman and the Chicago syndicate were more than casual acquaintances. Capone associates especially wanted to extend their racetrack wire operations in the St. Louis metro area for horse-race gambling. Wortman, already the leading rackets boss, appeared to be the best candidate to act as the Capone agent.

FBI records show that Wortman through the years made a number of trips to Chicago to confer with syndicate leaders.[72] Crime reporter Charles Stewart of the *East St. Louis Journal* never doubted the connection between Capone and Wortman. His sources on the streets of East St. Louis and in the back alleys of St. Clair County convinced him the Capone crowd and Wortman considered collaboration. Local witnesses gave Stewart persuasive anecdotal evidence.

In articles for the *Journal*, Stewart told how the people of East St. Louis learned about the Chicago invasion in 1946 and 1947: "Newspaper vendors along Collinsville Avenue are aware of the new move into our city. One vendor recently pointed out to a reporter that in the past several months, Chicago newspapers, which he formerly retained for several days now, are going as fast as he can place them on his stand."[73]

Although Wortman launched a serious campaign to control the action himself and keep Capone interests at arm's length, Stewart explained how the Chicago gang reorganized after the death of Capone in 1947 and focused on infiltrating East St. Louis and St. Clair County. Capone leadership sought downstate opportunities when Chicago and Cook County authorities turned up the heat and shut down many of the rackets during the early 1940s. By the mid-1940s, Chicago area officials aggressively arrested crime suspects and known members of the Capone mob. The police commissioner declared "all out war" in efforts to rid Chicago of the Capone connections. Unable to depend solely on gambling and rackets in Chicago, the Syndicate—the word used for Capone survivors—took over wire distribution of racing information across the country. The Syndicate controlled bookmaking information in Kansas City, Des Moines, Louisville, Dubuque, New Orleans, and Dallas.[74]

The potential for distributing racing information along with the enticement of money from large-scale gambling and cash-rich legal operations such as pinball machines, jukeboxes, and other coin-operated devices lured Capone interests to East St. Louis. The Chicago gang sent reconnaissance crews to scout for associates in 1946 and early 1947. Operatives tried to muscle in on gambling action. When that failed, they decided to find someone with local knowledge, familiarity with law enforcement agencies, and a base of support among racketeers. Wortman became their target. Although the Syndicate and Wortman flirted seriously, Capone interests never became major players. Wortman did not allow it, for he knew local officials would object.

Wortman had the run of the city and county, thanks to East St. Louis and county law enforcement officials. Trading on favoritism as a "local boy," Wortman stayed within view of the authorities and enjoyed their protection. To accomplish his objective of controlling gambling in the county, Wortman needed to lure St. Louis traffic to Illinois gambling spots. Aided by local law enforcement officials who looked the other way, vehicles from Missouri jammed parking lots at taverns and Wortman's gambling establishments throughout St. Clair County.

Wortman clearly had a finger in many pies, all of which generated cash and nurtured a sizable gang. The specific rackets changed over time and reflected his ability to shift with the winds of law enforcement and newspaper coverage. But he couldn't do it without the complicity of public officials. Eventually, the public responded to the corruption. Citizens of East St. Louis and St. Clair County could read, and they talked. They worried that the region might return to the days of the bloody Shelton era in the 1920s and 1930s, when the gang ran unchecked through the streets and residents could not tell the difference between hoodlums and cops. Citizens decided to take action.

Public indignation over reports of wide-open gambling and slot machines in December 1946 inspired the calling of a St. Clair County grand jury in Belleville, the county seat. Unable to get law enforcement officials to curtail the spread of gambling, the grand jury conducted its own investigation. In September, grand jury foreman George Wheeler solicited a petition from jurors to convene and to consider gambling indictments. He contacted reporters and editors at the *St. Louis Post-Dispatch* and the *East St. Louis Journal* for information about gambling locations.

The jury listened primarily to six witnesses. They included East St. Louis city judge Joseph Troy, city court reporter Rollin Moore, and East St. Louis attorney Saul Cohn. Perhaps the most informative testimony came from three newspaper employees who witnessed gambling firsthand and wrote about it in the *Journal* and the *Post-Dispatch*: Carl Baldwin, a reporter for the *Post-Dispatch*; Thomas Duffy, *East St. Louis Journal* news editor; and Stewart.[75]

To initiate such an investigation in an environment of disinterest by many law enforcement officials required considerable courage on the part of grand jurors. Gamblers never considered the citizen effort a threat. The Illinois gambling industry operated full blast in open defiance of the investigation. In East St. Louis, the "big stores," as newspapers called the horse-race gambling joints, were packed with customers. At one

location visited by a *Post-Dispatch* reporter, betting on horses occurred
in the open, three blackjack games held interest, and patrons kept thirteen slot machines busy while the grand jury met.[76] The defiant attitude
contrasted with the customary practice of "folding up" when a grand
jury showed interest in gambling.

The grand jury returned indictments against six public officials, including the mayor of East St. Louis, three city commissioners, and a
former sheriff of St. Clair County, and also against two known gambling
operators. Newspaper headlines shocked citizens of St. Clair County. The
indictment alleged two counts of malfeasance in office. The first alleged
that officials failed to suppress operation of slot machines and racing
handbook shops in East St. Louis. The second count listed eighteen
places in which slot machines operated in East St. Louis. If convicted,
those indicted of the misdemeanors faced a fine not exceeding $10,000
and removal from office.[77]

Within days of the indictments, four members of the grand jury requested presiding judge Edward F. Bareis and Illinois attorney general
George Barrett to name a special prosecutor for the case. Judge Bareis
refused the request, saying, "It would look bad to appoint a special prosecutor. It would appear as though I didn't trust [state's attorney Louis
P. Zerweck] or that I thought he was not qualified."[78] In turn, Barrett
denied the request, saying that he could enter the case only at the request
of the state's attorney, and he had received no request.[79] The matter died.
Zerweck, clearly not interested in prosecuting the officials and former
officials or the gamblers, fumbled the indictment process and paperwork
so badly that Judge Bareis dismissed the charges two months later. The
grand jury met into 1947 but failed to bring further charges.

The grand jury's action may have been inspired by Illinois attorney
general Barrett's appearance in Belleville and St. Clair County a few
months before the jury convened. He spoke at a downtown café surrounded on all sides by taverns containing slot machines and across the
street from a racetrack bookie operation. He spoke about his official
duties, but the session with reporters shed light on his attitude toward
local crime activity and suggested that he did not intend to do anything
about gambling in St. Clair County. When asked if he would look into
accounts of gambling activity, he said, "I have nothing to say." Told that
the Belleville City Council proposed to license slot machines, racetrack
handbooks, and gambling syndicate operators, he dodged again, saying,
"I have nothing to say."[80] He did observe that the council could be in

violation of state law if the measure passed. This was his standard answer
to questions about state government involvement in local criminal activity. He might have shown more interest if St. Clair County officials had
asked for help, but there was no indication that happened. This attitude
toward wide-open gambling became a reelection issue of consequence
for Barrett and Governor Green.

Citizen outrage at the coziness between police and gambling interests
and at the failure of the grand jury led to an uprising in the municipal
and county elections. Similar revolts occurred across the state where
veterans, with their fresh faces and reform attitudes, inspired citizens
to reject the business-as-usual approach of public officials to politics.
Returning veterans seemed to say, If the young men of East St. Louis
and St. Clair County could prove their valor on the battlefields of the
world, why not at home?

Alan Dixon, a native of St. Clair County who just a few years later
started a political career of forty-two years in elective office, including
two terms as a U.S. senator from Illinois, remembered those postwar
times: "It [veterans' involvement] was the culture of the time. The system
was full of young people who wanted to get rid of the bad. The recurring
theme was 'We'll do the right thing for the people.'"[81]

In that environment, and with encouragement from the local press,
citizens aimed to upset the East St. Louis and St. Clair County political
machine that coddled gamblers. They sought candidates for office in the
1947 municipal elections—similar to the timing for selecting a mayor
in Chicago—to challenge the long-standing bipartisan machine that
ran the city and county. The upstarts developed an independent slate of
contenders headed by Richard Thomas Carter, age thirty-one.

From 1947 until he retired as a senior regional judge thirty years later,
Carter pursued careers with the highest level of visibility and involvement
in county law enforcement. The degree to which Carter remained true
to the independent pronouncements of 1947 was the subject of public
and private arguments for most of those years. His story illustrates the
difficulty of moving from rhetoric and citizen anger to action in a corrupt
urban environment. On the Illinois side of the Mississippi in 1947, the
reform hopes of a region rested on the promise of an individual unen-
cumbered by the past and inexperienced in public office.

Born 9 July 1915 in East St. Louis, Dick Carter followed the family and
schooling route of so many others in his native city.[82] His father worked
for years at the Swift & Co. packing plant at nearby National Stock

Yards. Carter graduated from St. Joseph's parochial school in 1929 and with Central Catholic High School's first graduation class in 1933. He received a law degree from St. Louis University in 1938 and began practicing law in East St. Louis. In June 1941, Carter entered the U.S. Army.

Carter rose from a private in the infantry to a lieutenant colonel in the air corps, accumulating a hero's record. In 1942, he flew a fighter plane in North Africa and served in the Sicilian and Italian theaters of war. After being shot down and wounded, Carter returned to action after a week of hospital care. In 1944, he flew to India as a squadron commander and served in the China-Burma-India theater until returning to the United States later that year. The military discharged him in 1946 with the Distinguished Flying Cross, the Air Medal with three oak leaf clusters, the Order of the Purple Heart, and two campaign ribbons with battle stars.

Carter returned to East St. Louis an acclaimed hero to practice law. In a few months, friends and associates convinced him to become part of a challenge slate of independent candidates for East St. Louis municipal positions. Carter sought election to the city commission, to the surprise of many people. He had expressed no special interest in public affairs. His calm, almost passive personality hardly fit the brawling nature of East St. Louis politics. The *Journal* later said this about Carter in the 1947 election: "His demeanor in that knockdown, drag-out battle—probably the most vicious city election in history—was the same. Of all the candidates, Carter was the most placid; his attitude was credited by many with being the reason for the near-defeat he avoided only after a long court battle."[83]

Independent challengers to the machine presented a full slate for the commission and mayor's position. After the election, the old guard retained three commission positions, and newcomers claimed two. Joining Carter was Russell Beebe, who would serve many years as police commissioner. The commission battle is best described in hyperbole. One newspaper reporter exclaimed, "Never before (perhaps never again) have the people of East St. Louis witnessed a political fight parallel to that which has become known, in political jargon, as the 'Carter Case.'"[84] The "case" had intrigue and unpredictability.

The legal battle began when independents challenged the original election that Carter had lost by 100 votes. After hearings by a county judge, a revised tabulation showed Carter the winner by 34 votes. For the year following, Carter and his opponent contested each other in the courts. Appeals and political and legal maneuvers delayed and confused matters until May 1948, when an Illinois appellate court declared Carter the winner.[85]

No sooner had Carter won a seat on the East St. Louis commission than he set his sights anew. He announced he would run against St. Clair County state's attorney Louis P. Zerweck, a veteran of sixteen years in office and a product of the Democratic political machine. Reformers and independents who backed Carter for the commission looked at the state's attorney contest as part of a continuum—one race simply became another without pause. Carter, the conqueror of one machine candidate in East St. Louis, prepared to take on the icon of machine politics in the county elections of 1948.

A classic Democratic primary followed. Carter, running as an independent Democrat, had his veterans and anti-machine followers. Zerweck treated Carter with all the disdain of a cocky incumbent, and the machine backed Zerweck to the hilt. Carter knew the machine's soft spot—gambling—and he attacked. He said the county "abounded with gangsters and hoodlums like the Sheltons." Later he charged, "Gangsterism is again rampant in this general area," and repeated a pledge that he would wage constant war on the underworld. Carter attacked Zerweck's role in defending and supporting labor unions and accused the incumbent "of mediocrity in office."[86]

In at least one campaign appearance, Carter took aim at Governor Green, echoing accusations by Democrats running for state positions. He said Green "has done nothing to drive the gangsters out of the state despite the fact that he was elected on a lot of promises he made to that effect. That is why the gamblers and the gangsters are spending their money to re-elect Green."[87]

Carter thrashed Zerweck in the primary and went on to defeat Republican Curt Lindauer with ease in the general election.[88] In less than two years, Carter had slain the machine giants. Nevertheless, Carter found that ridding the county of evils that had grown and prospered over decades, as in Chicago, was easier said than done. Nevertheless, the triumphs of Carter and his followers helped feed an important groundswell that moved across the state in 1947 and 1948 and awakened an electorate tired of corruption and criminal behavior.

2. 1947: A YEAR OF DECISIONS

NATIONAL BATTLE LINES DRAWN

A case can be made that Democrats and Republicans alike were caught flat-footed at the end of World War II. Democrats, who had no better ideas than New Deal retreads, held fast to prewar concepts. Republicans, who prospered politically during the war, assumed that their anti–New Deal position and their policies of no foreign entanglements and less regulation would continue to attract voters.

Slowly in 1946, the public desire for a new, fresh life became evident.[1] This resulted in anger toward the same faces of elected officials and the same public policies, which offered little hope for change. Officials could see the signs but seemed paralyzed as to what should change. Meanwhile, the realities of unrest were plentiful: labor strikes, wage and price controls, unemployment, hesitation from clueless politicians, and a worsening postwar foreign environment. It did not help that the federal government appeared unable to produce meaningful laws. The new face in the White House, Harry S. Truman, seemed to prefer old Roosevelt programs designed to help the needy and to expand government involvement in the lives of citizens, but those had little traction with a Republican-dominated Congress. When President Truman tried his ideas, they gathered no momentum.

This season of unrest might have been little more than a mild rumble, a reaction to war's end, or a temporary case of nerves. As the symptoms persisted, however, political people saw the need to react. That is what made 1947 so important in the political outcomes of 1948 and well beyond. Political parties were in a race to see which could shed the doldrums and appeal to a demanding electorate. Nothing changed overnight, but people of vision made significant moves, new faces came forward, and old campaign slogans were dropped.

The baby boom that fueled an exploding economy began in 1946. This created a growing housing market. Marriages postponed during the war increased almost immediately, creating demands for goods to set up housekeeping to an extent never imagined or seen by a generation burdened with the Depression and world war. Government response to the challenges carried into the 1950s and 1960s, making the nation unmatched as to economic growth. In 1947, changes were just beginning.

Neither party did especially well in reading the public mind after the 1946 midterm elections, in which Republicans made major gains in Congress. Democrats, blistered at the polls, went into a funk. Republicans thought the vote was confirmation of their approach to less government and regulation. The public, the parties would learn the hard way, wanted more than the same old arguments and quarrels, especially in Illinois.

The Truman presidency had nowhere to go but up after the midterm elections of 1946. The Democratic Party hit rock bottom, and the president was part of the problem. Truman seemed ill at ease and appeared weak in the lingering shadow of FDR's overpowering persona, and the public sensed the condition. After four years of war, citizens wanted a new life to begin, but the federal government struggled. Unhappy union members took to the picket lines, and Congress thwarted every presidential initiative.

Adding to Truman's dilemma toward the end of 1946 was his confrontation with Henry Wallace, secretary of commerce and Roosevelt's vice president from 1941 to 1945. Wallace was the last thread holding the extreme liberal element to the rest of the Democratic Party. As 1946 developed, tensions between Russia and the United States increased, and the Truman administration developed a hard line toward the nation's adversary. Wallace feared that such a stance could lead to World War III, and he pleaded for a softer approach to relations with Russia.

Although Wallace did everything he could behind the scenes to derail Truman's approach to Russia, the president gave him the benefit of the doubt. That tolerance held until September, when Wallace made a speech before thousands at New York's Madison Square Garden. He expressed disagreements with the administration's policy, saying, among other things, "The tougher we get, the tougher Russians will get."[2] That was the last straw for Truman, and on 20 September, he fired Wallace. Truman's aides knew this would further alienate liberals from the president, but they had no idea how far Wallace would take his disagreements. He became the Progressive Party's presidential candidate and a major element in the fragmentation of the Democratic Party. Anticipating fallout in Illinois, newspapers and politicians kept a close watch on Wallace and his supporters.

Truman's prospects for 1947 did not look any better. For openers, expanded Republican control of Congress guaranteed trouble for Truman. In the Senate, Arthur Vandenberg held sway over matters of foreign relations. On the domestic side, Robert Taft, hard-core conservative elitist, considered Truman an intellectual weakling unfit for the presidency. Beyond that, Taft's ideas on public policy leaned sharply to the right, and he could count on support from southern Democrats to defeat the president's social agenda. Congress was the home of "powerful southerners [Democrats], powerful conservatives, and powerful old men."[3] With Republicans believing they could extend their election triumphs into 1948, the outlook for an "accidental" president appeared bleak.

However, Truman discovered during the first eighteen months of his presidency that he liked the job, in spite of his private and public statements about its trials and tribulations. He actually gained confidence in his ability to manage the office and lead the nation. Emboldened by increased comfort in the White House and surrounded by loyal staff, he headed into 1947 with a jaunty and positive perspective. True to his feisty nature, Truman would take the fight to Congress. When his efforts failed, he affixed the label of "good-for-nothing, do-nothing Eightieth Congress."[4]

The year had hardly begun when changes occurred. James Byrnes, whom Truman inherited from the Roosevelt administration, resigned as secretary of state. The president prevailed upon World War II hero General George Marshall to take the position.[5] Marshall had been in China attempting to negotiate peace between the communists and nationalist Chinese. While he failed in that mission, Truman and his aides were sanguine about convincing Marshall to take over the Department of State. An advocate of peace, and therefore not a hard-liner with Russia, Marshall was prepared to sit down with Soviet interests and attempt to hammer out agreements. He turned out to be more of an implementer of policy than a man with ideas of his own. As might be expected, Democrats and Republicans applauded the appointment.

Also early in January, Truman addressed a joint session of Congress to lay out his ideas for the year. He sounded a conciliatory note with his congressional adversaries, appealing to their conservatism by presenting a budget with a small surplus. He expressed concern about punitive labor laws and said he would not sign any bill attacking unions.[6] Before long, however, big-ticket expense items arose, drawing concern from members of both parties. Congress approved a food relief program costing $350 million. Another large request for $400 million was requested to thwart Russian-backed military threats in Turkey and Greece.[7]

Labor union strikes in 1945 and 1946 hitting the steel, coal, auto, and railroad industries disrupted the postwar economy and created animosities in Congress. Republicans believed some of the anger that had led to GOP gains in the midterm elections was a signal for legislation that would crack down on unions and prevent strife in the future.[8] Congress passed the Taft-Hartley Act in June 1947, calling for tighter regulation of activities and financial reporting by unions. Perhaps the longest-lasting impact over the following years was a provision that allowed states to pass "right-to-work" laws, forbidding forced union membership in organized shops. Obviously, labor argued against the congressional attack and pressured Truman to veto the bill. Aides argued that a veto could provide a political gain for the president by tying him closer to the Democrats' union constituency. On the other hand, they reasoned, if Congress overrode the veto, some good would come from the law. Truman issued his veto, and both houses of Congress overrode it by large margins: the House, 331–83, and the Senate, 68–25. The outcome was not a total loss for Truman, as he carefully played both ends against the middle. He pledged to carry out the law's provisions and embraced several of the mandates.

Truman's most expensive and expansive foreign policy proposal resulted from internal discussions and a speech in June by Marshall outlining a reconstruction program for Europe. It immediately became known as the Marshall Plan.[9] Truman called for a four-year program costing $22.3 billion, with $6.8 billion required in the first fifteen months. Congressional debate began early in 1948, and the plan ignited angry opposition from isolationists and those who believed Europe should get back on its feet without a huge outlay of U.S. money.

A volatile issue that carried over from 1947 to 1948 was civil rights. At the end of World War II, minority interests, spurred by victories during the war in behalf of oppressed peoples and fear of increased racial violence in the United States, pressured the Truman administration for action. In December 1946 he created the President's Committee on Civil Rights to study and report on ways "to safeguard the civil rights for people." Less than a year later, in October 1947, the committee submitted its report, titled *To Secure These Rights*, with thirty-five recommendations for action at the federal, state, and local levels.[10] This launched an intense debate. In February 1948, Truman sent a special message to Congress requesting legislative action. The Democratic Party, already split over the defection of Henry Wallace, now faced its most divisive issue just a few months before the national convention.

While the troubling issues piled up, Truman had decided to seek election. He named an informal strategic board to work on tactics for the campaign. His closest associates believed Thomas E. Dewey, governor of New York, again would be the Republican nominee. Nevertheless, influential Democrats, including some big city political operatives, had concluded Truman could not win. They read the Gallup poll numbers that showed a steady decline in Truman's approval ratings during 1947 to a low point around 35 percent.[11] A search had already begun to find someone who would push Truman aside and save the Democrats. Illinois political operatives would be deeply involved.

THE ILLINOIS PICTURE: MUDDLED

The Illinois political picture early in 1947 left no clear impression. The outcome of the 1946 election had not been fully digested, especially by the Democrats who had lost ground in Congress. Republicans could not wait for the 1948 slugfest to begin, although Governor Dwight Green had not indicated his intentions about a third term. Democrats had no names for candidates at the top of the 1948 ticket. Both parties prepared for the April 1947 mayoral and aldermanic races in Chicago and many downstate cities, such as East St. Louis, and wondered about the outcomes.

Democrats in Chicago normally would be confident of victories, with the well-oiled machine in place. However, prospects of a carryover of Republican fortunes from 1946 elections made city Democrats unusually jittery. Republicans usually went through the motions of nominating someone for Chicago mayor who would be crucified at the polls. This time they were giddy about the chances of electing a Republican as Chicago's leader. Optimism resulted not just from election returns but also from selection of little-known Martin Kennelly as the machine's candidate for mayor and recognition that the organization was depressed and out of favor. Republicans also took nourishment from President Truman's troubles with labor strikes, a sluggish economy, and a feisty Republican Congress.

The first months of 1947 shaped up as unusually intriguing, based on people's fears and expectations. The unpredictable events and revelations through April would be far more critical to outcomes in 1948.

Shortly after the 1946 elections, Republican leaders began a concentrated effort to win the Chicago mayoral election. Party officials—principally Green—selected Russell W. Root, who had never held elective office and had little name recognition, as candidate for mayor. He did have some exposure in Chicago and Cook County as a former assistant state's attorney. Next, the statewide organization received its orders to raise funds for the campaign and provide other kinds of necessary support. Throughout the Green administration, individuals from the highest to the lowest levels had valuable contacts with sources of funds, mostly corporations and businesses. Money and foot soldiers were needed to make Root competitive in Chicago, for he had little personal exposure to the resources necessary for a successful mayoral campaign.

A good example of how the administration's money system worked was fund-raising in the Department of Mines and Minerals, headed by longtime Republican Robert M. Medill.[12] His involvement with coal mining in Illinois reached back to 1898, when he went to work in a mine near Wenona. Ten years later, he earned his first supervisory position in what became a career of executive work in the mining industry that lasted almost forty years. Beginning in 1920, he served four years as director of the Department of Mines and Minerals under Republican governors Frank Lowden and Len Small. Based on this experience and other party activities, Medill referred to himself as a "GOP pet." Over the next fourteen years, Medill held executive positions with a number of coal mining companies outside the state. He returned to Illinois in 1938 and worked in Green's campaign for governor. His reward was directorship, once again, of the Department of Mines and Minerals in 1941, reporting to the governor and the State Mining Board.

Medill followed the mantra of the Green administration by running a tight ship that kept the party and administration closely aligned with high officials of coal mining companies. He also worked to keep regional and local officials of the United Mine Workers of America happy. The

UMWA supported his candidacy for director. Medill managed control of the department through a network of fourteen inspectors who spent most of their time moving from one mine to another, performing inspections according to procedures, and preparing reports that were filed with the department. Medill left the reading of reports to an assistant.

Coal was critical to the war effort of the United States, and from 1942 through much of 1945 the objective in Illinois was to keep mines producing at the highest levels, without regard for issues such as safety. The emphasis on production worked to the advantage of mine owners and to miners who had good paying jobs.

As political appointees, mine inspectors were part of the Green Machine and were expected to remember how they got their jobs.[13] Most inspectors complied with occasional political assignments or special requests from the department. An inspector's job was to make sure nothing stopped full production of coal. If safety complaints got out of hand, fixing them meant mine operators had to spend money and maybe face slowdowns. Medill's standing with Green and his associates depended on how smoothly the mines operated, how much they produced, and how little trouble they caused politically. If an inspector failed to toe the line, someone more amenable replaced him.

Given the department's attention to political matters, the request for help in raising funds for the Chicago mayoral campaign received a positive response. Medill eagerly joined the push for donations. Later, he explained his motivation in these terms: "I was sufficiently interested in the campaign to do whatever I could do to wipe out the Kelly-Nash machine and the New Deal down at Washington, and [felt] that the wiping out of the Kelly-Nash machine, if it could be done, would be a step in that direction."[14]

Medill called a meeting of mine inspectors and other department employees for 31 January 1947. They convened in Springfield at the mine rescue station, property owned by the state of Illinois. Most of the inspectors attended, including Driscoll Scanlan, who had been a pain in Medill's side for a number of years. Scanlan, one of the first inspectors appointed by Green, believed his duty was to perform inspections carefully and to report his finding without concern for the owner's pocketbook or for Medill's relationship with Green. He found multiple safety problems at Centralia mine No. 5, and he dutifully pointed out how lives were at stake. Additionally, he supported efforts by miners in Centralia to take their concerns to mine owners and department officials. Scanlan and

Medill clashed a number of times over the department's unwillingness to apply pressure to mine owners. At one point, Medill threatened to fire Scanlan. The state senator serving Centralia, a sponsor of Scanlan, refused to agree with Medill, and Scanlan kept his job.

Reports from the meeting claimed that Medill said his department had to raise $25,000 for the campaign, a figure demanded by "the boys."[15] Medill later admitted the $25,000 figure was his, not from campaign officials. He stated that the only way to reach that sum was to contact coal mine owners. Medill offered to contact the large mine owners for contributions but wanted inspectors to call on small and independent mine companies. The effect of inspectors making political contribution calls was to remind owners that state laws gave inspectors authority to close down mines for safety reasons. In the minds of some, this constituted a shakedown.

According to Medill's version of the meeting, he said, "I personally am going to contribute to that campaign fund. If you find anyone sufficiently interested in the campaign in Chicago that are willing to contribute, tell them to send their checks to the 'Root for Mayor' campaign in Chicago, to headquarters, not to me." Medill said that he did not direct anyone to call on specific owners and that "everything has to be voluntary."[16] Suggested amounts for contributions were $1,000 or more from large owners down to $100 for small operators. Scanlan had the impression that operators were being asked to make contributions to even the score for favors provided by the Department of Mines and Minerals.

The scheme backfired on Medill. On 2 March, Mark Saunders, director of the Illinois Department of Finance and a close associate of Green, called Medill to tell him of complaints received about the solicitations. Saunders said, "We have received complaints in the governor's office and I heard complaints on the floor of the House this morning that you are putting pressure and your inspectors are putting pressure on the coal companies for donations to the campaign fund. If you are doing that I want you to stop it immediately." Medill called a meeting for 7 March at which he instructed inspectors to stop soliciting contributions.[17]

Not all mine owners had appreciated the contact from inspectors, and one blew the whistle. Louis F. Lumaghi Jr., operator of a mine near Collinsville, wrote Medill on 15 March, and a copy of the letter went to the St. Louis Post-Dispatch. Lumaghi said a mine inspector told him he had been instructed to solicit contributions ranging from $100 to $500. Lumaghi wrote, "The state mine inspectors in Illinois are entrusted with the duty of enforcing the mining laws to protect the lives of the men who work in the mines. They have wide powers in keeping with these responsibilities, even to the power of closing a mine if in their opinion it is not being safely operated. Under these circumstances we do not consider it proper for them to solicit contributions from companies whose mines they inspect and we will not make any such contribution."[18]

Contacted by the newspaper, Medill admitted there had been complaints, adding, "A number of my men voluntarily sent in contributions. I told them if they found anybody who wanted to kick in, good. But I've never authorized any solicitations." The paper also asked Green for a comment, and he said, "This is the first I've heard of this matter." He promised an investigation, adding, "I consider acceptance of a voluntary contribution quite proper, but I would certainly frown on any attempt to put pressure on the mine owners." An article appeared in the *Post-Dispatch* on 19 March providing details of the solicitation request and result. Scanlan, suspected as the source of reports from the Medill meetings, said he found the contribution program offensive and he did not participate. He quoted Medill as telling inspectors that as long as the "boss" was satisfied, he had no worries about revelations. By the "boss," he meant Green.[19]

To the surprise of no one, Martin Kennelly won the February Democratic primary election in Chicago. Jack Arvey, party chairman, had nailed down Kennelly's selection shortly after the 1946 elections. Party leaders reluctantly accepted Arvey's choice, and the strategy behind it, so the only task remaining was to stiffen the resolve of the machine to elect the nonpolitical candidate. Arvey had concluded that the machine and Democratic dominance in the city would be at risk if Mayor Kelly sought reelection. To feed the public desire for someone without ties to the organization, Arvey completed the turnaround in record time. Historians concluded that he probably saved the organization from destruction by his bold choice.

Kennelly's election was anything but assured, however. The elections of 1946 revealed a serious lack of machine discipline and ability to turn out winning vote totals. Republicans believed they had Democrats on the run in Chicago, but Arvey had outfoxed the GOP. Against Mayor Kelly, the Republican candidate Russell Root presumably would have momentum and public sympathy. However, Republican chances would be diminished by attacking Kennelly, a civic-minded businessman whose claim to fame was building Allied Van Lines and serving as head of the

Red Cross with no visible ties to the history of the machine. In an attempt to reassure party regulars that the machine would survive, Mayor Kelly said they could support Kennelly because he "was not a reformer."[20]

What kind of instructions did Arvey give Kennelly on issues of importance to the organization as the campaign got under way? He said he told Kennelly: "The only thing I ask of you is that you help the Democratic Party as much as you can in a decent way. We want the patronage when a Democrat can fill the job. I am not talking about cabinet appointments or your own personal appointments. Get the best men you can for those. We want you to get the best. That's the way you can help the party the most. You're our showcase. If you do well, then we'll look good. All I ask is that you be loyal to the party—don't make an alliance with the Republicans."[21] That may not have reassured Kennelly, who had concerns when rubbing elbows with aldermen, precinct captains, and those who got out the votes.

With Kennelly having no past ties to the Chicago political machine, Republicans had less to say about corruption and graft than they would have if Kelly had been on the ticket. Instead, the GOP campaign focused on themes more suited to a campaign for federal office, such as would be heard often during 1948. Candidate Root told a radio audience that if elected, he would use his influence to elect a Republican president in 1948 and work against a third world war. He labeled Democrats the "war party" and said the Chicago election was a referendum on war. Republicans said a victory would indicate that citizens did not want a continuation of "war, waste, and broken promises." Kennelly, who for the most part ran a gentlemanly campaign that avoided contentious accusations, focused mostly on local issues and sidestepped discussions of national policy.[22] He won the mayor's job with 58 percent of the vote.

POLITICAL EXPLOSION IN CENTRALIA

For as long as anyone could remember, Centralia coal mine No. 5 had been dusty and dirty. Coal dust caused miners to choke and cough, and often their eyes watered and itched as the dust filled the air underground. Beyond personal irritations, coal dust was potentially deadly. If allowed to accumulate, dust could be ignited by a variety of means—cigarettes, lighted matches, explosives, malfunctioning equipment—causing an explosion that could carry throughout the mine, killing and injuring workers. With emphasis on production at all cost during the war, safety received low priority.

Everyone involved in mining coal knew the dangers. They could see them every day at work. Inspectors mentioned them in their reports. Mine supervisors listened to complaints. Miners talked about them and brought the subject up at union meetings. Owners knew they were courting disaster, and public officials crossed their fingers, hoping that nothing serious would happen.

After his appointment in 1941, state inspector Driscoll Scanlan had called attention every few months to serious safety problems at Centralia No. 5, especially dust but also including insufficient timbering in the mine roof and poor ventilation. Officials of the Mines and Minerals Department in Springfield paid little attention to his pleadings for improvements. They considered Scanlan a troublemaker and union sympathizer.[23]

In March 1946, Centralia local union members lost patience with disinterested officials and decided to write a letter to Governor Green. Little did the writers realize that the letter would resonate through the elections of 1948 and in history books. Union members asked fellow miner William E. Rowekamp, local recording secretary, to draft the correspondence. It contained complaints about poor treatment by officials and lack of response to safety concerns and summarized their fears to the governor. The first two paragraphs read:

> We the officers of Local, Union No. 52, UMWA have been instructed by the members of Local, Union No. 52 to write a letter to you in protest against the negligence and unfair practices of our Department of Mines and Minerals. But before we go any further, we want you to know that this is not a protest against Mr. Driscoll Scanlan, the State Mine Inspector in this district. Mr. Scanlan is the best inspector that ever came to our mine, he is honest, of good character and a good mining man, he writes his reports just as he finds the mine. But your Mining Board will not let him enforce the law or take the necessary action to protect our lives and health. This protest is against the men above Mr. Scanlan in your Department of Mines and Minerals.
>
> In fact, Governor Green this is a plea to you, to please save our lives, to please make the Department of Mines and Minerals enforce the laws at No. 5 mine of the Centralia Coal Company, at Centralia, Illinois, at which mine we are employees before we have a dust explosion at this mine like just happened in Kentucky and West VA.[24]

This became known as the "please save our lives" letter. After receiving it, one of the governor's three secretaries wrote a memo to Robert Medill, saying, "I have read the letter and the report of the State Mine Inspector very carefully and it is my opinion that the Governor may be subjected to very severe criticism in the event that the facts complained of are true and that as a result of this condition some serious accident occurs at the mine. Will you kindly have this complaint carefully investigated so I can call the report of the investigation to the Governor's attention at the same time I will show him this letter?"[25] Medill dismissed the letter as overly excitable and recommended that the governor tell the union local that he was referring the matter to the State Mining Board. That is what the governor did, along with sending a letter to union officials thanking them for writing.

More than a year later, on 18 and 19 March 1947, Scanlan, accompanied by supervisors, routinely inspected the Centralia mine. To his surprise, he learned a number of improvements in safety conditions had been made or were planned. In his report, Scanlan sounded optimistic, stating, "On my inspection . . . I found the mine in better condition than I had found it in a long time."[26]

A week later on Tuesday, 25 March, the routine at Centralia No. 5 for workers who came from all over the region began without incident and continued as usual until near the end of the day shift. As shift operations wound down after 3 P.M., drillers and shot-firers prepared to detonate explosives that would blast coal from the faces of the mine for the next shift of miners to process. Law required that no charges could be detonated until all normal face operations ended and men were headed toward the hoisting shaft or were already on top. Just before 3:26 P.M., operations ended and firers received the signal to light the fuses after safety requirements had been met. Workers knew they had at least ten minutes to reach safety before fuses were lighted.[27]

As 142 miners began moving to the shaft and the cage that took them to the top, an explosion tore through the mine. Days later, after countless rescue missions and endless hours of sorrowful waiting by relatives and friends, officials said 111 workers had died in one of the worst mine disasters in Illinois history. Among the dead were three of the four men who had signed the "please save our lives" letter to Green. Investigators later agreed the explosion had ignited coal dust and spread the blast throughout the mine.

One of the first to reach the mine after the explosion was Scanlan. He took charge of initial rescue efforts and spoke to relatives, friends, and newspaper and radio reporters. The press kept close watch for days and reported every rumor, conversation with survivors, and official reports.

Suffering from a severe cold, Green remained in Chicago, where he summoned state resources to care for survivors and injured. Medill hurried to Centralia by automobile. Federal Bureau of Mines officials assisted in rescue operations, as did employees of the state mining department. Political reaction occurred quickly, giving a hint of what was to come. State representative Paul Powell, in Springfield for the legislative session, said Democrats would demand an investigation by Green.

Emotional reactions closely followed first reports of an explosion and casualties. The *St. Louis Post-Dispatch* said in an editorial, "The blood of the men who lost their lives in the mine disaster at Centralia is on the hands of the mine operators who continued to run the mine in the face of repeated warnings of an 'explosion hazard.' Gov. Green cannot bring back the lives of the entombed. He cannot comfort the grief-stricken survivors. But there is one thing he can do: He can find out why this mine was not closed in accordance with repeated warnings."[28]

It did not take long for elected officials in Washington to react. Republican senator C. Wayland Brooks cosponsored a resolution demanding an inquiry into the failure of federal officials to enforce safety regulations at No. 5. The target of this partisan approach was President Truman. In support of his resolution, Brooks said the government "has become so all-powerful in the last 15 years" that it should be held accountable for the dead. Taking a decidedly different approach, Democratic senator Scott Lucas said safety violations were nothing new. The resolution, toned down a bit by Democrats, passed on a voice vote.[29]

Two days after the explosion, public disclosure of documents, including the "please save our lives" letter, prompted Democratic state representative Carl Preihs of Pana to call for impeachment of Green if it was determined that the governor had "neglected or refused to act." Green, still sick in Chicago, said he had turned the miners' letter over to the Department of Mines and Minerals and "as far as my office was concerned, that seemed to end it right there."[30]

After all the bodies had been identified, the official toll of 111 killed was announced on Friday. Families and survivors began the grim business of funerals and burials, overflowing local churches and resulting in days of back-to-back services. These solemn moments were interrupted periodically as the political situation warmed. Three separate investigations and inquiries were announced within a few days of the tragedy:

(1) Green formed a governor's fact-finding committee; (2) legislators agreed on a public inquiry; and (3) a special subcommittee of the U.S. Senate scheduled hearings, including three days in Centralia. The circus was about to begin.

Anticipating these opportunities for testimony, Medill and Scanlan began a bitter exchange in public statements, interviews, and press conferences. With the official toll established, Scanlan attacked Medill in an interview published by the *Post-Dispatch*.[31] He expressed resentment about the use of mine inspectors as political campaign fund-raisers and accused Medill of mishandling the use of rescue workers. Medill defended his actions.

Shortly after the exchange, Green sent a telegram to Medill directing him to conduct a survey of all coal mines in Illinois to determine whether any were violating safety regulations and Illinois law. The governor said, "In the meantime I direct that you communicate immediately with each mine inspector in the 14 districts of Illinois. If in their judgment there is any mine in their district which is not now operating with proper protection for workers, you will advise the Federal Coal Mines Administration of that fact and request that the federal operators not permit those mines to open Monday."[32]

Sometime during the weekend after the disaster, Green decided Medill had to go. However, he did not tell the director immediately. Green went to Centralia on Tuesday, 1 April, for the first time after the explosion to address the initial session of his fact-finding committee. He told the group to "pull no punches." Afterward, Green announced that Medill had resigned "for the good of the service."

Free of restraints, Medill stepped up personal attacks on Scanlan, only to be followed by Scanlan's rebuttals. All of this occurred as the fact-finding committee began deliberations and U.S. senators—Guy Cordon of Oregon, Henry Dworshak of Idaho, and Joseph O'Mahoney of Wyoming—started subcommittee hearings in Centralia. Green did not appear at any of the inquiries, nor was he summoned to testify. Fact-finders exonerated almost everyone from blame, except Scanlan, who they said had held the authority to close the mine and should have used it. Scanlan told the committee, "If I had closed the mine, Director Medill would have sent someone here to reopen it."[33] That did not satisfy the fact-finders, who were looking for a scapegoat.

For the Centralia hearings, the U.S. senators called dozens of people to testify, asked pointed questions of Scanlan and Medill, and in the end called for Congress to take action on a few suggestions. The senators avoided placing blame, and Congress ignored the recommendations.

The state legislative investigation provided political fireworks, as might be expected with both Republicans and Democrats on the committee. From the beginning, partisan bickering prevailed. Republicans controlled both the House and Senate and decided to put fewer Democrats on the committee. Democrats said representation should be equal if the inquiry was to be nonpartisan. House Democrats included Powell and Preihs, whose earlier statements about the GOP administration left little doubt of their attitudes. Powell, assuming the role of vocal leader of the committee minority, called the process a Republican "whitewash." Democrats called for Green to appear, but Republicans issued no request.

The most dramatic moment of the legislative committee sessions occurred toward the end of deliberations when Scanlan read a prepared statement. This was to be the last opportunity to state his case before investigating panels. His comments drew on personal files that included nonpublic records, correspondence, inspection reports, and public statements, many of which he had provided to newspapers. Scanlan saved his most aggressive comments for Medill, claiming that the director's motivations in dealings with inspectors and mine owners were political and had no relationship to concern for miners.[34] Regardless, every observer knew that Medill worked for Green. The governor could not avoid being implicated.

Before the committee closed its investigation, Democrats walked out, primarily because the majority refused to allow testimony about political contributions to the Chicago mayoral race. Powell responded, "We should be permitted to find out if politics played a part in this disaster so we can make laws to correct those conditions. If we can't do this I'm walking out."[35] Democrats issued a minority report, which took issue with only a few of the majority's recommendations for legislation but provided plentiful partisan rhetoric.

The majority's reaction to injecting "politics" into the investigation prompted the *St. Louis Star-Times* to address the issue on its editorial page. After stating that politics had been involved in the case of the No. 5 mine, the editorial added, "The State Department of Mines and Minerals, which was chiefly responsible, is politically organized, after all; its members are appointed not without considerable regard for partisanship. Evidences of political strings are plain. How can this committee be so sure they weren't pulled? How, in fact, can they possibly ignore the politics written in screamingly tall letters all over this disaster?"[36]

While Medill and Scanlan grabbed most of the headlines about controversies, the underlying political story was about Green. As became obvious later, he remained an inviting target of newspaper editorial pages and Democrats.

1948 LINEUP TAKES SHAPE

Nearly lost during the Centralia mine saga, at least outside of Chicago, was that Martin Kennelly became the thirty-eighth mayor of Chicago in the 1 April election, crushing the Republican Russell Root, 58 percent to 42 percent. Jack Arvey and Kennelly had helped restore the Democratic machine's election prowess. After Kennelly's victory, the next objective was the 1948 election. There was little time to rest. Having succeeded with the selection of non-machine candidate Kennelly, Arvey could see the importance of choosing other candidates with similar backgrounds as a means of winning elections and energizing the machine.

Arvey had not missed the campaign by Paul Douglas for a position on the 1948 Democratic ticket, preferably for U.S. senator. In fact, Arvey had his eye on Douglas from earlier experiences. The two had been Chicago City Council members together before each served in World War II. Arvey recalled, "I served in the city council with Douglas. I loved him. We exchanged affectionate greetings. I had every confidence in him. There was no man I knew of who had a higher sense of integrity, but he was not a practical man. In the council he was not open to compromise. He was an advocate more than he was an administrator. He had an academic background which was marvelous. He was intelligent, knowledgeable. . . . I worked with Douglas as an alderman [and] . . . at times he would turn to me and say, 'Does the chairman of the finance committee assure me that this contract is in the best interests of the city?' Invariably, when I gave him my word, he would do it. But Douglas was an advocate. He'd take a position and he'd hold to it tenaciously, stubbornly."[37]

That statement, and Douglas's long-standing image as a non-player with the Chicago machine, gave proof to the claim that Arvey could see Douglas in the Washington environment but not in Springfield as governor. A freshman U.S. senator had no seniority, no patronage, and limited political power, which was fine with Arvey. However, trying to do business with Douglas as governor on such matters as patronage and open housing would have been impossible for the party organization.

His unwillingness to compromise might be a matter of principle in Washington but in the state capital would bring deal-making to a halt. He also knew that Douglas made others in the organization extremely nervous based on their recollections of him as an alderman.[38]

With Douglas as a candidate for the Senate against the *Chicago Tribune*'s favorite Curly Brooks, Arvey believed that the Democrat's background before he was on the Chicago City Council could be an embarrassment.[39] Douglas had a distinguished academic record, including selection as Phi Beta Kappa at Bowdoin College, where he graduated in 1913. He earned a master's and a PhD degree in economics at Columbia University and built a reputation as a productive scholar, excellent teacher, and civic activist. He became intrigued with communism in the 1920s, although he rejected the movement's extremism and leaned more toward socialism and pacifism. In 1932, Douglas supported socialist Norman Thomas for president but embraced much of the Roosevelt public policy agenda. During that time, he published widely on social issues in support of the Social Security Act, the Wagner Act, and the Fair Labor Standards Act. He was a longtime friend of labor and associated with organizations that leaned far to the left philosophically. Such were the issues that Robert McCormick and his *Tribune* would parade before the paper's readership with cries of alarm.

Arvey had Douglas picked for the Senate nomination long before many others reached the same conclusion. He explained, "I was sure that Governor Green could be beaten and I thought Brooks could if we got the right man. I had made up my mind in 1946 that it should be Paul Douglas against Brooks. In 1946, Douglas came to a mass meeting in uniform. He did not make a speech but he waved a greeting to the crowd. I saw his withered [left] hand. Brooks never made a speech without saying, 'I got shrapnel in my back at Chateau-Thierry and I learned what it means to serve our country.' I knew the shattered hand would dispose of that."[40]

Douglas had his objective clearly in mind, too: politics. He had returned from the military to his position on the faculty at the University of Chicago, where he found that changes in the department had put conservative economists in the majority. His discontent cast doubt on a future in the classroom and increased Douglas's determination to enter politics.[41] During the school year early in 1947, he began a routine of making public appearances in the Chicago area on weeknights and in downstate Illinois on weekends. In the summer, he used vacation time to pound the pavement. He discovered support outside Chicago and friendly audiences in ethnic parts of the city. Arvey noticed and recognized the determination and promise in Douglas.

That left the question: Who to slate for governor?

Before 1947, Adlai E. Stevenson II had hardly flirted with running for public office in Illinois. In fact, he barely had been in the state. He had received an undergraduate degree at Princeton University and a law degree from Northwestern University in 1926. In the following twenty years, Stevenson spent about half his time practicing law in Chicago and the other half in Washington. In 1942, his name was kicked around in Illinois as a possible Democratic candidate for the U.S. Senate; however, it was little more than wishful thinking. He had no standing with the state Democratic organization and had not been particularly active in party affairs. In 1944, he expressed interest in running for governor against incumbent Dwight Green. A few newspaper people and friends circulated his name, but nothing happened. An officer in the Marines, Paul Douglas of Chicago, wrote Stevenson with encouragement. Stevenson responded that he was "still very indecisive" about a political career.[42]

The closest Stevenson came to public affairs activity in Illinois between 1926 and 1946 had nothing directly to do with local politics. Soon after graduation from law school, Stevenson joined the Chicago firm that became known as Sidley and Austin. From 1927 to 1933, he practiced law and enjoyed a position of political royalty in Illinois. His grandfather, Adlai E. Stevenson I, had served as a downstate congressman from Illinois, then as vice president in the Grover Cleveland administration from 1893 to 1897. Stevenson's father, Lewis, had held the office of Illinois secretary of state from 1914 to 1917. By virtue of Lewis's marriage, the Stevenson family owned a minority interest in the *Bloomington Pantagraph*, which circulated in his hometown.[43]

Stevenson first spent time in Washington from 1933 to 1936, working in the Agricultural Adjustment Administration and other minor roles during the early years of the New Deal. He returned to the Sidley firm in 1936. Beyond practicing law, Stevenson's primary interest was in foreign affairs, which stemmed mostly from involvement with the Chicago Council on Foreign Relations.[44] Another Chicago-based activity occurred in 1940 with the United States at arm's length from the growing war in Europe: he became an official of the Chicago branch of the Committee to Defend America by Aiding the Allies, otherwise known as the White Committee. Kansas newspaper editor and publisher William Allen White directed the national organization. The committee fought to have the nation's Neutrality Act revised to allow support of Allied resistance to Germany.[45]

As war drew closer, Stevenson's interest in his law practice lagged, and he lobbied for a position in the Roosevelt administration. After interviewing for several jobs early in 1941, he joined the Department of the Navy, headed by Republican Frank Knox, part owner of the *Chicago Daily News* and vice presidential candidate in 1936.[46] Knox appointed Stevenson principal attorney in the secretary's office. For the balance of the war years, Stevenson traveled extensively abroad on diplomatic assignments. In 1943, he took a leave of absence from the Department of Navy to head an economic mission to Italy.

With the war's conclusion, Stevenson's administrative duties in Washington ended. Preferring not to practice law in Chicago again, at least not immediately, he sought a role in the development of the United Nations.[47] Early in 1945 he became a special assistant to the secretary of state and served as press officer at the United Nations Conference on International Organization. In September, President Truman appointed Stevenson as deputy to Edward R. Stettinius Jr., the American delegate to the U.N. Preparatory Commission. When Stettinius fell ill, Stevenson served as delegate, earning applause for efforts to finish the commission's work successfully. Stevenson hoped his experience would qualify him as a delegate to the first U.N. session in 1946. However, in spite of good marks and support within the Truman administration, he failed to be selected. Instead, he was chosen as a "senior advisor." Truman later appointed Stevenson as an alternate delegate to the second part of the first session. At the end of 1946, Stevenson returned to Illinois and rejoined the Sidley law firm.

Stevenson wanted to run for the U.S. Senate in 1948. His lack of contacts within the Chicago machine, specifically Jack Arvey, presented one obstacle. Also, he had little exposure across the state. Still committed to a run, Stevenson turned down job offers outside Illinois, saying he wanted to "try out" the political situation in the state.

Stevenson had other liabilities that worked against a statewide candidacy. His frequent absence from Illinois would certainly be a target for Republicans wanting to belittle his qualifications. Isolationist and anti–New Deal factions would concentrate on his ties to the Roosevelt and Truman administrations. Those same parties, likely led by the *Tribune*, would sneer at Stevenson's internationalist leanings. Stevenson thought those potential negatives actually were positives for his Senate candidacy.

Political friends of Stevenson—some who would be allied with him through the presidential races of the 1950s—began talking up their man for the Senate about mid-1947. They had a long way to go. Arvey, commenting later, said he knew little about Stevenson. The first mention of Stevenson to Arvey as a possibility for any position on the 1948 ticket occurred in the spring, when Arvey met with a number of people in Washington.[48] That does not mean Stevenson's name was a complete blank to Arvey. His name could have come up in private conversations.

While Arvey was in Washington, Senator Scott Lucas arranged a meeting with the express purpose to hear from people who had firsthand knowledge of Stevenson's government experience.[49] Invited to participate in the luncheon were James Byrnes, who had recently stepped down as secretary of state, Senator Thomas Connally of Texas, and Senator Arthur Vandenberg of Michigan. With the group gathered, Lucas posed the question about Stevenson's fitness to serve in the Senate. According to Lucas, all assembled spoke well of Stevenson. Arvey recalled a private moment with Byrnes at lunch, during which the Democratic statesman said, "I have had many dealings with him. He is an ideal man for this job."

Following promotional efforts by his friends in Illinois, Stevenson became increasingly vocal about running for the Senate. In October, recognizing that the Democratic Party apparatus would make decisions on candidates toward the end of the year, he issued a statement saying he would accept the nomination if offered. Interestingly, he made the announcement from New York City, not Chicago.[50] Stevenson also made it clear to anyone who would listen that he was not interested in seeking the governorship.

By this time, a small group of Illinoisans, including prominent Republicans, were working their connections in behalf of Stevenson's candidacy. These included Hermon Dunlap "Dutch" Smith, a North Shore insurance executive active in Republican Party affairs. Democrats at work included Laird Bell, Louis Kohn, and Stephen A. Mitchell, none of whom had a record of Democratic Party activism.[51]

Paul Douglas, on the other hand, adopted a tactic he felt would scare machine Democrats sufficiently to put him in line for the Senate seat. He mentioned broadly that he might be interested in running for governor. Douglas knew that party leaders who feared him as governor would become allies in pushing him toward the Senate.

Arvey had Douglas slated for senator well before asking the state Democratic Central Committee for a decision, but he was less settled on a candidate for governor. Arvey knew what he wanted but had not enough familiarity with Stevenson for a recommendation: "I wanted someone of his [Stevenson's] type. I wanted a Democrat who had not been involved in what you call machine politics, but with the organization. . . . I knew we had a tough fight and I looked around for people to bring in to add to the organization, to enhance the image of the organization. I hardly knew Stevenson, but I knew of him. I knew what he stood for."[52]

When Arvey spoke of a "tough fight," he did not need a crystal ball to understand the hill Democrats had to climb in 1948. As he watched the national political picture, Arvey had reached a conclusion that the party needed someone stronger than Truman running for president. The national picture made Democrats uneasy about state chances in 1948. This defeatist attitude actually strengthened Arvey at the moment he made a recommendation, because officials had no better ideas. He knew something had to change for Democrats to win, and party officials gave him full authority to pick the candidates.[53]

Although Arvey naturally focused attention on Chicago and Cook County, he was a realist who knew the party's fortunes depended on an alliance with downstate Democrats. He could not afford to ignore the likes of Paul Powell and John Stelle, who knew how to trade needed votes for political favors. Arvey had no intention of turning his back on what the two men could deliver—votes.

John Stelle had not won an elective office since 1936 and had suffered an ignominious loss for governor in the Democratic primary election of 1940. By all measures, he should have been politically dead and fully retired at his home in McLeansboro. However, events occurred in the early 1940s that helped rebuild his political reputation in Illinois.

After service in the military during World War I, Stelle became active in the American Legion, a strong force in state and national political affairs. Through contacts in the Legion, he played a major role in passage of the GI Bill by Congress in 1944.[54] That work opened the door to his selection as national commander of the politically potent organization in 1945.[55]

Another 1945 victory for Stelle occurred in concert with Paul Powell of Vienna, who served as assistant minority leader for Democrats in the House of Representatives. Working across the partisan aisle—the only way for Democrats to pass any legislation in those days—and with the help of Stelle, Powell rounded up enough Democrats and Republicans to pass the Illinois Harness Racing Act.[56] Until passage, harness racing was

restricted to downstate county fairs and the annual state fair in Springfield. The law changed harness racing forever, legalizing race meetings
and pari-mutuel betting in all months but July and August. Governor
Green signed the bill and was applauded by the state organization of
county fairs. Stelle and Powell made fortunes together in racing venues
over the next twenty years.

With Democrats in such disarray across Illinois, why did Stelle hang
around and why did Powell bother with the ex-governor? It was because
they shared interests in public policies that benefited southern Illinois. They
knew the winds of change would blow again and Democrats would hold
positions of power. No single party dominated the state scene for long.

There were other political realities at work. The 1901 apportionment
of legislative districts made it possible for downstate Illinois to be a full
participant in power politics, despite a declining percentage of state population. For more than fifty years, rural parts of downstate lost population
while Cook County and urban areas such as Peoria, Alton, and East
St. Louis gained heavily. Downstate interests of both parties benefited
from the old provisions that distributed seats based on a much more
agrarian society than existed in the 1940s and 1950s. This meant Chicago
organization interests could dominate local politics and influence statewide contests, but when it came to getting favorable state programs and
appropriations, the organization needed help. That is how Stelle came
to power in the early 1930s. He represented votes that gave downstate
interests leverage far beyond the area's strength of population. He told a
Horner biographer, "There I was three hundred miles south of Chicago.
I had to have a foothold in Chicago. Without it I would have been dead
as a mackerel."[57]

The partnership of Chicago and downstate Democratic legislators
meant benefits in patronage and programs. Democrats in southern Illinois could do little on their own and were always on the lookout for
cooperative ventures. Stelle thrived in this environment, and he believed
his role should be as organizational head of downstate Democrats during
the campaign. In 1947, downstate pro-Horner Democrats sought a leader
who could stifle Stelle's ambition. The logical choice was Lucas, a downstate resident who also had been a strong supporter of Henry Horner. A
showdown for leadership came in the fall of 1947.

Party leaders met in Springfield to find a leader who could bring
cohesion to the party riddled by Republican gains since 1940. When
Stelle made his move at a meeting of the Democratic state committee,

members rebuffed him by appointing a downstate organization committee consisting of men loyal to Lucas.[58]

At the same committee meeting, members voiced support for Mayor Kennelly as a candidate for governor. While they knew Kennelly had no interest in running for governor—before slating was completed, he repeatedly turned down the party bid—leaders told newspaper reporters they wanted a gubernatorial candidate without ties to the Chicago organization. Powell, Stelle, and other southern Illinois Democrats began beating the drum for the U.S. attorney for eastern Illinois, Howard L. Doyle, as the favored candidate for governor, although they knew Doyle had no chance of being chosen.[59] Instead, Powell and Stelle wanted a deal with Arvey to slate downstate candidates for attorney general, lieutenant governor, treasurer, and auditor. With downstate residents in those job-rich positions, everybody would work to elect the top of the ticket, and Stelle and Powell would share in the spoils.

While Stevenson's advocates worked their connections—all outside the Chicago organization—he left Illinois in September for another session of the United Nations as alternate delegate. During that time, Stevenson believed that Lucas favored him for a Senate run. Actually, Lucas had begun thinking of Stevenson for governor, and in September he and Stevenson met in New York to discuss the campaign. Lucas recalled, "I presumed that he wanted to talk to me about the governorship of Illinois. However, after a brief exchange I learned to my great surprise that he wanted me to become a candidate for the governor's job, and at the same time he wanted to be the candidate for the United States Senate." Lucas said he would serve out his Senate term and would not be a candidate for governor, declaring, "Adlai, you are the man who should become the candidate for governor." Stevenson gave Lucas a flat "no."[60]

Except for an occasional appearance in the state during the next three months, Stevenson left Illinois political fortunes in the hands of others. They followed Stevenson's wish to run for the Senate. Until 15 November, none of Stevenson's backers had met with Arvey. When a few of them sat down with the political boss, he spoke glowingly of Paul Douglas as the logical candidate for the Senate, pointing out his campaign work downstate during the summer and his growing name recognition, all in contrast to Stevenson. Arvey did not mention the governor's race, leaving the delegation stunned and depressed.[61]

Arvey then asked for and got a meeting with Stevenson and Lucas, at which he suggested Stevenson run for governor. Stevenson said he was not interested. In a statement on 29 November, Lucas declined to be considered for governor. That left Arvey with few choices. He could twist Stevenson's arm, plead with Lucas, or find someone else.

In what appeared to be a stressful game of chicken where neither Stevenson nor Arvey backed down, the process moved into December. In less than a month, Arvey had to recommend a ticket to the slate-making committee. In another conversation, Arvey asked Stevenson's people for a casual meeting at a suburban home away from the party seats of power where he could talk to Stevenson's spouse, Ellen. While Stevenson played tennis, Arvey went to work on Stevenson's wife. Arvey commented, "I had to go convince his wife that he should run for governor."[62] However, when the social affair concluded, the parties were no closer to an agreement.

The moment of truth arrived on 30 December. The central committee planned to meet that afternoon and announce the slate the next day. Arvey and Stevenson conferred in the morning, with virtually no time left on the clock. Stevenson finally realized he had no chance of being chosen for the Senate. Others told him of the reality of his situation, including Ed Sidley, Stevenson's mentor at the law firm, and Lucas. Stevenson capitulated.

At 10 A.M. on 30 December, Lucas recalled in a memoir, he received a telephone call from Barnet Hodes, corporation counsel for the city of Chicago and an intimate of Stevenson. Hodes said Stevenson had called and wanted to be released from the commitment as the candidate for governor.[63] Hodes told Lucas, "You're the only man who can bring this fellow back into the fold." Both men were shell-shocked at Stevenson's about-face. Reached by phone, Stevenson agreed to meet with Hodes and Lucas. Lucas confronted Stevenson and declared, "You shouldn't do this. You can't do it and keep your self-respect. You can't let the Democrats of Illinois down at this late hour."[64] The discussion continued for some time, and Stevenson finally agreed to accept the endorsement. Lucas and Hodes stayed with Stevenson until the central committee met, to make sure another change of mind did not occur.

Arvey had his candidates. At the slating meeting that afternoon, the committee unanimously approved Paul Douglas for the Senate, and all but one person, an alderman, voted for Stevenson for governor. A few didn't vote. While the members bowed to Arvey's wishes, most had no hope that either man could win against incumbent Republicans. They had approved two candidates who had no ties to the organization, who had no record of successfully running for elective office statewide, and who offered no assurances they would do what the organization wanted. Arvey admitted the party's desperation worked to his advantage: "That helped me put him [Stevenson] across. There's no question about it, I took advantage of it. The same with Douglas. They figured it's a losing year. But I had my way because of it."[65]

The full slate of Democratic candidates contained intriguing choices, considering the territorial issues within the party. Three men chosen for state office resided in southern Illinois, validating the tactics of Powell and Stelle. They were Fred Harrison, a banker from Herrin, for treasurer; Ivan A. Elliott, a lawyer from Carmi, for attorney general; and Benjamin O. Cooper of East St. Louis, Secretary of State Edward J. Barrett's chief clerk and formerly head of the politically potent East Side Levee and Sanitary District, for auditor. Harrison, who fell ill, was replaced on the ballot by Ora Smith, a six-term member of the state House, from Biggsville in western Illinois. John Sherwood Dixon of Dixon, a lawyer and longtime Democratic Party worker in northern Illinois, was selected for lieutenant governor. Also on the ticket was incumbent secretary of state Barrett, of Wilmette, with a record of statewide election victories stretching from 1930.

Chicago Sun political columnist Milburn P. "Pete" Akers, writing with more than a little sarcasm, said, "Little Egypt, where John (100 Days) Stelle still prowls, did right well, thank you, in the Democratic slate-making. The far southern third of the state, with less population than three or four Chicago West Side wards, got three candidates endorsed." He added, "Eddie Barrett, seasoned campaigner and the party's best vote getter, who runs again for secretary of state, has to carry the load. Without him, the ticket would stand no more chance (on the basis of the downstate selections) than a snow ball in a blast furnace."[66]

The tough guys of Chicago politics who made up the slating committee agreed to support as candidate for governor Adlai Stevenson, who was more at home on the social circuit than in an election campaign, whose friends were more likely Republicans with large homes and bigger bank accounts than backroom deal makers with precinct captains as close associates, and who had spent so little time in Illinois that he hardly knew one Chicago ward from another. In Paul Douglas, they chose a candidate who had an anti-organization record in Chicago politics, whose background included a flirtation with communism and a level of comfort with socialism but also an enviable war record, and who probably supported public housing ideas that would bust Chicago's ethnic neighborhoods. Democrats had chosen candidates for the top two spots on the ticket who had not paid any serious political dues and had not worked their ways up in the seats of government. They had never worked the precincts. There was little hope that the two candidates liked each other and would coordinate campaigns. No wonder political experts expected the worst.

Meanwhile, on the Republican side, Dwight Green had his hands full of angry party members who believed they should have a shot at governor and Green should vanish after two terms. Some believed a messy primary election for governor could wreck the appearance of a smooth party operation. The result would be that Green would win, but a contested election would open wounds to public view and provide Democrats with campaign issues.

Adding to the public discussion of dissatisfaction with Green were newspapers around the state with Democratic Party leanings. They identified issues that might either disqualify Green for a third term or make him vulnerable to a strong Democratic challenger. Among subjects for Green's opponents, the *Chicago Sun* listed these: "His political conduct of the state's welfare institutions makes him vulnerable. So does his default on veterans' housing. His failure to achieve constitutional revision is of the same pattern as his unredeemed pledge to take the sales tax off food. His insistence on hoarding a huge state surplus while rejecting the pleas of distressed municipalities for aid is akin to his callous disregard of the needs of the public school system. There are other questions on which the governor, by action or by inaction, has created issues. His prostitution of civil service is one. His creation of a political machine, in direct violation of his 1940 campaign pledge, is another."[67]

As autumn passed, the early names for a Republican gubernatorial primary faded. Replacing them were two serious contenders: Lieutenant Governor Hugh Cross, who had split from the governor's camp after serving nearly two full terms with Green, and Warren Wright of Springfield, who was treasurer from 1941 to 1943 and who had run in the party primary against Senator Brooks in 1942. Cross and Wright both knew that neither could win a three-way race that included Green. From Green's standpoint, the more dangerous of the contenders was Cross, who for seven years had watched the governor at work and had been the Illinois Speaker of the House in 1939–40. The governor could expect Cross to launch a series of slashing attacks.

Further down on the Republican ticket, Green had another headache. State treasurer Richard Yates Rowe, an ally of Green who could not succeed himself in office, announced for secretary of state.[68] That brought Rowe in direct conflict with aspirations of at-large U.S. representative William Stratton, a strong vote-getter statewide with a record of several run-ins with the governor. Green had not greeted Stratton's previous candidacies kindly, believing him to be a soldier in the army of Brooks and likely to listen to the senator rather than to the governor when it came to patronage. In 1946, Green told Stratton that if he ran for the at-large congressional seat against Emily Douglas, Stratton would be slated for secretary of state in 1948. But Green had reneged before on promises, and Stratton was not reassured.

As expected, the Republican state central committee endorsed Green for governor and Brooks for the Senate.[69] While Brooks had the full support of the Republican organization, he was the only candidate on the primary ballot with opposition, token though it was. His opponent, William J. Baker, had run for several offices without much support and no victories. Chosen for other state offices were Rowe for lieutenant governor; Stratton for secretary of state; George F. Barrett for a third term as attorney general; incumbent auditor Arthur C. Lueder, who became ill before the primary and was replaced by Sinon A. Murray, a Chicago lawyer who had been administrative assistant in the auditor's office; and James Simpson Jr. of Lake County for treasurer.

Acting as if nothing threatened him for a third term, Green announced his candidacy in a 500-word statement a few days after the state committee endorsement. He said, "I invite the support of all the men and women of Illinois on my record as governor and on my pledge to continue a sound and progressive state government founded on experience, efficiency and economy." Green also addressed an issue on which he and Cross disagreed: distribution of state treasury money to needy communities. Cross believed the state should share its funds with municipalities. Green said in his statement, "We must meet the challenge of those who seek to cure the woes of inflation with New Deal measures which would raid the State Treasury, destroy our state's solvency, and inevitably increase the tax burden of the people of Illinois."[70] He would stress that point many times during the campaign.

With a few minor adjustments still to be made, both party lineups were in place for the fateful year of 1948. If Governor Green could convince Cross and Wright to drop out, it would be a primary election in April that would hardly draw flies.

NEWSPAPER WARS AND POLITICS

Daily news happenings in Illinois and surrounding states in the years leading to 1948 appeared primarily in newspapers. Television, in its infancy, had no impact. WGN television in Chicago first went on the air during 1948 with much ballyhoo from its parent, the *Tribune*, but few people had sets. Radio provided mostly a mixture of entertainment, national news, and rewrites of what appeared first in newspapers. The networks carried occasional live speeches, such as in October when Truman and Dewey campaigned in Chicago. The focus of magazines leaned toward photographs and snippets of news from across the nation. As for commentary, newspaper editorial pages got the heaviest reading and carried the most weight at election time. By any standards, daily newspapers in and around Illinois played a sizable role in the 1948 election outcomes.

The political leaning of a daily newspaper with large Illinois circulation often influenced the news content. Some of the hardest-hitting editorials followed staff-written stories that were designed to favor friendly candidates and disparage those deemed unworthy. Slanting the political news to suit an owner's or editor's taste reflected earlier trends in competitive American journalism, where increases in circulation sales were directly related to big black headlines. Street sales in urban centers accounted for large percentages of circulation, leading papers to use the boldest headlines with dramatic photographs. The word "objective" rarely was used to describe the work of editors and reporters.

Competition for advertising and circulation was fierce in cities where more than one newspaper existed. Publishers and editors made personal attacks on competitors and savaged their rivals in print. Newspapers had progressed somewhat from the days of the penny press and yellow journalism in the nineteenth and early twentieth centuries, but not greatly.

Newspapers serving Illinois readers in 1948 had well-known and opinionated owners. In the 1940s, few of the papers were parts of large chain operations. That meant owners, or their offspring, often lived in the cities where the papers were published and circulated. They were routinely involved in news and editorial decisions.

Characteristically, the largest papers with healthy circulation numbers had celebrity political reporters whose high visibility generated widespread attention to what they wrote. In general election years such as

1948, bylines of these writers appeared frequently, often slanting articles toward their paper's favorite candidates.

As 1948 began in Chicago, four influential daily newspapers served readers in the region, and in at least one instance well beyond the state's borders. The *Chicago Sun-Times* was owned by Marshall Field III.[71] Blessed with a large personal fortune, he started the *Sun* in December 1941. Field wanted to provide a different slant on the news in the morning field against the dominant *Tribune* and had sufficient personal funds to withstand losses. After running a deficit of $10 million, in 1947 Field bought the *Chicago Times* and merged it with the *Sun*. One chronicler of Chicago journalism wrote, "He [Field] possessed gilt-edged White House connections, the sympathy of organized labor, and a Chicago electorate in tune with his message."[72] While the *Sun-Times* provided an editorial slant counter to that of the *Tribune*, it did not have the circulation reach of its competition or the content heft.

The *Chicago Daily News*, owned by Knight Newspapers, was led editorially in Chicago by principal owner John S. Knight.[73] His organization bought the afternoon paper in 1944 after the death of publisher Frank Knox, who ran for vice president with Alf Landon in 1936. During the 1930s, the paper developed a reputation for aggressive reporting and won two Pulitzer Prizes. The *Chicago Herald-American*, owned by the Hearst chain of newspapers, was a lesser factor in political coverage and circulation in the 1940s.

The *Chicago Tribune*, owned by the family of Joseph Medill since 1855, was run by Medill's descendant Robert R. McCormick, also known as Colonel McCormick and by some members of his family as "Bertie." Of all papers in Chicago and surrounding territory, the *Tribune* had the largest circulation—more than 1 million daily and 1.3 million on Sundays—and advertising revenue. On several occasions in 1948, the paper announced new records in advertising and pages printed. By virtue of its wealth and the strong will and ego of McCormick, the paper also had a louder, strongly conservative voice than any of its competitors. Covering a huge territory promoted by the paper as "Chicagoland," news and editorial coverage reached from Kansas and Nebraska on the west, to the Canadian border on the north, to Ohio on the east, and to Kentucky, Tennessee, Arkansas, and Oklahoma on the south. The *Tribune* outsold all competition across the state of Illinois, except in some southern Illinois locations covered by St. Louis papers.

A common trait among Chicago newspapers was a continuous carping about competitors, especially owners and top editors. Because of its size and influence, the *Tribune* held the dubious honor of Enemy No. 1. Other Chicago papers ridiculed the *Tribune*'s sharp-edged and right-leaning editorials, but mostly they attempted to characterize McCormick as a mean-spirited scoundrel. The *Daily News* published a popular comic strip called "Colonel McCosmick," which ridiculed McCormick. The strip was discontinued after Knight purchased the paper. Unmoved by the attacks, McCormick spewed his own invective against competitors.[74]

This intramural warfare constituted a small percentage of time and effort among all Chicago papers. Major energy was devoted to coverage of and commentary on politics, reflecting the nature of life in Chicago and the desire of owners and editors to influence public officials. Hardly a day went by during 1948 without a page 1 headline devoted to politics in all of the city's papers. The runner-up usually was a crime story or a natural disaster. Considering the levels of creative politics in Chicago, Illinois, and the nation, there was no shortage of material. Throughout elections, the papers cast highly favored candidates in the best light and, conversely, published articles and editorials hinting at the darkest of intentions of the least favored. The *Sun-Times* had little good to say about Green or Brooks, making its preference for Stevenson and Douglas obvious. The *Tribune* disparaged Democratic candidates with labels such as "liberal," "New Dealer," and "internationalist." It frequently referred to Paul Douglas as "professor," assuming the word belittled the candidate. Meanwhile, the *Tribune* lavished praise on Green and Brooks.

Each of the papers put its top political writers on the front lines as campaigns expanded, often with determined editors providing support and guidance. Candidates knew the reporters' political proclivities and sought them for advice and counsel while hoping for favorable stories. They rewarded certain reporters with exclusive interviews, advance copies of speeches, and inside information about opponents. In 1948, there was nothing subtle about it, and no apologies were offered.

At the *Daily News*, the principal political reporter was Charles Wheeler, a longtime Chicagoan familiar with the ways of Illinois politics.[75] Wheeler's favoritism for Stevenson as governor comes clear in John Bartlow Martin's biography of Stevenson. Martin relates several instances where Wheeler wrote articles promoting Stevenson's candidacy before party officials chose him.

Stevenson and Douglas had favorite reporters and columnists in Chicago who were aligned either by personal persuasion or by newspaper loyalty to any candidate not favored by the *Tribune*. During the weeks when Stevenson could not make up his mind about running for governor, he consulted Pete Akers, managing editor and political columnist for the *Sun* before it merged with the *Times* and former worker in the Democratic administration of Governor Horner.[76] The *Sun* leaned more than slightly toward Democrats, especially those independent of the Chicago political machine. The paper's editorials in the last months of 1947, before selection of Stevenson and Douglas, claimed Green had a shoddy record as Illinois chief executive. The *Sun* exulted with a huge banner headline when the Democratic slating committee chose Stevenson and Douglas and provided a primer on issues that degraded the Green administration.[77]

Among the best-known political editors of the day was John Dreiske of the *Sun-Times*. He served as the paper's political editor during most of the 1940s and drew applause from colleagues, competitors, and politicians for his informative and incisive political commentary built on solid sources. While Dreiske had his favorites, they did not fall into carefully crafted partisan categories.

Editors at the *Tribune* had many resources from which to choose for political coverage. On Illinois subjects, two reporters got choice assignments. George Tagge was anointed by the *Tribune* hierarchy to carry torches for Green and Brooks. Tagge worked among legislators in Springfield for McCormick's agenda or on the stump for candidates who spoke the *Tribune*'s language. He began his journalism career in Chicago with the City News Bureau, home base for many of the city's notable reporters. He graduated to the *Tribune* and shortly became its political editor.[78] His favorite subject beyond Green was Jack Arvey, whom Tagge and the *Tribune* respected and feared for his political agility. Tagge's stories on Arvey often were designed to paint the operative as unprincipled.

Sharing political assignments with Tagge was Robert Howard, who joined the *Tribune* just before the 1948 campaign after acclaimed reporting for the Associated Press and the *Sun*.[79] The *Tribune* opened a full-time office in Springfield before the 1948 elections with Howard in residence. During 1948, he worked out of Chicago frequently, covering a variety of political stories, sometimes backing up Tagge on Green and writing about Brooks and other Republicans running for state office.

Walter Trohan, long associated with the *Tribune*'s Washington staff, wrote extensively about the paper's favorite candidates during 1948. He began a journalistic career in Chicago with the City News Bureau. As a young reporter, he was first on the scene of the infamous St. Valentine's Day Massacre when Al Capone's gang gunned down members of the rival Bugs Moran outfit. Part of Trohan's role in 1948 was to write articles that kept Senator Brooks in the paper on a positive note. He also wrote frequently on the prospects of Truman. During the campaign, he chose not to cover the candidates for president on the campaign trail. He explained, "I went around to the key areas and talked to various people and wrote situation stories and wrote how I thought they were going to go."[80] His articles usually found their way to page 1 of the *Tribune*.

St. Louis had its own colorful newspaper history. The city across the Mississippi River from southern Illinois had its crime gang wars, political machines, syndicated mob activity, and celebrated newspaper characters, of the sort familiar to most urban centers. With the southern half of Illinois outside the circulation reach of Chicago newspapers except for the *Tribune*, St. Louis dailies directed coverage toward the suburban cities and rural towns of Illinois, focusing primarily on politics and crime. There was no shortage of either. Although central Illinois was not in their strong circulation territory, St. Louis papers kept correspondents in the state capital of Springfield.

By the 1940s, St. Louis newspaper readers were down to three daily papers. Most U.S. urban newspapers existing after World War II had survived lengthy wars of attrition that drained capital and human resources. The *St. Louis Globe-Democrat* had the morning field to itself. The *St. Louis Post-Dispatch* shared the afternoon with the weaker *Star-Times*. Few in number, the papers offered a clear choice of attitudes and approaches to politics. The *Globe-Democrat* took a strident conservative approach, usually favoring Republicans for office. At the opposite end of the spectrum, the *Post-Dispatch* spoke in behalf of liberal candidates, which placed the paper mostly in the camp of Democrats. None of the papers tolerated candidates with doubtful credentials or suspicious backgrounds. Famously, the *Post* became a vocal critic of President Truman, citing his support by the Pendergast political machine in Kansas City. Although headquartered in Missouri, the opportunities for the three papers to sell papers in Illinois provided incentive for heavy coverage of that state's news.

The *Globe* and *Post* had both prevailed in bitter competitive warfare and remained well financed. The morning *Globe* traced its beginnings to

1852, when the *Daily Missouri Democrat* began publication. In an article on its 125th anniversary, the paper claimed the *Democrat* as "the only major pro-Union newspaper in a slave or border state, during the Civil War."[81]

Joseph Pulitzer, born in Hungary in 1847, eventually found his way to St. Louis after holding a series of jobs in the eastern United States. He purchased the *St. Louis Post* for $3,000 in 1872, then bought the troubled *St. Louis Dispatch* at a sheriff's sale for $2,700 and combined it with the *Post*, establishing the paper as a fighter for progressive causes. His will established the school of journalism at Columbia University and financed the Pulitzer Prizes. Shortly before his death, Pulitzer named his son Joseph II to head the *Post-Dispatch*.[82] Joseph II was successful in St. Louis, continuing his father's outlook and policies on the editorial page and battling in news columns against crime and mobsters. During the 1940s, an editorial writer, Irving Dilliard, became the paper's leading intellectual and liberal thinker. A resident of Collinsville, Illinois, he was a champion of Adlai Stevenson.

St. Louis papers devoted substantial resources to coverage of organized crime activities across southern Illinois. The band of investigative staff members who worked the St. Louis metropolitan area's crime beat had profiles higher than their colleagues' on other news assignments. To hoodlums, law enforcement officers, public officials, and citizens, the names of crime reporters became as common as soap brands. For the era including the 1940s, the star was Theodore "Ted" Link, who built an image as the prototype seeker of truth in the *Post*'s crusade against mobsters.[83]

Crime reporters were a strange lot, often with peculiar personal habits and obsessions. They competed against each other for exclusives and developed sources who whispered only to them. They seldom shared information with associates on the same paper and never with competitors. Some crime reporters, such as Ted Link, crossed legal and ethical lines to obtain and use exclusive information, actions that their newspapers defended. Link maintained an aura of mystery and intrigue created by his erratic behavior and solitary habits. His close connections with and alleged sympathies for the Shelton brothers gang gained him notoriety and built suspicions about his motives and loyalties. Some critics believed he hated corrupt politicians more than criminals.

Link became a major factor in the development of official corruption as a theme in the 1948 campaign for governor. His research and reporting broke fresh ground, but true to form, his behavior became part of the story, too. His reporting work and the *Post*'s relentless editorial campaign brought the paper in direct conflict with the *Chicago Tribune* over the worthiness of incumbents Green and Brooks. Although the two papers were not direct competitors in a financial sense, they competed in efforts to promote candidates for Illinois offices.

Other newspapers in Illinois contributed to partisan coverage of political campaigns, although their impact remained mostly local. An example was in Springfield, where one morning newspaper and one afternoon newspaper, owned by the same company, had viewed the state's politics from opposite sides since the days of Abraham Lincoln. The *Springfield State Journal* circulated in the mornings and leaned editorially toward Republicans, especially conservative Republicans. In the afternoon, the *Illinois State Register* counseled with Democrats. Because of common ownership, competition was tamer. Other large cities across the northern half of the state had substantial local influence. That was the case in Peoria, Rockford, Bloomington-Normal, Champaign-Urbana, and Decatur. Candidates sought the favor of these large local papers, but nothing compared to what occurred in Chicago and St. Louis.

3. Opening Blows

In the opening days of January 1948, ten months before the general election in November, both major political parties had finished their slates. According to the unofficial rules of Illinois political engagement, that should have been the final word, but it wasn't. Even though the slates were fixed—if not permanently, at least firmly—quarrels in private and in public meant party leaders had more work to do.

Adlai Stevenson, a balding, mild-mannered man most at ease on the tennis court or at a diplomatic reception, was an easy target for critics. Some called him the "gentleman in politics," but no one was sure whether that was a compliment. He was contrasted with Paul Douglas, who bore the scars of battle for all to see. Stevenson had neither name recognition nor photographic familiarity with citizens across the state. His record as a lawyer did not set him apart from others, and his duties in Washington and even with the United Nations struck people on the street as "so what." The editorials and newspaper columns that had praised the selection of Stevenson could offer no credentials or achievements that would make him sound as if he were ready to run the state. They made him appear like a bit of a stuffed shirt, a minor-league bureaucrat. To say he started at ground zero in the campaign was an understatement. Republicans couldn't wait to take him on. Grumblers in the Democratic Party, wishing they had a candidate with gravitas, shrugged their shoulders. A few complained publicly.

Regardless, most Democratic commentators and editorial pages heaped praise on the Stevenson-Douglas ticket. The *Chicago Sun* quickly showed its support of the twosome, because the paper wanted to get rid of Dwight Green and Curly Brooks: "Adlai Stevenson, the Democratic leaders' choice for governor, is an exceptionally qualified citizen who has never been a cog in the machine. The issues of the state campaign will be Gov. Green's record of profligate expenditures, his refusal to help meet the pressing financial problems of Illinois cities and local school systems, his debasement of the state administration by the crudest spoils politics. Mr. Stevenson can offer Illinois the refreshing contrast of integrity, competence, political independence and progressive leadership. The state would be foolish indeed not to avail itself of his rare abilities."[1]

Although most arguments over the Democratic slate had been put to rest, Mayor Martin Kennelly let it be known he didn't think much of putting Stevenson on a track to the governor's office. He preferred Judge Thomas J. Courtney of the superior court, a man who had been tossed aside by Jack Arvey and other members of the slating committee.[2] Kennelly had helped with Courtney's failed campaign for governor in 1944.

Kennelly did not have anything personally against Stevenson, just that he wasn't qualified to be governor. He wanted someone closer to the mayor's office. What really bothered Kennelly was that the party professionals who made up the slating committee represented the political machine. Kennelly, elected in April 1947 with little political experience and no participation in the party organization, felt obliged to show his independence. Earlier in the fall, he had turned down offers to be the gubernatorial candidate—three times he publicly said no—saying he was elected to the job of mayor and intended to finish it. He acknowledged that some Chicago politicians might want him to run for governor just to get him out of the mayor's position.

Arvey had played the Kennelly game carefully during December, when most of the decisions were made about candidates. After Kennelly first said early in December that he was not a candidate for governor, Arvey noted the downstate interest in the mayor. Party officials outside Chicago liked Kennelly because of his independence of the machine. Arvey gave Kennelly two more chances to reconsider. Whether Kennelly had tried to persuade Arvey of Courtney's value before the final strokes of slating is not known. Arvey had been working long and hard to find candidates for the two top jobs, and it seemed unlikely he would back away from Stevenson and Douglas at the last minute. Instead, Arvey let

Kennelly demonstrate his independence of the machine. When Kennelly realized the deal was done, however, he withheld public support of Stevenson until a month before the election, refusing until then to campaign for the Democratic slate. He feared being too closely attached to a failed campaign.

The sniping about Stevenson's candidacy continued off and on through January, mostly in a few newspaper editorials and columns. On 22 January, the *Chicago Daily News* commented on rumors of a deal between Arvey and Green to slate candidates so as to minimize competition for positions at the state and Cook County levels. The paper said, "It is no compliment to the slate-makers, however, that their handiwork was cut to the pattern that would have been followed if there had been such a deal. The Democrats weakened their chances of electing a governor when they made Adlai Stevenson the candidate, instead of Paul Douglas for that place. Stevenson is a man of first-class character and ability, but he is not experienced in the local public life of Illinois as Douglas is."[3] The rumors of a deal must be chalked up to the continuous gossip about politics in Chicago because it had no basis in fact that anyone could detect. However, it was easier to complain when the conventional wisdom of January was that Stevenson would lose.

To show he intended to engage Republicans in the battle, Stevenson on 7 January made his first campaign speech in Chicago, ahead of a meeting in Springfield with downstate party officials and candidates for other positions. He wasted no time confirming his ties to Democratic international policies that had little to do with Illinois issues. Speaking as if he were a candidate for the U.S. Senate, Stevenson said the Marshall Plan had to be supported even though its success could not be guaranteed and despite questions on whether the United States had adequate resources to place $17 billion in western Europe. He stated, "The problem of western Europe is not one of people who do not work, but of people who do not have the material or the fuel and power with which to produce, or sufficient food to sustain their strength."[4]

Untying the Republican slating knot proved a greater challenge. Throughout the latter part of 1947, Republicans opposed to Dwight Green seeking a third term increased the level of criticism in an attempt to encourage other candidates and to embarrass the governor. Most of the time, Green ignored the intraparty quarrels, intending all the while to be the party's candidate again. This reveals how Green and his followers confidently believed the governor was the probable winner against any

Democratic candidate—and that eventually he would convert those who argued for a new face on the ticket. While Democrats believed defeat was inevitable in November, Republicans thought they would win in a walk. Why not? Many in both parties believed President Truman had little chance to be elected, and Illinois Democrats did not seem to have candidates for state office that appealed to voters.[5]

The *Chicago Tribune* led cheers for Green and Brooks when they announced as candidates for reelection. The paper wanted its readers to be impressed with the formal declaration. In a lengthy story that did not quote either candidate directly, the paper shared its feelings on page 1 under the headline "Green and Brooks to Run Again."[6] The first mention of Democratic candidates for the two positions occurred in the last paragraph of the article. The *Tribune* perhaps also was making an announcement that the paper would be stating the case for the two incumbents throughout 1948 in news columns and on the editorial page.

None of that stopped two Republicans from announcing that they would seek the nomination for governor against Green. Few seemed surprised at the candidacy of Lieutenant Governor Hugh Cross, who had been in Green's doghouse for some time in spite of being in the office since 1941. They disagreed on a range of state issues, and Cross had witnessed aspects of the Green Machine that he did not like.[7] Additionally, Cross's philosophical sympathies were closer to Senator Brooks's than to Green's. Cross believed it was his turn to run for governor and that Green should be satisfied with eight years. The surprise candidate was Warren Wright, a former state treasurer and vice president of the Michigan Avenue National Bank. In his announcement, Wright said, "I figure I have a good chance of being nominated and elected. My action is not at the request of any group, faction or clique. This is in line with my background of independence in Republican politics."[8] In other words, Wright had no ties to the Green Machine. If Wright had remained on the sidelines, Cross might have gained enough traction to stay in the race against the governor.

Cross and Wright laid low through December while party leadership, directed by the governor, announced support for Green and Brooks. As soon as that was accomplished, Green issued his statement of candidacy for a third term. Pete Akers, managing editor of the *Sun*, which already had announced its support of the Democratic candidates, laid out his arguments against Green. Surely, Cross and Wright were paying attention. Akers began his criticism of Green by reminding readers of the governor's pledge in 1940 that he would not install a political machine. Akers stated, "Today, the Green machine outdistances the old Kelly machine." He then argued, "Candidate Green pledged he would remove the sales tax from foodstuffs. Gov. Green did not do so. Instead, he claims credit for reducing the sales tax from three to two percent. He did neither. The original sales tax act, passed in a preceding administration [Horner's], provided for the reduction." Akers attacked Green's declaration that he had balanced the state budget without a tax increase: "That is not so. The governor has increased and has added taxes. He has increased the liquor tax. He has added, and then increased, the cigarette tax."[9]

Green ignored attacks by Cross and Wright. However, both Republicans prepared to contest the governor regarding issues that were at least a year old or more. Green had addressed them in January 1947 and held his ground in January 1948.

According to Illinois tradition, the sitting governor met with all members of the General Assembly at the beginning of the biennial session, which occurred in January of the odd-numbered years. Unlike the State of the Union message delivered by the president to Congress, it received little newspaper attention. The only lasting impact of the moment was for legislators to welcome the governor and perhaps shake his hand. The presentation by Green to the Illinois General Assembly on 8 January 1947 was notable for the issues that would make their appearance during the 1948 election campaign. Green followed the formula by offering a positive picture of state finances and programs that had been enacted and by identifying unresolved issues. He emphasized laws that had been passed to aid returning veterans. There were no grand schemes or reforms presented by the governor. He accurately identified the challenge ahead, saying, "Ours is the task to provide for the transition of state government from the unusual conditions which resulted from the greatest war in history to a permanent basis of operation."[10]

Green identified a large surplus of state funds on hand for the 1947–49 biennium but was quick to dash any hopes of new spending. He said, "Those balances and the fact that during most of the war years the state's receipts exceeded its expenditures have resulted in a common misconception that the state's revenues are larger than necessary." He added that most of the surplus would be needed to fund capital expenditures that were postponed during the war. That led him to declare, "We will impose no new taxes on our people." He cited increased expenses due to inflation, higher labor costs, and more expensive commodities for everyday use as burdens facing citizens and said the state should not add to them.[11]

Perhaps the most explosive issue addressed by Green was the demand by municipalities for a greater share of revenues from the state retailers' occupational tax and other resources. Green rejected that idea based on constitutional questions and denied that it would deprive the state of needed revenues. He stated, "The long-range problem is not one of devising means whereby cities may gain more revenue from the state treasury, but rather it is one of putting the cities on a self-sustaining basis." During the 1948 campaign, issues of how to relieve municipalities' revenue shortages, and specifically whether the state should provide more funds, became a contentious point between Green and his Republican challengers, and later with Stevenson.[12]

In his first campaign appearance on 21 January, Green ignored his Republican adversaries and aimed his comments at the Democrats. Without providing details, the governor said the state faced a $47 million deficit for the biennium ending 1 July 1949, although just a year earlier he had predicted a positive balance. He blamed the shortfall on legislative expenditures over the state's estimated income and increased cost of government. Republicans controlled both houses of the legislature. He charged Democrats with "voicing new demands and making fresh promises of something-for-nothing should they be elected."[13] He also may have been giving notice that further demands on state finances, such as grants to counties and cities, would endanger fiscal conservatism.

Once Green announced, Cross and Wright took off the gloves and began pounding him. Green's supporters became annoyed at the two, and talks began about how to remove them from the competition. Cross charged Green with attempting to perpetuate himself in office. He said, "The people of Illinois are not asking him to run. It is the payroll spokesmen of a vicious political machine who have been asked to perpetuate him in office."[14] Cross made it clear he would campaign against the machine that had excluded him.

As the month progressed toward the deadline for filing candidate petitions, Cross and Wright increased their attacks on Green. Cross was the first to file his petition, on 21 January 1948. He gave an indication that he would have plenty to say about the governor's conduct. He vowed to expose Green's "entrenched power of organized patronage and money. I have seen the incredible alliance of the Republican machine with the unspeakable Kelly machine in Chicago. And the third-term menace springs from, and is, the creature of these machines." Cross predicted no Republican could be elected to a third term and claimed he could save the party at election time. He concluded, "I will battle against party stagnation and oblivion in Illinois. It is time for Republicans to nominate a Republican—and a Republican who can win in November."[15]

A few days later, Wright became an official candidate, taking a swipe at Cross as well as at Green. He said, "You, Mr. Cross, are still stooging for the administration. As lieutenant governor, you had the power to gavel down bad legislation, but instead you gaveled the bad bills through the Senate."[16] By virtue of the constitution, the lieutenant governor presided over sessions of the state senate. However, authority for setting the chamber's agenda rested largely with the majority leader, regardless of party affiliation.

Few expected Cross and Wright to remain in the fight, given the lack of campaign funds and the likelihood of Green's overwhelming victory in the primary. Republican party pressure mounted for the two to withdraw. Four hours before the 31 January deadline, Cross backed off. Two days later, Wright withdrew.[17] (Traditionally, the secretary of state, who controlled state elections, allowed extra time for withdrawals.) That left Green alone at the top of the state ticket, and only slightly bruised. The claims against Green by Cross and Wright did little more than provide ammunition for Democrats.

No party insiders confessed to forcing the withdrawals, but Robert Howard, a *Chicago Tribune* reporter during the campaign, expressed his opinion in an oral history years later: "I was sure that [city editor Donald] Maxwell arranged the next move in the newsroom. I was there watching him, but I couldn't hear what was said."[18] Anyone speaking for the *Tribune* publisher, Robert McCormick, as did Maxwell, could have made it clear to Cross and Wright that they would suffer the consequences if they insisted on running against Green. Howard, by then an experienced reporter familiar with the role of the paper in Republican affairs, did not miss much, even if he did not have a full transcript of the conversations.

Reflecting the need to help Cross and Wright save face, party officials gave Cross a gift by having his opponent for Republican National Convention delegate withdraw. Wright received a meeting with Green to discuss his concern for legislation to help veterans. Green was reported to have expressed his concern for the same issues.

In the end, Green got his way, and the path was cleared to a third-term campaign. As newspapers proclaimed, the likely maneuver by Green advocates of sending Wright into the contest after Cross announced his intentions was a calculated scheme designed to make it impossible for Cross to have a chance of defeating Green.

Evidence that party slating of candidates left no room for independent candidacies occurred in a change of the Republican lineup at the eleventh hour before the filing deadline. Until that point, James Simpson Jr., a wealthy businessman from Lake County, believed he had received Green's blessing for candidate as state treasurer. Assuming he was the chosen person, Simpson had circulated petitions early, waited for the deadline to pass, and had not started forming a campaign organization.

However, party officials had other ideas, presumably to put more geographic balance on the ticket and appear more competitive with the Democratic slate. A last-minute decision was made to drop Simpson and add Elmer H. Droste of Mt. Olive for treasurer.[19] Droste, a farmer, had stepped down as deputy director in charge of downstate payments to the Illinois soldiers' home. The two men were advised by Leslie P. Volz, administrative assistant to Green, of the change on Friday before the Monday filing deadline. Simpson withdrew immediately. Because of the timing, officials recruited state employees and volunteers to complete a petition drive for Droste over the weekend. The deadline was met, and Droste joined the Republican slate. The process for getting Droste's petitions signed and filed and the legitimacy of signatures later became public issues raised by the *Chicago Daily News*.

After the ballot shakeout, here is how the two parties lined up for the primary in April:

Republicans
Senate: C. Wayland Brooks, incumbent, versus William J. Baker
Governor: Dwight Green
Lieutenant Governor: Richard Yates Rowe
Attorney General: George F. Barrett
Secretary of State: William G. Stratton
Auditor: Sinon A. Murray
Treasurer: Elmer H. Droste

Democrats
Senate: Paul Douglas
Governor: Adlai E. Stevenson
Lieutenant Governor: Sherwood Dixon
Attorney General: Ivan Elliott versus Joseph B. Burke

Secretary of State: Edward J. Barrett
Auditor: Benjamin O. Cooper
Treasurer: Ora Smith

The two political machines had worked their magic, and the contested races did not threaten incumbents or those slated by the organizations. In the absence of continuous public opinion polls—a common occurrence yet to come—speculators on newspaper staffs and among experienced politicians left no doubt that they expected the Republican ticket to prevail in November, probably by large majorities. Did they know how voters lined up in January? Probably not, but incumbent Republicans looked strong, had plenty of money, and were full of confidence. Democrats looked like losers.

FEBRUARY 1948

Consider a baseball team arriving at the ballpark hours before an important game. No players are in uniform. Throwing arms are stiff. No one is watching, and the ballpark is empty.

That is an apt description of the Illinois political campaigns in February 1948. The final lineups for the April primary election were not widely known. Raising serious money had just begun. Issues and campaign styles were untested with the public. Early in the month, the Republicans said they would not conduct a campaign caravan across the state before the meaningless primary, thus demonstrating their confidence in winning. In contrast, Democrats, with everything to gain, announced an ambitious caravan with all candidates on the ticket participating. In the contest for governor, both Green and Stevenson made their first major speeches, defining the issues as they wanted them defined. Whether anyone listened beyond party loyalists is doubtful. Most of the rhetoric was for newspaper reporters. The opening guns were fired, even if few heard them.

Behind the scenes, intraparty tussles occurred as new and old candidates met and talked tactics for the first time. Since many of the Republicans on the ticket were incumbents and had campaigned together earlier, major spats were few, or else simmered quietly. Nearly everyone was a stranger on the Democratic ticket. Only Edward J. Barrett and Paul Douglas had run statewide campaigns. All the rest were beginners. This applied especially to Stevenson, who had never before run for elective office.

On the surface, Stevenson and Douglas had much in common. They were thoughtful, intellectual men familiar with formulating ideas and articulating them. Both had solid reputations in "good government" circles. By making a few compromises, they should have been able to work and campaign together. However, something happened that caused a rift between them.[20] Douglas approached Stevenson with a proposal to pool campaign contributions. Stevenson said no; pooling would disadvantage him. Such a proposal seems naive for someone like Douglas. Trying to organize and control the pooling of revenues and dispersing the funds fairly would have been a nightmare, leading to internal squabbles. Douglas was a man of modest means who had lived essentially on income from teaching at the University of Chicago. His ability to reach and persuade wealthy individuals and companies for funds was limited. Presumably, he expected to benefit from the money network available to Stevenson.

From Stevenson's standpoint, the idea of pooling money had no merit. Among his financial supporters were wealthy Republicans from the North Shore near Chicago. Convincing them to let Douglas use their contributions would have been difficult. Also, Stevenson had sufficient personal wealth if he needed more campaign funds than were otherwise available. Spreading that money on Douglas would have been improbable. This inevitably led to the two running separate campaigns in terms of contributions and messages. From the outset, Stevenson rarely mentioned Douglas on the stump, except before union audiences and at Democratic Party rallies. Douglas, on the other hand, graciously mentioned other Democratic candidates, including Stevenson.

In his autobiography, Douglas said of the situation, "The fact that he kept his campaign separate from mine and only referred to me before union audiences . . . cost me votes. No doubt this strategy was based on attracting Republican voters who would not support me." Douglas resented Stevenson's posture that left the impression Douglas was not a "real Democrat."[21]

Both candidates had their idiosyncrasies, and they confused and confounded associates, friends, and observers. Senator Scott Lucas, a strong supporter of Stevenson for governor and active in the 1948 campaign for several candidates, later wrote critically of Stevenson's behavior in his unpublished autobiography: "During the campaign, I have never seen a candidate so worried and fidgety. At various times he indicated he couldn't be elected; that money for carrying on the campaign was short; and that he wished he had never consented to go into the race."[22] That probably could have been said about any number of candidates during the campaign. Also, Lucas wrote these comments years after he and Stevenson had a parting of the ways politically. Stevenson's hesitancy in making critical decisions was often mentioned by his detractors, while others said it was just Stevenson being politically crafty.

Although thrown together on occasions that neither could dodge, differences in campaign styles added to the irritations. Stevenson's biographer, John Bartlow Martin, wrote:

> Douglas was expert at sidewalk campaigning, standing at factory gates early in the morning, shaking hands. He was a burly vital man, stronger physically than Stevenson. Stevenson studied his technique but never learned to do it so well as Douglas. Douglas would move into a crowd, shake a voter's hand, say a word or two, then move invincibly on, like a tank, smiling, listening, speaking a few sentences to each, making sure he missed no one but spending little time with any. If, on the other hand, something a voter said struck Stevenson as interesting, he would stop and carry on a long conversation with him, while the rest of the voters waited and his campaign aides fidgeted.[23]

Another reason for Stevenson's actions, especially during much of the campaign, might have been that even his strongest backers had doubts about beating the incumbent Green. Speaking of the attitude of party officials during 1947, Lucas also wrote, "Our party in Illinois and nationally was at a low ebb in 1947. I recall a conversation with [former] mayor Kelly, one of Illinois' most astute Democratic leaders of all time, when he said, 'Scott, we are going to be hard-pressed to elect state-wide any Democrats in 1948.'"[24]

By necessity, Douglas and Stevenson campaigned together occasionally. One of those moments came at the official beginning of the Democratic campaign early in March, which was announced in February. The schedule called for candidate presentations in 130 towns and villages across the state, beginning in the south. During the day, separate groups would spread out over an area and converge each evening for a rally.[25] Douglas committed to forty-two sessions during the sixteen days, and Stevenson agreed to forty-one. On days when Douglas had another commitment, his wife, Emily, planned to join the caravan. All Democratic candidates, when offered a spot on the ticket, pledged an active campaign and promised to hit downstate locations during the tour. Douglas said he would speak in every county, in every community, and at every factory gate in the state. No one would keep track, but it sounded good to Democrats. The itinerary for night meetings of the caravan included Carmi, Effingham, East St. Louis, Decatur, Danville, Kankakee, Joliet, Dixon, Rock Island, Peoria, Quincy, Springfield, Bloomington, and Waukegan.

Before the gubernatorial campaign began, both candidates for governor outlined the issues in major speeches, which drew widespread newspaper coverage. As is the case in almost every election campaign, events closer to November dramatically changed the array of issues. Green, the incumbent, already had a record as governor, and defending it early was the appropriate place to start. Consequently, in his 6 February speech in Waukegan, Green did not introduce any new ideas for a third term.[26] Stevenson, without a record as governor, spent most of his first major speech outlining how he would govern and speaking of differences between him and his opponent.

Green may have surprised his supporters in the audience with commentary on national public policy, especially foreign relations. This choice of subject underlined his interest in being chosen as vice president on the national Republican ticket. His ambition had been carefully controlled until 1948, but close associates knew he had no great enthusiasm for a third term. Green called for a halt of any foreign policy that drained the "nation's resources and threatens more regimentation." Specifically, he attacked the Marshall Plan as an evil instrument of socialism by remnants of Roosevelt's New Deal administrations. The governor stated, "We must not peacefully submit to the program of the New Dealers who propose more to stop communism in Europe by establishing socialism in the United States."[27]

The *Tribune* responded to Green's attack on the Truman administration with a headline that read "Green Hits Democrat Socialism." From that paper's point of view, an attack on the Marshall Plan took precedence over comments about state issues. Also indicative of the *Tribune's* slant on news coverage was a comment in a story the day before Green's speech. George Tagge, the paper's lead reporter for the gubernatorial campaign, referred to Stevenson as "a delegate to the United Nations general council" and an "internationalist" in the same sentence. Labeling the Democratic candidates was a telltale sign of the *Tribune's* not-so-subtle strategy.[28]

When Green turned his attention to Illinois issues, the subject was how Republicans had governed effectively. He also reaffirmed his position on one of the campaign's hottest topics, distribution of state funds to counties and cities, saying the "New Dealers want to raid the state treasury." Green struck at the heart of Democratic arguments, declaring, "It is obvious that their state campaign will be based on reckless promises of huge state expenditures, particularly for the relief of local governments." The governor predicted that approach would lead to new taxes. "It will not take long to get back in the red again."[29]

Green offered a list of accomplishments, having mentioned them periodically before the campaign. He took credit for a reduction in the sales tax, although others pointed out that had been built into the law under the previous Democratic administration. He mentioned aid to dependent children, a 55 percent increase in state aid for common schools, aid to veterans at Illinois state colleges and universities, a building program to relieve overcrowding at state hospitals, a state housing program partnership with builders, and development of farm-to-market roads. Based on earlier comments from Democrats and the newspapers, the state financial picture, aid to counties and cities, education, and taxes were the most likely issues to be debated.

More than two weeks later, Stevenson gave a Jackson Day Dinner speech in his hometown of Bloomington, vowing to smash the Green Machine: "This unconscionable spoils machine must be destroyed beyond the possibility of repair." He used much of his time to accuse Green and associates of unethical behavior, shakedowns of government appointees, and waste. He declared, "I want servants not solicitors on the state payroll." There were few specific proposals, which is not surprising for a candidate who had been in the hunt only about six weeks. On education, he called for "a thorough and efficient system of free schools." He promised to preserve gains made by unions under Presidents Woodrow Wilson and Franklin Roosevelt. Stevenson made a pointed reference to Green ignoring appeals from inspectors about safety issues at mines and using the inspectors to raise campaign funds, points raised by the Centralia mine disaster a year earlier.[30]

The *Tribune* and *Daily News* each gave Stevenson's speech important location in the next day's papers, but the headlines and writing made it appear that reporters attended two different events. The *Tribune* did not mention Stevenson's promise to destroy the Green Machine, while the *Daily News* placed that in the banner headline. The *Tribune* chose to feature a statement by Stevenson that he would use state government as a testing ground for new ideas, which, without a direct quote from the candidate, the paper called "New Deal ideas."

Senator Brooks was on the attack in February, pursuing two of his favorite subjects. The *Tribune* demonstrated early that it intended to follow Brooks everywhere he went in order to record his speeches and trumpet his talking points. Two events in February followed that plan. Before a friendly Lincoln Day audience, Brooks chose one of his favorite punching bags, the Marshall Plan. He blasted promoters of sending large appropriations to Europe while not providing funds for the "free enterprise system of production in America" and declared that the U.S. budget could not afford the requested $17 billion for the Marshall program: "It means higher prices for everything we buy in America." Throughout the campaign, he never let up in criticism of the foreign aid program.[31]

Late in the month, Brooks spoke in Philadelphia to the annual meeting of a manufacturers' association, where he offered another campaign theme, the U.S. government as "a monopoly preying upon the American people." He cited the federal government's expansion of bureaus, agencies, and commissions as evidence of the "monopoly" label. Brooks declared, "We constantly hear the demand for more power, more controls and more regulators," which increased costs and caused higher taxes. These were familiar targets of the incumbent senator and played into his consistent call for a smaller federal government and restraints on international spending programs.[32]

Few people thought President Truman could win the presidency in 1948, and a growing number of Democratic high-profile individuals, including Illinoisans, worked behind the scenes to find another candidate for president. According to the Gallup polling organization, New York governor Thomas E. Dewey led Truman 46 percent to 41 percent in a January poll. By early presidential campaign standards, that was not a huge lead.[33] The poll registered 7 percent for Progressive Party candidate Henry Wallace, whose efforts to get on state ballots had barely begun. If pundits needed anything to back up their predictions about Truman's fate, the January numbers provided slim evidence. However, that did not quiet them. On the contrary, reporters for newspapers across the land jumped on the bandwagon of negative speculation about Truman's troubles.

Due to newspaper headlines in papers serving the state, Illinoisans began learning of a subject that would gain momentum with state officials as the Democratic National Convention neared. Truman unveiled his call for civil rights legislation in a message to Congress on 2 February.

The essence of the proposal came from a report made public in October 1947 titled "To Secure These Rights." At the beginning of 1947, Truman had appointed a committee to study various aspects of cries for equal rights legislation and to make recommendations to him. The committee called for laws to eliminate forms of legal segregation and discrimination. The report sought an end to discrimination in education, a ban against discrimination in the armed forces, fair employment practices laws, prohibition of lynching, repeal of poll taxes and voting restrictions, an expanded civil rights division of the Department of Justice, and creation of various commissions at the state and federal levels. The report constituted a total rejection of the concept of "separate but equal."

Reaction to the October report had created an uproar in southern states that would become a political revolt in 1948. One of the loudest cries against the report came from southern protectors of states' rights. Ralph McGill, editor of the *Atlanta Constitution* who had opposed federal intervention—and who became one of the outspoken "southern liberals"—wrote, "The plain truth is that national public opinion is against us. We have allowed enough evil to make the rest of the nation look upon us without sympathy. We have plenty of laws against violence, such as lynching. We have not enforced [them] well in Georgia. We have allowed local pride to cover up the most ghastly crimes."[34]

Other moderates in the southern press voiced skepticism over the recommendations, reflecting caution in dealing with cultural issues. Hodding Carter Jr., winner of a Pulitzer Prize for editorials attacking bigotry, opposed outlawing lynching, poll taxes, and discrimination in hiring. He believed the poll tax and hiring issues were state matters, not federal ones.[35]

McGill's and Carter's remarks were some of the mildest. James Eastland, a Mississippi senator, stated, "I am going to fight it to the last ditch. They are not going to Harlemize the country." Other politicians from the South fell in line behind Eastland and issued calls for an alternative to Truman as the Democratic presidential candidate. The authors of *The Race Beat: The Press, the Civil Rights Struggle, and the Awakening of a Nation* said the electorate "was harder to read than usual. From the tobacco roads to the statehouses to the Potomac, there was much posturing."[36] And all that was just about a proposal. Those complaining loudest hoped to frighten Truman and kill any chance of a legislative initiative.

Taking such a calculated risk in a presidential election year meant that Truman believed he had little to lose and thought perhaps it might help him. Shortly after receipt of the civil rights report in October, Clark Clifford, one of the president's closest political advisors, gave a lengthy memorandum to Truman arguing that the civil rights issue and the black vote were important elements in a winning strategy for 1948.

Truman did not immediately support any specifics or offer a proposal of his own, although there were internal White House discussions, and many of his key aides urged him to respond with a plan. That came in February, when the president offered an abbreviated version of the committee's recommendations. His plan would lead to a serious split in party ranks and give rise to a political movement in the South that further threatened the president's chances to win.

Truman asked Congress to enact these ideas: strengthen existing civil rights statutes and establish a permanent commission on civil rights, name a joint congressional committee on civil rights, establish a civil rights division in the Justice Department, provide federal protection against lynching, protect the right to vote, outlaw use of the poll tax and other restrictions, name a fair employment practices commission, and prohibit discrimination in interstate transportation facilities.[37]

The Truman recommendation to Congress endeared him to the liberal wing of the party, and primarily to those who had lobbied hard since the end of the war for steps to increase equality for blacks. Truman needed those loyalists because southerners and conservatives in the party felt betrayed by the man from Missouri. After all, Truman was the nephew of a southern veteran of the Civil War. Truman might have underestimated the reaction that followed his recommendations.

Illinois newspapers gave the president's proposal space on page 1 and vocal editorial expressions. Reactions tended to follow the papers' political leanings. The *Chicago Daily News*, often presenting a moderate to conservative political alternative to the liberal *Sun-Times* and the ultraconservative *Tribune*, viewed Truman's presentation as a political move that would not receive enough support from Congress. The editorial said, "However political the purpose of the message may be, however insincere in some respects, we have at least reached the point in American politics where gestures in this direction are considered good politics in a presidential year." On balance, the paper's editorial called for changes: "Perhaps we can go on from here, beyond the stage of gesturing, to the actual consideration of specific measures on the basis of merit and demerit, practicality and impracticality."[38]

The same newspaper, after reporting southern outrage, ran an ana-
lytical news article by Henning Heldt, who was attending a meeting
of the Southern Conference of Governors in Florida. His take on the
uproar was that it should be expected, and history indicated that after
a period of complaining, southerners would rally to vote for the Democratic Party, while holding their noses. Heldt wrote, "What makes
futile any threat of a party revolt by southern governors is the fact
that the masses of voters in their states are still firmly wedded to the
party and will vote for it in the presidential election, regardless who
the candidate may be." He added, "Another angle that makes southern Democratic chiefs squirm is that they're stuck with a party which
depends for victories largely on votes of labor and liberal intellectuals."
Heldt concluded that after the fuming and whining, officials "in all
probability [will] do no more than formally protest the civil rights
legislative proposals."[39]

After a few days of reporting by the *Tribune* on the fulminations of
southern officials—the paper's headlines almost seemed to express joy
over the president's troubles—its veteran Washington correspondent,
Walter Trohan, offered a history lesson. He observed that Truman's
place on the 1944 ballot for vice president had occurred because the South
refused to take former vice president Henry Wallace as a fourth-term
running mate for Roosevelt.

Trohan recalled that the South threatened revolts against the New
Deal in 1940 and 1944 and was doing it again in 1948: "Nothing came of
the 1940 and 1944 revolts and few observers expect anything to come of
the 1948 uprising." Trohan pointed out that Governor J. Strom Thurmond
of South Carolina had convinced other southern governors to send an
ultimatum to Truman demanding he "cease attacks on white supremacy"
or else face political revolt. Toward the end of February, angry southern governors said they would carry their protest to the Democratic
National Convention.[40]

Aside from recognition of an old-fashioned regional political fight in
a presidential election year, what did this intramural party conflict mean
to the Illinois political picture? For many party leaders, such as Jack
Arvey, the conflict elevated concerns about the ability of Truman to be
nominated and, if so, to win the election. With Republicans controlling
virtually every state office of consequence, Democrats in Illinois feared
the worst with a politically weakened president at the top of the ticket.
The civil rights battle increased concern over party apathy and poor voter

turnout in Illinois, which could dampen enthusiasm for Democrats on the state ticket.

Arvey, along with political leaders in many large cities and state capitals, had begun talks to rally support for Dwight D. Eisenhower as the Democratic nominee. As the possibility of third party candidates appeared more likely, Arvey figured the president should stand down and let a familiar leadership face come forward. However, Arvey and allies did not know of a meeting Truman and Eisenhower had in Washington late in 1947. According to Eisenhower, Truman said if the general would accept the Democratic nomination, the president would be willing to run as the vice presidential candidate. Eisenhower declined Truman's offer, if indeed it was made.[41]

Political observer and author Michael Barone called the movement toward Eisenhower "a quixotic enterprise." Barone wrote, "In 1905 Eisenhower's brother Arthur had been one of Truman's roommates in Kansas City, so Truman had known the family for years; he knew that Eisenhower was a Republican and also knew that he was not interested in running in 1948."[42] Nonetheless, the quest to get Eisenhower on the Democratic ticket for president had much more time to run, with Illinois in the forefront.

The first of several newspaper reports during 1948 that featured questionable activities by the Green administration appeared on 9 February in the *Chicago Sun-Times*. The paper accused Green of accumulating a million dollar campaign "slush" fund involving civil service state employees primarily associated with state hospitals and prisons. The paper said the fund was illegal under Illinois law and claimed Pontiac warden Arthur Bennett had served as the principal collector in behalf of the Green campaign.[43]

Providing much of this information was Michael F. Ryan, attorney for the Civil Service Protective Association. He sent a letter to Green demanding a stop to the alleged forced collection from 30,000 state workers and a return of funds already collected. Ryan charged the contributions were made "under coercion."[44]

Ryan said Bennett and Green had violated civil service laws and were subject to legal action. Ryan and the newspaper cited laws that prohibited soliciting campaign contributions from civil service workers by state officials or employees and said state buildings could not be used for accepting contributions, even if they were offered voluntarily. The laws provided fines and imprisonment for violations as well as removal from office of persons convicted of collecting or soliciting. Ryan's letter to the governor cited eight instances of violation of the law at specific state institutions—Jacksonville State Hospital, Anna State Hospital, Manteno State Hospital, Kankakee State Hospital, Peoria State Hospital, Pontiac Penitentiary, and Lincoln State School—and included names of those who had done the collecting.

Predictably, Democrats running for office demanded action by the governor to stop the practice and return funds. Stevenson turned the report into a campaign statement. He said, "This sort of shakedown racket must stop. Gov. Green will probably do nothing to stop it. However, when I am elected in November, I will do something about it. I do not want campaign fund solicitors on the state payroll. I want only conscientious workers, devoted to the public service."[45] However, he did not promise to stop contributions from state employees who were not under civil service, nor did it appear he had any independent information on which to support his accusation.

In spite of newspaper articles and editorials, nothing came of the investigation in terms of legal action, which often was the outcome of political corruption claims. Nevertheless, the *Sun-Times* refused to leave the subject alone as the campaign developed. As an example of the paper's tenacity, a series of articles published in October 1948 about state finances under the Green administration included two on the subject of alleged civil service abuse in raising campaign funds.

While the October *Sun-Times* articles, by reporter David Anderson, did not add further details to the February allegations, they repeated comments by Green after his election in 1940.[46] Green was quoted as saying, "Since the power and prestige of a political machine is maintained by jobs, every extension of civil service is a blow to bossism. The merit system is no longer a subject of controversy. It is a permanent and beneficial element of our government." He added later, "The new administration will comply with the civil service statute." The articles repeated Michael Ryan's accusations, adding that changes in the law as late as 1947 made it impossible for an employee "to defend himself before a trial board before discharge." Ryan also accused the Green administration of installing "personnel officers" whose job it was to get rid of certain state employees. *Sun-Times* columnist Pete Akers jumped on the subject in October with a column reinforcing points in the Anderson articles.[47]

The issue of department bosses asking non–civil service government employees to contribute in a general election year had its roots in earlier decades, and both parties had their version of what was called "the lug." The critical point was to leave civil service employees alone and let them contribute of their free will. As if it were a badge of courage to solicit non–civil service employees, an article appeared in the *Tribune* by reporter George Tagge explaining how the Republican process would work in the 1948 campaign.[48] This article would not have appeared without the blessing of the Green administration.

Tagge referred to the Democratic "lug" from the days of Governor Horner. He reminded readers that Democrats assessed employees 2 percent of their salaries for campaign purposes. Higher-paid employees were expected to provide a higher percentage. The reporter provided this Republican scale for the 1948 primary and general election:

$15 for employees paid from $2,100 to $2,399 a year
$30 for those getting $2,400 to $2,999 a year
$35 for those receiving $3,000 to $3,599
$50 for salaries from $3,600 to $4,199
$75 for salaries from $4,200 to $4,799
$100 or more for those paid $4,800 and higher

Quoting party officials, Tagge said that with the exclusion of civil service employees, 10,000 of the 29,472 state employees would contribute to the party campaign. He estimated an average contribution of $30, which would provide $300,000. Department heads in the administration agreed to the scale. Paul C. Rosenquist, Republican state chairman and head of the Department of Revenue, said there was nothing compulsory about the contributions.

MARCH 1948

The political pace quickened in March. For the first half of the month, Democratic candidates campaigned across the state in an organized caravan, slashing their way with thrusts at Republicans in what can only be described as combat. The gloves were off. Republicans, who had not planned to campaign aggressively against Democrats until after the April primary, or even later, rose to defend their records and return the blows. The attacks got personal and specific, especially in the race for governor, and lasted for most of the month.

An explosive issue during March came in the form of an article by John Bartlow Martin in *Harper's Magazine* titled "The Blast in Centralia No. 5: A Mine Disaster No One Stopped." The article resurrected the explosion that had killed III miners a year earlier and provided Democratic candidate Adlai Stevenson with fresh material for his stump speeches through central and southern Illinois. While most political people expected the disaster to be a prime issue, Martin's work lifted the subject to the status of current event.

The effort by leaders in the Democratic Party to enlist Dwight Eisenhower as a presidential candidate in place of President Truman grew, with an Illinois factor of consequence. Jack Arvey continued as a rallying point for those who believed the party's chances of retaining the presidency were nil with a Truman candidacy, but he was greeted with mixed reactions among Illinois party leaders. The issue placed Arvey and the Senate candidate, Paul Douglas, at odds with former Chicago mayor Edward Kelly. Truman announced he would run if nominated, causing the *Tribune* to comment, "It is indeed an extraordinary state of affairs when an incumbent President has felt compelled to announce that he will run for re-election."[49]

The Centralia coal mine disaster of March 1947 was rehashed thoroughly. St. Louis newspapers kept the political story alive with editorials condemning Governor Green and his appointees in the Department of Mines and Minerals. However, the story lost steam as the months passed. With the first anniversary of the disaster on 25 March 1948, those sensitive to its political potential braced for the inevitable newspaper commemoration. Republicans hoped it would be over in a few days. Democrats couldn't wait to use the anniversary for gain. All of them were blindsided by publication of Martin's article in the March issue of *Harper's Magazine*.[50] It was a shot heard around the nation and throughout Illinois.

Martin, of Chicago, a former newspaper reporter, had built a reputation as a freelance writer. The 18,000-word article in *Harper's*—the longest in the magazine's history to that point—gained a national reputation for Martin that led to political advocacy and diplomatic appointments by Democratic presidents. The article provided Stevenson with material to pummel Governor Green. In 1952, Martin went to work for Stevenson as a speechwriter during the presidential campaign. He later wrote an 800,000-word, two-volume biography of Stevenson, which served to burnish the subject's reputation in spite of his holding elective office for only four years.

The article provided a dramatic version of the explosion's force and aftermath by focusing on individual miners who died and on those who survived. Martin recounted the fear and longing experienced by women and children who waited for hours to learn the fate of their husbands, brothers, and fathers. He told of miners working with danger every day in a mine where conditions were unsafe and how no one in authority would listen to their complaints. Martin's descriptions of working conditions in the mine, punctuated by quotations such as "I used to cough up chunks of coal dust like walnuts after work," jarred readers unfamiliar with details of the disaster.

As powerful as the story was from a human standpoint, Martin wove a compelling tale of political intrigue that landed squarely at the feet of Governor Green. The governor entered the picture in March 1946 when Centralia members of the United Mine Workers of America local wrote an impassioned letter to him, pleading with him to make the mine safer: the famous "please save our lives" letter. Green again appeared in the article during the account of Robert Medill asking inspectors to get campaign donations from mine owners for the Republican candidate for Chicago mayor in 1947.

Stevenson quoted one phrase from the article time and again, to keep Green's name in his remarks about improving mine safety and reforming the selection of mine inspectors. Martin's often-used commentary read as follows: "Here lies Green's responsibility—not that, through a secretary's fumble he failed to act on the miners' appeal to 'save our lives' but rather that, while the kingmakers were shunting him around the nation making speeches, back home his loyal followers were busier building a rich political machine for him than in administering the state for him. Moreover, enriching the Green machine dovetailed nicely with the personal ambitions of Medill and others, and Green did not restrain them."[51]

Stevenson made a point of being in the Centralia area for speeches on the first anniversary of the explosion. He mentioned the Martin article prominently, urging those in the audience to read the piece because "it recounts in sequence all the reports that were made over a period of years by a conscientious inspector, Driscoll Scanlan, to the state Department of Mines and Minerals about that mine and what happened to those reports that the mine was unsafe." Throughout the speech, Stevenson read from the article, quoting the *Post-Dispatch*'s criticism of Green and Martin's statement about Green's responsibility. The candidate concluded the remarks, "It is the disease, not only the symptom, that must be eradicated. We must attack that malignant growth on the body politic, the cynical cold-blooded sale of privilege. And I hold that the governor is responsible for the system whether he personally condones, actively solicits, or passively permits the sale of governmental favors. There will be no bold and no furtive solicitation of campaign funds for me at the risk of human life in the coal mines or anywhere else."[52]

Adding to public attitudes toward the Centralia disaster, and helping Stevenson, were newspaper articles on the anniversary that tugged at the heartstrings. One example, in the *Sun-Times*, an avowed backer of Stevenson, were interviews with a number of surviving spouses of the 111 dead coal miners, pointing out how they had coped with the tragedy. The paper reminded readers that many wives were mothers of large families and faced difficult times finding a hopeful path. The article stated, "The widows are fitting into new patterns of life. They know that, although the mist always will come occasionally to their eyes, the future demands more of their devotion than the past."[53]

Democratic and Republican candidates for Illinois offices had campaigned in some form of caravans before 1948, but nothing with the intensity of the Democrats' effort in March. In the first seventeen days of the month, all state candidates spread themselves from bottom to top of the state. During the day individuals fanned out to the smallest of towns and in the evening gathered for a big rally in one of the larger communities. This onslaught across downstate Illinois, covered extensively in daily and weekly newspapers, was designed to reach the party faithful deep in the strongholds of the Republican Party and to test campaign themes.

The tour's first rally was in Herrin on 1 March, where a driving rain cut attendance in the auditorium to 300 from an expected 800. Stevenson, according to the *Chicago Daily News*, provided "a blistering review of the Centralia mine disaster" in an area of the state heavily dependent on coal mining jobs. The explosion became the poster for Stevenson's campaign in central and southern Illinois for most of the campaign, but it got a first test in March. He attacked the practice of political appointments of mine inspectors as "the cynical, cold-blooded sale of privilege" and pledged "no more Centralia tragedies—no more sales of privilege." He added, "I want public servants on the payrolls. No solicitors need apply." His assault included an indictment of the whole Green record.[54]

An early but characteristic example of local political curiosity about the caravan occurred in the hamlet of Goreville in northern Johnson County. State representative Paul Powell of Vienna, downstate campaign director for the party, produced 200 people for the meeting. The county normally voted Republican 3 to 1, so the turnout delighted the Democratic candidates.[55]

Paul Douglas provided a sample of his campaign "theme song" by extolling the administration of Franklin D. Roosevelt. He stated, "I pledge the people of this state that when elected senator I will try to walk in the steps of Franklin Roosevelt and be faithful to his spirit."[56] His comments met with approval as southern Illinois voters had favored Roosevelt in all his presidential elections. Douglas assailed communists in the United States along with extreme reactionaries in the labor movement and Republican Party. He voiced full support for the Marshall Plan and enforcement of federal coal mine safety laws.

Before the next evening rally in Carmi, Douglas campaigned in several coal mining districts, commenting on the need for increased mine safety and getting the attention of union members with criticism of the Taft-Hartley Act. He admitted satisfaction with one or two provisions of the law but said the whole "will do more harm than good" to organized labor. Douglas also spoke during the day and at the rally about the need to extend electrification to a greater extent in farm areas. He said, "Private utility interests prevailed upon the Republicans in the current session of Congress to slash appropriations for this work by 25 million dollars. As a result, thousands of Illinois farmers who want this service extended to their farms have been denied their hopes."[57]

Stevenson, addressing an overflow crowd of 300 cheering partisans in Carmi, opened a second line of criticism of Green's administration, claiming, "It is shockingly apparent that the schools have not been treated very generously in the distribution of what Mr. Green has called inflationary dollars." Stating he would place education at the top of his priority list as governor, Stevenson added, "I shall not treat education as a secondary issue." He said Green had "piled up dollars in the state treasury so that he can present himself as an expert in economy and thus be considered eligible at next June's Republican convention for the vice presidential nomination."[58] Stevenson would claim throughout the caravan tour that Green's national ambitions had diminished his attention to state issues.

Reporters covering the first days of the caravan noticed that speakers avoided a subject that had been identified by both parties as likely to inflame the state campaign. This was the matter of diverting sales tax revenue to cities. Governor Green had defended his position not to increase funds to cities, even if they appeared to need an infusion of revenues. During the caravan, Stevenson complained about Green's allotment of funds to education but did not talk of diversion to cities. Charles Wheeler, political correspondent for the *Chicago Daily News* who covered much of the tour, wrote of a meeting in Carmi at which Democratic speakers agreed to "give the diversion issue the silent treatment downstate." Wheeler said the decision occurred because members of the Illinois Education Association were opposed. He wrote, "They are said to be relying on sales tax surpluses for larger appropriations to the distributive [educational] fund."[59] He also said the Illinois Agricultural Association opposed diversion because it feared a business recession might require new taxes and a large surplus would be important.

The caravan headed to the industrial centers of East St. Louis and Alton, where Douglas was expected to increase criticism of the Taft-Hartley law, as he had in coal mine communities. Thomas Morrow, reporting for the *Tribune*, wrote that the candidates had visited forty towns in fourteen counties and "have spoken to approximately 14,000 persons." Morrow added a critique of Stevenson's style on the stump, recognizing that this was the candidate's first political campaign for anything: "Stevenson, gaining confidence as he travels the vote-getting circuit, is making better use of his voice but needs a loud speaker. Audiences yield to his personality but those seeking burning utterances are disappointed."[60]

East St. Louis and Alton were key cities in the second largest and most effective Democratic political machine in Illinois, with Chicago and Cook County being first. The candidates spoke to the choir, the audiences heavily populated with union members who cheered almost everything said by the candidates. Some of the comments were predictable. Douglas stated again how the Republican-controlled Congress had stacked the deck in the Taft-Hartley bill with antiunion elements designed to punish labor. Stevenson denounced the previous General Assembly, which was heavily controlled by Republicans. He pictured the governor's budget approved by the legislature as loading the machine-building payrolls and denying the common schools of what

Stevenson considered a proper share of revenues. He said a report on the condition of state hospitals, citing poor living conditions, failed to mention "one important factor: graft."[61]

Cutting across central Illinois to Tuscola, Urbana, and Danville, Stevenson kept up his attacks on corruption and graft, characterizing Green as a man "who says on Monday a third term is wrong, and on Tuesday that a third term is fine." Reporter Morrow noted that Stevenson seemed tired after a week of steady campaigning. He quoted the candidate as saying, "I am no corn stalk orator, but I plan to discuss the issues calmly throughout the state." Stevenson had begun using frequent anecdotes in his talks, which Morrow said sounded like the "chatty style employed by Mayor Kennelly in the Chicago campaign." Stevenson had continued a stream of increasingly caustic comments about Green in a part of Illinois where "people usually vote Republican and forget about it," one reporter wrote.[62]

Meanwhile, Green made few campaign appearances while the Democrats chiseled away at his image. During a joint appearance in Chicago with Senator Brooks on 6 March, Green paid no attention to the Democrats, preferring instead to sound more like a candidate for national office. Both candidates ripped sixteen years of the New Deal administration of Roosevelt and Truman and referred to Democratic foreign policy as "a scrambled jig saw program."[63] Either the Democratic tour clippings had not reached Green or his mind was elsewhere. He left on vacation, only to return after a few days to respond to Stevenson's tongue-lashings, obviously concerned by the drumbeat of the Democrat's campaign.

Green counterattacked with vigor. On 10 March in Fairfield at the first of several downstate appearances, he said in a speech (termed an "uppercut" by the press) that Illinois voters "are in no mood to extend the power and the scope of the New Deal Democrats and bunglers." Then turning on Stevenson, Green said the Democrat was "apparently on leave from the striped pants brigade of the Roosevelt-Truman state department while he carries the New Deal torch in Illinois." This began Green's earnest attempt to hang the labels of internationalist and diplomat on his opponent. Stevenson took up the challenge. In Rock Island he criticized the 1947 legislature as the handmaiden of Green. He said legislators were "guilty of a crime against the people of Illinois, for betraying the trust placed in them, for accepting their legislative salaries under false pretenses, for squandering the money bestowed on them, and for bringing dishonor on the state that honored them." He said Green's comment about the "striped pants brigade" missed the campaign issue: "Power-drunk political spoilsmen, pseudo-Republicans with temporary authority, created the issue of this campaign. This issue is Illinois."[64]

Coming to Stevenson's defense in Chicago was the pro-Democratic *Sun-Times*, which stated editorially, "When Gov. Green talks about striped pants, he is trying to cover up his own record at Springfield, which is the real issue of the state campaign. So it doesn't hurt Adlai Stevenson to be identified with the U.N. idea. The talents which he devoted to its work—the intelligence, the deep human conscience, the incorruptible patriotism, the awareness of world realities—are precisely the qualities which fit him for the governorship."[65] This statement, and others repeated by the paper, attempted to balance the *Tribune*, which applauded Green's choice of words.

A day later, Green fired back at Stevenson's comments about the General Assembly and governor as coming from a man who had no knowledge of work done by the legislature: "The man who delivered that tirade against the General Assembly wasn't even in the state of Illinois during most of the time the assembly was in session." Green pointed out that Stevenson had spent much of the last decade outside Illinois: "His interests have been elsewhere—in Washington and New York, in London and Paris on first this and then that assignment he received from various agencies and bureaus of the New Deal government in Washington."[66]

The "striped pants" issue hung around the gubernatorial campaign through the rest of March. Green beat the drum repeatedly in an attempt to stick the label on Stevenson, who felt obliged to defend his record. At the same time, Green had difficulty focusing on Illinois issues, preferring to speak about matters of national concern. He concentrated on Roosevelt and Truman during appearances at Aurora, Elgin, and Wheaton. This statement summed up his approach: "In three short years the Roosevelt-Truman diplomacy has lost the peace. Its weak and shameful compromises with the communist dictatorship—compromises which violated our American ideals of freedom, justice and decency— opened the way for the communist aggression which now threatens to engulf all Europe."[67]

Throughout the caravan tour, reporters praised Douglas as the orator among the Democratic candidates. In contrast to Stevenson, he aimed criticism at Republicans in Congress, and any barbs thrown at incumbent Brooks were incidental. On the domestic side, he spoke mostly as a liberal who wanted to extend government services and opportunities to low income families. An example of his domestic proposals was an initiative to build 12 million homes over the next decade. He said, "Land can be obtained more readily if large, unused tracts of delinquent property are returned to tax rolls. Interest rates can be reduced by increasing the government guarantee on private building."[68] On other domestic matters he called for repeal of the Taft-Hartley law, price supports for farmers, expanded social security benefits, and improved civil rights protections for racial minorities.

Douglas came across as adamantly opposed to communism and Russia's reach into internal affairs of other nations. Knowing that his opponent and Republican-leaning newspapers continued to associate him with socialism and communism, he mentioned his position at almost every campaign stop. Based mostly on his experiences during World War II, he argued for a strong national defense, a position he maintained throughout his three terms in the U.S. Senate. His support of the Marshall Plan was unstinting, flying in the face of his opponent, who was just as firmly opposed. Douglas said the Cold War with Russia was a moral struggle between the forces of good and evil. At every step, Douglas praised the Roosevelt record. On this point alone, he separated himself from Senator Brooks.

During the caravan tour, Douglas gave other Democrats and citizens across the state a good taste of the campaign style he would maintain until November. He worked long hours every day, stopping at factory gates and shopping centers, walking miles on the streets of towns of all sizes, and shaking hands and speaking to anyone who would listen. When addressing audiences at formal campaign events, he forcefully reiterated his themes. His wife, Emily, maintained a full schedule of appearances before women's groups and in private homes. The network of contacts across the state during her years in Congress provided opportunities to spread the word for her husband. Before a crowd of Democratic women in Chicago late in March, Douglas said he was running on his wife's coattails.[69]

Brooks, on the other hand, attended to business in Washington, making only a few appearances in Illinois during March. He occasionally issued press releases. The *Tribune* kept Brooks's name before the public, publishing his remarks delivered before the Senate. On 13 March, he told his colleagues he would vote against the $17 billion Marshall Plan spending bill, calling the plan a taxpayer subsidy of socialistic regimes in Europe. "The people of Illinois are as charitable as any people on earth and they want to help in every constructive way, but I am sure they would not want to drain the resources of America to perpetuate conditions which will make their efforts futile and their high purposes a failure."[70] He reminded Illinoisans of his opposition to the United Nations and made no mention of his opponent. Brooks wanted to appear as a hard-working senator. His attacks on Roosevelt and Truman programs were relentless as he pushed his brand of isolationism and concern for the burdens on taxpayers, points he had made countless times during his eight years in the Senate.

If the campaigns of candidates for governor and senator during March were any indication, the fight to November would be memorable. Regardless of Stevenson's aggressive words across the state and Douglas's pronouncements about issues facing the nation, they were far behind their Republican opponents by all measurements available. Green and Brooks campaigned with the confidence gained from the 1946 elections and from the fact they faced amateurs when it came to reaching Illinois voters. Also, it was so early in the campaign that potential voters had not paid much attention. The opportunity for false confidence existed. Although each candidate staked out his basic premise for the campaign in March, the months ahead would provide unforeseen issues and significant shifts in voter interest.

Throughout the Democratic candidates' caravan, Adlai Stevenson praised the work of Franklin Roosevelt but never mentioned Harry Truman. When Kentucky senator Alben Barkley was honored at a Chicago event, Stevenson spoke, mentioning Paul Douglas, Edward Kelly, Martin Kennelly, and the other state candidates, but not the president. Stevenson's icy attitude toward Truman lasted well into the fall campaign season. Stevenson believed Truman would lose if nominated, and he worried that Republicans would attempt to tie him to the president.

On this issue, Stevenson represented a sizable segment of Democratic officials in Illinois. His running mate, Paul Douglas, opposed Truman's nomination, thereby voicing approval for Arvey's behind-the-scenes work to enlist Eisenhower. Others in the state publicly voiced disapproval of Truman and said if Eisenhower was not available, others should be sought, such as Senator Barkley or Supreme Court justice William O. Douglas.

The biggest split over Truman among high-ranking Illinois Democrats was between Arvey and former mayor Kelly, who served as

Democratic national committeeman for the state. Kelly's friendship with Truman dated to the 1944 Democratic convention, when he helped in the movement to keep Henry Wallace from being nominated for vice president. Practical politicians in the Illinois party expected Kelly to support Truman.

Late in March, Arvey consulted with Democratic national chairman J. Howard McGrath on Truman and other issues related to the campaign. Upon returning to Chicago, Arvey told George Tagge at the *Tribune* that Truman was "not as strong as he was two months ago." Presumably, since Arvey thought Truman was a loser two months before, his opinion had not changed. A day after Arvey's return to Chicago, Kelly told Tagge he favored Truman's nomination. Tagge quoted Kelly as saying, "Personally I'm for Truman until such time as it would be unwise. Most Democrats will be for Truman, upturn or no upturn. He's in the ditch right now, but keep in mind that these things run in cycles. We don't nominate or elect a president in March."[71] He also said he would run for reelection as committeeman. Meanwhile, Arvey consulted national union leaders and close friends of Truman about alternatives to the president.

In the same article, Tagge quoted Arvey about an Eisenhower candidacy. Arvey said, "I'm no more for Eisenhower than for any of the other men who might be considered. I consider him the kind of a liberal I could vote for. I'd be almost as willing to vote for Justice William O. Douglas, Sen. Barkley, or Sen. Lucas. I'm not beating the drums for Eisenhower."[72] Of course, he was "beating the drums" for Eisenhower, and the others were simply convenient names. Within days, two of Franklin D. Roosevelt's sons, Elliott and Franklin Jr., announced their preference for Eisenhower. But even among the family members there was a split. James, the eldest son, and the only daughter, Anna Roosevelt Boettiger, backed away from support for Eisenhower, although neither voiced a strong "yes" for Truman. In the end, three of Roosevelt's sons—James, Elliott, and Franklin Jr.—supported Eisenhower. This turn of events occurred after news surfaced of an Eisenhower declaration that he would not seek the presidency as a Republican. He did not mention the possibility of running as a Democrat, giving hope to liberals opposed to Truman.

As a windup to the month, Eisenhower's press aide, Major General Floyd Parks, said "under no conceivable circumstances" would the general consent to be drafted as the Democratic candidate for president. Parks added, "The general means his no politics announcement of some weeks ago to apply to all parties and groups of voters. What he said about wanting to have nothing to do with politics applies to the Democrats as well as the Republicans."[73] As everyone would learn, a statement by an aide to Eisenhower did not serve as a statement by the man. Eisenhower thought the movement would die if he refused to address the matter publicly, and besides, as his biographer Stephen Ambrose wrote, "With no party identification, no political experience of support or base, no record, and no organization, he doubted that there was any reality to an Eisenhower boom."[74]

John H. Stelle *(left)*, governor for a tumultuous ninety-nine days, accompanies governor-elect Dwight Green to inaugural events in 1941. (Courtesy of the Abraham Lincoln Presidential Library and Museum)

Senator C. Wayland Brooks *(left)* and Governor Dwight Green *(right)* meet with *Chicago Tribune* editor and publisher Robert McCormick at a Springfield event. (Courtesy of the Abraham Lincoln Presidential Library and Museum)

(From left) Jack Arvey, Senator Scott Lucas, and longtime Chicago mayor Edward J. Kelly discuss Democratic Party campaign strategies. (Courtesy of the Abraham Lincoln Presidential Library and Museum)

George F. Barrett, Illinois
attorney general, 1941–49,
was a controversial figure
in newspaper accounts of
gambling and corruption.
(Courtesy of the Abraham Lincoln
Presidential Library and Museum)

Governor Dwight Green announces the firing of the Department
of Mines and Minerals director after the Centralia coal mine
disaster, April 1947. (Courtesy of the *Centralia Morning Sentinel*)

Senator Scott Lucas *(left)* tried to persuade Adlai Stevenson to run for governor during meetings in Springfield in November 1947. (Courtesy of the Abraham Lincoln Presidential Library and Museum)

Senator Scott Lucas *(left)* and Mayor Martin H. Kennelly *(right)* greet President Truman on his visit to Chicago in June 1948. (Courtesy of the Abraham Lincoln Presidential Library and Museum)

Candidate Adlai E. Stevenson II meets with reporters at a
Springfield airport in 1948. (Courtesy of the Abraham Lincoln Presidential
Library and Museum)

President Truman's stop in Herrin drew thousands more people than
the town's population, September 1948. (Courtesy of Herrin City Library)

President Truman visits Abraham Lincoln's tomb during a campaign trip to Springfield, October 1948. (Courtesy of the Abraham Lincoln Presidential Library and Museum)

State representative Paul Powell *(left)* accompanies President Truman to the podium for a speech in Springfield, October 1948. (Courtesy of the Abraham Lincoln Presidential Library and Museum)

Democratic candidates gather with President Truman at a Springfield campaign event, 1948. *From left:* Edward J. Barrett, Paul Douglas, Truman, Adlai Stevenson. (Courtesy of the Abraham Lincoln Presidential Library and Museum)

Theodore Link, *St. Louis Post-Dispatch* investigative reporter, became a public figure during late stages of the 1948 campaign. (Reprinted with permission of the *St. Louis Post-Dispatch*)

Senator Paul H. Douglas works at his Washington, D.C., desk early in his first term. He served in office from 1949 to 1967. (Courtesy of the U.S. Senate Historical Office)

4. A Time for Ceremonies

April was the first of four consecutive months that could be called ceremonial in terms of formal political activity: in April came the primary election; in May, the state party conventions; and in June and July, the two national political conventions. Most eyes were on the national conventions, where both parties promised fireworks and intrigue.

The election was a "boss's primary," created by Republican and Democratic political machines that squeezed out any meaningful opposition. The election had only two competitive races for state and federal offices, and both were considered uneventful. Opposing Senator C. Wayland Brooks was William J. Baker, often a candidate but never elected. On the Democratic side, Joseph P. Burke of Chicago, a former Cook County assistant state's attorney, opposed slated candidate Ivan A. Elliott of Carmi for attorney general. Burke had withdrawn from the race but waited too long for his name to be erased from the ballot.

Without any election drama, the essential objective for each party was to use the primary election as a preliminary to the main event in November. As *Chicago Tribune* reporter Bob Howard wrote in one of the preelection roundup articles, "The primary is like spring training for big league baseball players. It is important only as a means of getting in shape for the summer and fall grind that will end with the all-important election November 2."[1] In essence, it was a trial run, a chance for precinct workers across the state to work out kinks before the outcome mattered.

As newspapers laid out the backgrounds of all candidates in lengthy articles, readers had an opportunity to see between some of the lines. The *Tribune*, notorious for loading political articles to put its favorites in a good light, led stories with information about Republicans, burying Democratic candidates with less detail on inside pages. From the first paragraph of some stories, the *Tribune*'s images determined the play. One article began, "Heading the rival party slates in Illinois this year as candidates for governor and senator are two Republicans, experienced in public office, and two Democrats with background as New Dealers and internationalists."[2] Technically, the statement was correct, though it leaned decidedly toward the Republicans.

Searching for something to write about in a mostly dull election period, newspapers gave prominent mention to the candidates' service records. With the war still in the minds of most people, time in the military—those who served and those who did not—had meaning. A few men had served in World War I, and some in both wars. If wounded, the candidate got special attention. Accounts for those who did not serve in either war were conspicuously bare. Republicans with a war record included Dwight Green, Curly Brooks, Richard Yates Rowe (lieutenant governor), William Stratton (secretary of state), and Elmer Droste (treasurer). Those without a mention of service included Sinon Murray (auditor) and George Barrett (attorney general). Democrats with war records were Paul Douglas, Sherwood Dixon (lieutenant governor), Edward Barrett (secretary of state), and Ivan Elliott (attorney general). No military record was given for Benjamin Cooper (auditor) or Ora Smith (treasurer).[3]

With about 30 percent of registered voters casting ballots in the primary, all the slated candidates in both parties won. The surprise occurred in the Democratic race for attorney general where Elliott squeaked by Burke, the noncandidate, by 10,000 votes.[4] Republicans made much of vote totals for governor and senator, although they were meaningless for November. Green received about 200,000 votes more than Stevenson, and Brooks slipped past Douglas by about 50,000.

Before the primary, Jack Arvey pleaded with precinct workers to turn out a healthy vote for Democrats. His cheerleading did little to inspire election workers, who newspaper reporters claimed were depressed by slim chances of victory in November. Before the primary, *Chicago Daily News* columnist Madison West said Democratic leaders were "glum" about primary activity. He commented on a general feeling of "we're licked in November."[5] However, Arvey's other motive was to frustrate organizational attempts by the Progressive Party. If the party was able to get on the Illinois ballot, everyone assumed liberal Democratic voters would drift to the group headed nationally by Henry Wallace.

Most of the action involving the Progressives occurred in state and circuit courts just days before the primary election when the state supreme court proclaimed the group a legal party in Cook County. A day before the vote, a county circuit judge denied the party's petition to force election officials to put Progressive candidates on the ballot. The judge ruled that timing "will not permit such an action to be carried out."[6] He said it would be a physical impossibility as ballots had already been delivered to polling places a day earlier. Progressive Party officials requested its followers to boycott the primary so they could remain eligible to sign independent petitions to place Wallace and state and local candidates on the November ballot.

With public interest in election politics lagging during the month, newspapers, especially those in Chicago, gave major attention to the Progressive Party's candidate for the U.S. Senate, Curtis D. MacDougall of the Northwestern University School of Journalism, in Evanston. While MacDougall hardly had name recognition across the state, he had familiarity among journalists, many of whom had attended his classes. He also had a record as an activist for liberal causes and a failed run for Congress from a North Shore district in 1944.

After the primary election, papers learned that Kenneth E. Olson, dean of the School of Journalism at Northwestern, had advised MacDougall "in a friendly way" that he should withdraw from the Progressive ticket to avoid "a red smear" that would damage the university's image. Campaigning in nearby Iowa, Wallace said he thought MacDougall should be free to decide whether to run without interference from university officials. In an editorial comment, the *Daily News* stated, "We do not know all the facts, but the counsel Dean Olson says he offered sounds friendly to us. If the friendship were close enough to permit complete candor he might have added that Prof. MacDougall would probably not make a very good senator, anyhow."[7] The MacDougall saga would continue well into the campaign season.

In a continuing soap opera with many Democratic Party officials hoping to find a way to replace Truman on the ticket, Dwight Eisenhower again voiced his refusal to run. After a twenty-five-minute conversation with President Truman at the White House on 10 April regarding alleged non-presidential matters, Eisenhower said to reporters, "I made up my mind to say nothing more. I wrote a letter and I meant every word of it. I told my aides they could do the talking from now on. I'm not talking any more. I find it doesn't do any good."[8] But by not adamantly stating in person to reporters that he was not a candidate for either party, he continued to leave the door open.

Meanwhile, Arvey devoted new energy to a drop-Truman campaign. After the primary election, he traveled to Palm Springs, California, for a conference with former Chicago mayor Edward Kelly.[9] Arvey intended to tell Kelly it was unwise to hang onto the president. As Arvey left Chicago, newspapers reported that black political leaders in the city had issued a statement backing Truman. As it turned out, Arvey's attempt to dissuade Kelly failed. A few days after the meeting, Kelly repeated his support of Truman, adding he believed the president would be chosen on the first ballot at the convention. Kelly took some of the sting out of Arvey's rebuke by saying, "Jack Arvey and I don't agree on the Truman matter at present, but we're still friends."[10] Kelly had criticized a speech a few days earlier in California by James Roosevelt in which he did not mention Truman and indicated support for Eisenhower.

Dwight Green's consuming interest in being the Republican vice presidential nominee in 1948 was never artfully concealed. Everyone in Illinois politics knew about it. He had a distinguished background as federal prosecutor, had served eight years as governor, and had spent countless days outside the state developing contacts that would be valuable at the appropriate time. He went through the motions of filing for a third term as governor but demonstrated a lack of enthusiasm for the campaign in the first three months of 1948.

A vice presidential nominee from the key state of Illinois looked to many like a natural placement on a ticket with Thomas E. Dewey, governor of New York. Dewey would need someone from a large state with connections distant from the northeast to assure election as president. A number of Illinois Republican power brokers thought that made sense and began working toward the goal. Although a severe critic of the New Deal years, Green had developed a moderate image on domestic affairs that fit well with Dewey.

If there was a fly in the ointment, it was the candidacy for president of Senator Robert Taft from Ohio. Taft, the darling of conservatives and President Truman's severest critic, did not seem such a good fit for Green. Also, the geographic proximity of Ohio to Illinois discounted the governor's value to the ticket. In the overall picture of Republican presidential politics by April, Dewey, in spite of his loss to Roosevelt in 1944, looked like the favorite in a convention showdown with Taft.

The saga of Green's attempt to land on the national ticket involved a multitude of suspicions about backroom deals at the Illinois and national levels of the Republican Party. Some were designed to get Green his wish, others to deny him anything but running for governor.

One of Dewey's closest advisers was Herbert Brownell, the New York governor's campaign manager and former chairman of the Republican National Committee. He fashioned the idea of a ticket headed by governors of two of the nation's largest states, New York and Illinois.[11] Before Brownell took the idea to Dewey or Green, he conferred with Republican officials in Illinois, who raised no serious doubts. On the state level, Green's behind-the-scenes backer for vice president was Donald Maxwell, the politically active city editor of the *Chicago Tribune*.

With plotting in full bloom, Green aided his case by frequently attacking the Roosevelt-Truman record and New Deal policies in place or pending. He tried to mix Illinois issues in the speeches, but as often as not newspaper editors gave the headlines to Green's national aspirations. Noticing the trend, Stevenson called attention to Green's presumed preoccupation with a bigger picture than Illinois. Watching all this with interest, and a degree of concern, was Brooks, who did not trust Green and believed an Illinois ticket without the governor would work against him. If Green were to succeed as the vice presidential nominee, his place on the Illinois ticket would be filled by the Republican State Central Committee. Of course, nothing much would happen regarding Green's future without the concurrence of Robert McCormick, a stalwart supporter of Taft.

The work of schemers for Green produced a major achievement. On Tuesday, 20 April, Republican National Committee members meeting in Philadelphia unanimously chose Green as temporary chairman and keynote speaker for the national convention in June.[12] The governor would have a national stage on which to gain the kind of attention others lusted for. While announced candidates for president were not considered as keynote speakers, there was no such standard for possible vice presidential nominees. Party officials in Illinois and Green made the appropriate comments of appreciation.

As Adlai Stevenson's campaign gained strength early in 1948, he and advisers knew they had to embrace the southern Illinois Democratic team of state representative Paul Powell and former governor John Stelle. If

Stevenson delayed that action too long, it could seriously damage his chances of defeating Green. Making nice with Powell and Stelle, especially Stelle, must have been unpleasant, but Stevenson had no other choice. Stelle and Powell considered Stevenson an inexperienced elitist, which made a connection with him uncomfortable, to say the least.[13]

Stelle was anathema to those who revered former governor Henry Horner, among them Stevenson, whose warm feeling for Horner was obvious. Stevenson used the former governor as a counterweight to the Green administration, making it clear in public statements that he wanted to be viewed as Horner's logical successor. Stevenson's posture irked Stelle.

Powell, free of any alliance with the Horner crowd, had a political style precisely the opposite of Stevenson's. Furthermore, Powell had shown his disdain for "good government" types, who often were active in the Stevenson campaign. That attitude would prevail long after the election. Powell and Stelle were political compatriots by 1948. They had joined in passage of legislation favorable to their horse-racing interests and traded favors with Chicago Democrats and Republicans whenever that might boost their interests in southern Illinois. This was not the way Stevenson viewed political affairs. Given his inclinations, Stevenson would have ignored the two. Given their preference, Stelle and Powell would have favored someone like Edward Barrett as a candidate for governor.[14]

Practical politics being what they were, however, Stevenson could not ignore them. Powell was the downstate Democratic campaign director, and that meant he could influence the degree of enthusiasm for Stevenson among hardcore Democratic workers and officials outside Cook County. Stevenson needed Powell, who had standing with lawmakers as minority leader in the state House. And if Stevenson wanted Powell working for him, he had to do something to mollify Stelle, who was fully capable of supporting Green, as distasteful as that might be.

Winning over Powell and Stelle required more than greeting them warmly on the campaign trail or making staff people available for strategy meetings. A good example of Stevenson's tactic in this regard was a speech he gave to an audience in McLeansboro, Stelle's hometown, on 10 April.[15] Stevenson had campaigned through the region in March as part of the Democratic caravan tour, but he needed a more direct encounter with Powell and Stelle to ensure their support.

Stevenson opened his talk by stating three reasons for appearing in McLeansboro. First, he wanted to talk about what he would do as governor. Second, he wanted "to pay my respects to your distinguished fellow townsman and the former Governor of Illinois, John Stelle, whose name and fame, whose vitality and enterprise, are as well known in other parts of the state as they are in Hamilton County." Stevenson carefully sidestepped the negatives of Stelle's reputation across the state.

Stevenson continued on his mission, stating, "But my third reason is most important, for I came here to pay my warm regards and my respects to Paul Powell of Vienna, who is seeking re-election as representative of this district in the state legislature." Stevenson had just begun to ring Powell's bell. "Paul Powell's remarkable talents as a political speaker have not gone unnoticed in Chicago—or anywhere else for that matter—and I would far rather sit here and listen to him speak than speak myself. I'm sure you would, too." Stevenson had a way of self-deprecation that endeared him to audiences across the state. He continued, "And I am also sure that we would both be the wiser, because this man from Johnson County has been in the legislature for 14 years and has not been asleep in Springfield for the eight long years of the Green plague, and when it comes time to write the obituary of the statehouse gang next November Paul Powell will be able to embellish it with all of the sordid details of the Green Gang's more prosperous days."

Stevenson painted a picture of himself as governor arm-in-arm with political powerhouse Powell:

> Perhaps everyone here does not know that Paul Powell is not only a member of the House, but also minority floor leader. And that is a position of great importance to me personally, since with your help, I expect to move to Springfield next January. And when the 66th General Assembly convenes we are going to start on the long road back to the position of preeminence among the states which Illinois is entitled to by virtue of the quality of her people, her resources and her great traditions. That is why I hope you people will give me Paul Powell as my co-worker in the 66th General Assembly.

In reality, Powell was a shoo-in for reelection. Even though Johnson County usually elected two Republican legislators, Powell won his seat term after term because one representative from the minority party was elected, according to provisions of the state constitution. In 1949 Powell would be chosen speaker of the House, over Governor Stevenson's objections.

Stevenson had learned there were certain buttons to push in southern Illinois, and most of the speech related to those. In discussing Green's campaign funds from special interests, Stevenson alluded to the Centralia mine explosion: "I can well understand why, after Centralia, he might have trouble collecting campaign contributions in the coal industry. In the face of editorials charging 'prostitution of the mine inspection service,' and with national magazines such as *Harper's* and the *Reader's Digest* exposing his administration's responsibility for the tragic disaster a year ago, I don't wonder that he looks, as the newspapers suggest, to a new source of campaign revenue."

At the conclusion of his remarks, Stevenson returned to mention his "friends," saying, "With your help, with the help of capable, sincere men like Paul Powell, like your fellow Townsman, John Stelle, and other southern Illinoisans who have served our party with honor, we will have a state administration of which the whole state—Democrats, Republicans and independents alike—can be proud." Time would reveal Powell and Stelle as only temporary friends of Stevenson, but for the election campaign they stayed on the same team. Commenting on the Stevenson-Powell relationship, *Tribune* reporter Howard said, "Paul never could understand Stevenson because Stevenson was a moral man who didn't think that there should be any shenanigans going on. Powell would claim that after all there ought to be a little for the boys someplace along the line."[16]

In a month light on state campaigns, Paul Douglas took an opportunity to respond to an editorial with an outline of his approach toward federal expenditures and taxation. A characteristic of the campaign for the U.S. Senate was *Chicago Daily News* editorials criticizing Douglas for his support of foreign aid and opposition to tax cuts. These were issues on which Senator Brooks attacked Douglas throughout the campaign. On 9 April, the paper's editorial page criticized Douglas for opposing a $5 billion tax cut while supporting a $5.3 billion appropriation for the Marshall Plan. Douglas responded in a few days with a lengthy letter to the editor, which the paper headlined "Paul H. Douglas Explains His Stand for High Taxes."

Douglas obviously did not agree with the editorial, or the headline. After an analysis of federal costs and revenues, he concluded the government had between $12 billion and $13 billion for three purposes: foreign aid, which, with China, Greece, and Turkey added to the Marshall Plan and occupation costs in Germany, Korea, and Japan, would total $8 billion; debt reduction; and tax reduction. Douglas preferred foreign aid and debt reduction, saying, "I favor foreign aid because I believe it is necessary to relieve acute human distress, to build up the economies of the European countries so that they can again become self-supporting and also to reduce the dangers that communism may move westward to the Atlantic Ocean."[17] In contrast, the Republican-controlled Congress favored a tax reduction.

MAY 1948

Once chosen to be the public face of the Republican Party's national convention, Dwight Green spent much of the month of May preparing for his moment in the spotlight. His principal activities included a speech at the state Republican convention with remarks about his responsibilities, conferences with national convention officials, and drafting the speech he believed would elevate him to nomination as vice president. The state campaign for governor took a temporary backseat.

Before the state convention convened in early May, the *Tribune* editorialized in defense of Green's selection as keynoter.[18] Some newspapers, and Republicans of a moderate leaning, had disagreed with the selection. More than an opinion about Green's philosophy, the editorial staked out the differences between "real" Republicans and pretenders. It characterized those the *Tribune* believed did not act in the best interests of the United States.

The commentary argued for Republicans as the true liberal defenders of the constitution "for a century or more and as it produced the society in which we live." It stated, "They are for the political and social organization made possible by the Bill of Rights, under which the government is the servant of the individual, and the individual is not the slave of the government."

Having defined "liberal" in the paper's terms, the remainder of the editorial was devoted to assorted Republicans: "It is not the liberalism that these self-styled liberal Republicans are talking about. They are not Republicans; they are New Dealers trying to interfere in the management of the Republican party and to frustrate the desire of the majority of its members. They are for socialistic controls that make the state all-powerful and thereby eventually will destroy the Bill of Rights. They are neither liberals nor Republicans, but socialists and war mongers in masquerade." The significance of the *Tribune*'s argument was its imprint on the campaign comments of Brooks and Green as they integrated statements on national policies with defense of the party's record in Illinois.

In their speeches at the state convention, the two incumbents continued lashing Democrats at the national level in familiar language. Green blasted "New Deal theorists who have taken over the Democratic party," adding, "Their method is to get elected and then run hog wild with spending, leaving the people to pay the bill for countless years to follow."[19] Brooks unleashed his rhetoric against the Democratic executive branch "and more than two million payrollers." He said the Republican Congress "has put an end to presidential purges. We have succeeded in part in breaking up the Communist coalition control of our economic life that was dragging us to destruction."[20]

Green used the state convention pulpit to brag about Republican leadership of the state, which was predictable before a captive audience. An example: "By strict economy we met all the increased costs of wages and materials, resulting from the war and post-war inflation, and still maintained and expanded every state service." In defending his handling of state finances, Green reaffirmed his pledge not to take additional money from the treasury for counties and cities. Green also asked Illinois delegates to the national convention to remain uncommitted to any presidential candidate in order not to embarrass him: "I trust there will be no effort to commit the Illinois delegation to any candidate before we reach Philadelphia. I shall be particularly careful to take no part in the campaigns, before or at the convention, of any of the splendid Republicans seeking the presidential nomination." Speculation among reporters gave Taft the bulk of Illinois delegate votes after the first ballot, when all would be pledged to Green as "favorite son."[21]

Following the state convention, Green left for Washington to confer with party officials about the national event and his role as temporary chairman. By that time, work had already begun on the draft of Green's speech. Speaking years later, former *Tribune* reporter Robert Howard provided his recollection of the drafting process:

> Obviously [Green] needed a masterful oration and nobody in the inner circle felt competent to write this speech. So they contacted Raymond Moley, who had been a Roosevelt braintruster and had left the Democrats, a great professional writer. Moley agreed for a sum—I don't know what it was—to write the keynote speech. The boys passed the hat and took up the collection. The speech arrived, and they passed it around in the inner circle for comments.

It was a little too liberal for Illinois Republicans, so everybody would make a change in it. In time, there was no Moley left in it.[22]

In his book about the life of Robert McCormick, Richard Norton Smith provided some of the same information but got more specific about the editing. Green turned it over to the *Tribune* editor and publisher. "Instead of vetting the mildly internationalist text, McCormick gutted it, thereby closing the door to Green's vice presidential ambitions," Smith wrote.[23] This in fact had been McCormick's intent all along. A stalwart backer of Taft for the presidential nomination and a firm opponent of Dewey, he was the immovable object in Green's way. Those planning to put Green on the ballot with Dewey had forgotten about the Colonel. Without the assurance of an editorial endorsement by the *Tribune* for vice president, Green had no practical choice but to forget his ambitions.

On 10 May, just before the state Republican convention, the *Chicago Daily News* shouted in headlines from page 1 "Primary Petition Forged by State G.O.P. Machine/Fake Signatures Total Thousands." The paper had investigated petitions presented to support placing the name of Elmer Droste on the ballot for state treasurer. Droste, of downstate Mount Olive, was a last-minute choice of Green to give the state GOP ticket geographic balance. The action bumped James Simpson Jr., of Wadsworth in Lake County, from the slate. The paper claimed the decision to choose Droste was made on Friday, 23 January; the deadline for filing petitions was Monday, 26 January. Over the weekend, the paper said, "trusted" government employees worked in an organized effort to forge thousands of signatures on petitions. They were filed before the deadline, and Droste was placed on the ticket.[24]

Droste claimed he knew nothing of any forgery effort. The *Daily News* wrote, "There is no evidence that he was aware of the fraudulent methods used to obtain his petitions in the brief time available." The paper's articles did not name anyone as having organized or carried out the forgery plan. Cook County state's attorney William J. Tuohy promised a thorough investigation and presentation to a grand jury. However, the timing of the paper's revelation and the fact that Droste had been nominated in the primary made legal action unlikely. Enough legitimate signatures were found to justify Droste's name on the ballot, regardless of forgeries.[25]

Most of the peccadilloes that newspapers uncovered evaporated because of official inattention, deliberate attempts to bury the issue in evasive talk, or lack of evidence. Few were resolved with an investigation and action. One exception was the issue of whether signatures on Droste's petitions were forged, and if so, how many. Officials brought the case to a Cook County grand jury.

Prosecutors subpoenaed 125 state employees to recite their experiences with the petitions in question. Almost all, fearing self-incrimination, refused to testify. One testified that he had circulated a petition honestly and that the signatures were legal. Leslie "Ike" Volz, administrative assistant to Governor Green, talked at length to the grand jury, acknowledging that some of the signatures were false. On the Sunday before the deadline, Volz had received petitions with as many as 15,000 signatures for his review. "I took an hour to try to determine the good ones. I picked out between 7,500 and 8,000 and sent them on to Springfield. I knew some would not be bona fide. In my long years in politics I learned some circulators are careless, indifferent or lazy. I don't think forgery, if it took place, should be condoned."[26]

One other witness, John J. Dillon of Chicago, an employee of the state revenue department, reportedly told the grand jury his name had been forged as circulator. With no further witnesses willing to discuss the matter, an assistant state's attorney said, "We haven't enough evidence to indict anybody." The jury dropped the case.[27]

The *Daily News* was indignant on its editorial page. The paper's commentary criticized Attorney General Barrett, Treasurer Richard Yates Rowe, and Green for ignoring the case and refusing to uphold state election laws.

Newspapers had for years delighted in writing about Green loading the state employee roster with friends and political associates, some of whom drew salaries for little or no work. Before the month was out, the *Daily News* found another subject that raised an issue about Green administration mishaps. An example of a state employee drawing two paychecks from public entities appeared in the 7 May *Daily News*.[28] It provided no accusation or intent to defraud, nor did it point the finger at a culprit. However, it left an impression that the man may have been able to draw two paychecks because he was a Republican.

Of all the early 1948 campaign issues, one of the most persistent involved Illinois Democrats in pursuit of an alternative to President Truman as the party's nominee. Historians have concluded that the push for Eisenhower was doomed from the start and that derailing Truman was never going to happen. In May 1948, Illinois newspapers watched the effort closely, mostly because Jack Arvey had assumed leadership and Illinoisans familiar with Arvey's record figured if anyone could pull off the switch, it was the commander of the Chicago machine.

With just two months until the Democratic National Convention, pressure mounted on everyone, although few minds were changing. Early in May, former Chicago mayor Kelly reiterated his commitment to Truman for at least a third time. He said, "I'm still for Truman up to this moment. We've got to wait and see what the race looks like when we get to the wire. Right now it's Truman against the field. The Democratic convention comes after the Republican. Let's see whom the Republicans pick. Then we'll pick the man to beat him." About Eisenhower, Kelly added, "No man is big enough to refuse this job."[29] Each time he spoke, Kelly seemed to leave more doors open.

At almost the same time, Arvey said after meetings in New York, "I still have an open mind, but I don't think Truman is the strongest candidate of the party. I believe Eisenhower would electrify the country. Much of our fear would be eliminated if Eisenhower were our candidate. He certainly would be elected." The words meant little except to provide answers to reporters' questions and a buildup to Eisenhower's address to the Chicago Commercial Club later in the month. The general appeared as scheduled and evaded reporters' questions and any mention of a presidential candidacy in his talk. In asides, Eisenhower said he could not remember ever voting during his thirty-eight years in the army. A reporter said he voted by postcard in 1918. "If I did, I don't remember it," he responded. The general said he wasn't aware of the boom for him as president and claimed he did not know Arvey. "I have never heard of the name that I know of," he said.[30]

Meanwhile, newspapers followed Arvey's steps everywhere in search of something to indicate momentum or lack of it. Prior to the state Democratic convention late in the month, Arvey spent several days in Philadelphia during meetings of the national convention committee and stayed in a hotel suite. This gave rise to a story in the *Tribune* that Arvey "tried to throw a monkey wrench in plans" for the convention by attempting to persuade committee members of the need for Eisenhower. The paper quoted Arvey as saying, "I'm sure Eisenhower will be nominated. We Democrats would go to town with him." Adding that the loss of the presidency would cause the loss of thousands of Democratic offices across the nation, he said, "What we need is a candidate who will help us to win locally. Eisenhower is our best bet. He will get more votes for the party than any other candidate."[31]

While those direct quotes would indicate that someone at the committee meeting had provided an account to the paper, Arvey said the following day he did no plotting against Truman in Philadelphia. The *Tribune* quoted Arvey as saying, "Sure, I had a suite at the Belden-Stratford hotel but no national committeemen visited me there and no politics was talked. If you want the truth I entertained an army buddy and his wife and we spent the afternoon playing bridge. There were no deals talked and I haven't asked anyone to exert his influence for or against President Truman."[32] So went the cat-and-mouse game.

A few days later at the state Democratic convention in Springfield, Arvey attempted to eliminate any discussion of Truman or Eisenhower in order not to distract focus on state issues and candidates. The *Tribune* headline said, "Arvey Hangs Up 'Quiet' Sign on Nomination." Former governor John Stelle said, "I'm for Truman and you can put that down." When asked later for further comment, Stelle stated, "Arvey told me not to talk to you boys."[33]

Senator Scott Lucas, chairman of the convention, made opening remarks that alluded to the national campaign but mostly avoided using Truman's name except in context with Roosevelt and New Deal achievements. At one point, Lucas said, "The only program of practical liberalism is the program of Franklin D. Roosevelt and Harry S. Truman. To insure peace throughout the world and continued prosperity at home, we must have a Democratic congress and a Democratic president." In another reference, Lucas praised Truman by name, saying, "Harry Truman has been confronted with problems on the domestic scene and on the international front which would tax the wisdom of a Solomon. Time after time he has met his problems with calm deliberation and sound judgment." Still, Lucas had not given an unqualified endorsement of Truman.[34]

When it came to the presidency, and in particular the fate of Truman, Lucas was an enigma in May. Although a devoted Democrat and supporter of Truman's version of the New Deal, Lucas avoided the issue of Truman's nomination whenever asked. Arvey and Senate candidate Paul Douglas both pushed for replacing Truman, while other Democrats up and down the state stayed with Truman or kept quiet. Surrounded by divisions in Illinois over whether Eisenhower should be pursued to replace the president, silence on the issue may have been a prudent act on Lucas's part.

Nevertheless, observers in Washington and Illinois considered Lucas a supporter of Truman, but for some unexplained reason the senator wanted to hold his public support until closer to the national convention in July. Increasing the Lucas quandary, an article a few days later in the *Sun-Times* said Lucas had described himself as "more or less the personal representative of the president" at the state convention.[35] Some thought Lucas's cautious behavior reflected the mention of him as a prospective vice presidential nominee.

Adding intrigue to Arvey's activities for the presidential nomination was a protocol predicament related to a scheduled appearance in Chicago by Truman on 4 June. Arvey was in charge of arrangements for a small dinner for Truman of about forty persons. That may have been reason enough for putting up the "quiet" sign.

Otherwise, the state convention held no surprises and served mostly as another opportunity for candidates and party officials to continue their criticisms of Governor Green. Lucas termed the Green administration a "state government which has no equal in all our history in extravagance, waste and corruption." Stevenson, who had campaigned in East St. Louis, Belleville, Alton, and Edwardsville before the convention, followed with his own characterization of the Green organization, calling it "an enormous rapacious political machine to serve the ends of political pirates in the state house. Corruption and moral poverty have invaded every department of the state government."[36]

While mainstream political party people paraded and prepared for the campaigns ahead, the specter of the Progressive Party lurked in the background and occasionally surfaced as a reminder of its threat. Republicans appeared happy that Henry Wallace's assault on the Democratic Party promised to erode support in November. After a Cook County judge rebuffed Progressives' efforts to get on the April primary ballot, Progressives temporarily dropped out of the headlines. At the same time, Professor MacDougall of the Northwestern University faculty ended his candidacy for the Senate, presumably the result of pressure by university officials.

However, strange things happen in politics, and apparently that was the case with MacDougall. By early May, the Progressive Party announced that he would be its Senate candidate after all. A full slate of Progressive candidates for state and Chicago offices was also made public.[37] MacDougall said he gave thoughtful consideration to the concerns of his boss at Northwestern, who preferred that he go back to teaching rather than incur embarrassing questions about communist sympathies. The journalism professor said he had applied for a leave of absence to campaign.

Political columnists and editorialists speculated that something more than MacDougall's principles were at work. Columnist Madison West of the *Daily News* claimed to have information that Republican officials had contacted Northwestern leaders and convinced them that to infringe on MacDougall's academic freedom was a serious mistake. West gave his opinion on why the Republicans were active in MacDougall's cause: "They didn't want MacDougall out of the race. They thought he would take votes away from Paul Douglas. With the opposition split, [Senator] Brooks would benefit."[38]

Early in May, Douglas took another of his extensive campaign tours downstate, visiting eighty towns in thirty-two counties. He had found these excursions outside Cook County fruitful in providing support of his candidacy, and he knew victory over Brooks would come only if downstate voters helped. After he left on the tour, the *Tribune* published an article suggesting Douglas had more than a passing interest in communism. Cornelius C. Cole, vice chairman of the Illinois Republican Veterans League, made the accusations. Cole did not label Douglas a communist but implied that the candidate had expressed interest in Soviet Russia or support for its causes.[39]

On the tenth anniversary of the Russian revolution in 1927, Douglas had been a member of a trade union delegation to the USSR, the itinerary of which was organized by Soviet officials. Although he had shown interest in socialist ideas, Douglas insisted that no known communist party member be included in the delegation. The group spent several weeks exploring socialist programs put in place by the government and participated in interviews with Soviet leaders Joseph Stalin and Leon Trotsky. Upon return to the United States, a report was prepared for publication. Douglas wrote the section on Soviet violation of civil liberties in which he spoke harshly of Russian government actions and attitudes. In his autobiography years later, Douglas said his article was watered down considerably by the delegation's leader and when published did not represent his strong feelings as presented in the original draft.

As a result of the trip to the USSR and subsequent sympathy with socialist leaders and ideas in the United States, Douglas became an advocate of the United States officially recognizing Russia. That took place during Roosevelt's presidency. Douglas later had second thoughts about that action and expressed them in his memoir: "When a nation is in fact reaching for your throat, it may not be wise to give it the facilities that recognition inevitably gives."[40] As a U.S. senator, Douglas voted against diplomatic recognition of the communist regime in China.

Douglas's sympathies for socialist programs in the early 1930s were well known before the 1948 campaign and were highlighted frequently by Republicans and supporters of Senator Brooks. The *Tribune* often reminded its readers of Douglas's support of socialist Norman Thomas for president in 1932 and of the candidate's book that called for a third party to espouse liberal ideas. Douglas did not deny any of these facts.

Regardless of candid admissions about his earlier associations, service as a World War II veteran, and frequent anti-communist statements, Douglas remained vulnerable to conservative assertions of doubts about his patriotism and whether his comments about communism were framed simply for his political campaign. After a litany of Douglas's activities, Cole said, "Here we have a professor who couldn't see the dangers of dictatorship then, or was willing to sacrifice liberty to an all-powerful bureaucracy. Now he is for getting tough with the Frankenstein he helped to create, unless he is merely saying so to get votes."[41]

Douglas also took his lumps from the left, primarily from Progressive Party partisans who believed he was not liberal enough. Liberal commentators supportive of Douglas fretted that the progressive attitude might help reelect Brooks. Pete Akers, the *Sun-Times* political columnist, made this point: "Illinois progressives should re-examine their opposition to Douglas. That opposition, if continued, will cost their party in other local contests many a vote as that opposition fits too closely the known communist pattern. . . . For no matter the allegations made regarding the degree of liberalism held by Douglas, the record demonstrates him to be far more acceptable to most American liberals than Brooks."[42] This issue would continue to be of concern to Douglas.

President Truman needed to get out of Washington and connect with potential voters at the grass roots. To accomplish that goal, he announced an extensive journey by rail in June from Washington to the West Coast and back, arriving just in time for the Democratic National Convention. He hoped the trip—a forerunner of the whistle-stop tours he would make in September and October—would put him back in the race after serious drops in his approval rating, months of disappointing experiences with the Republican-dominated Congress, and efforts to dump him by leaders in the Democratic Party.[43]

The manner and style of the tour would become familiar: short speeches from the train's rear platform and a few major presentations in large cities. A writer for the *Tribune* described Truman's informal style: "These will be impromptu, extemporaneous talks on the homey, just-among-us-folks order in which he is always at his best—except when he puts his foot in it by some ill considered remark. But generally he makes a good impression by his good natured personality and unaffected manner."[44] Truman and his handlers hoped this approach would put an end to talks of replacing him on the ticket.

Truman's itinerary called for a northern trip, excluding any stops in the South, where he was likely to receive an unfriendly greeting. The southern revolt, inspired by Truman's proposal for civil rights legislation, showed no signs of abating as the two party conventions approached in June and July. In spite of appearances, Truman said this was not a campaign tour. No one believed him because of similar experiences with President Roosevelt during campaigns for his third and fourth terms. FDR had also labeled those trips "nonpolitical."[45]

Truman's first stop for a major speech was Chicago on 4 June. Others were planned for Omaha, Seattle, the Berkeley campus of the University of California, and Los Angeles. That was as far as trip plans were made at the time of the announcement. None of the appearances would create as much of a stir as in Chicago, a hotbed of anti-Truman sentiment among Democrats who feared the president's name on the national ticket would mean disaster for party interests in Illinois. One of the main greeters of the president would be Jack Arvey.

The controversy raging over abandoning Truman was almost without precedent in recent U.S. political history. Normally, no matter how unpopular a president had been, the party would not think of denying him nomination. The rumble in 1948 was not restricted to a few party officials. Southern Democrats wanted Eisenhower—perhaps they wanted anyone but Truman. In New York and other places in the Northeast, usually supportive of Democrats, the talk of replacing Truman thrived. At the Illinois state convention, party members refused to pass a resolution of support for Truman. To say the least, Democrats feared the worst, and many wanted to do something about it. The Illinois Democratic candidates for governor and Senate did little to discourage the anti-Truman sentiment. Paul Douglas openly hoped for Eisenhower, and Adlai Stevenson almost never mentioned the president during his campaign. Truman's visit on 4 June promised to enliven Illinois politics.

JUNE 1948

Serious politics—the kind that influences election outcomes—broke out during June. While the Republican National Convention in Philadelphia made headlines for a week or more in Illinois newspapers, the Democrats were not loafing. President Truman appeared in Chicago to launch the national whistle-stop swing, and city Democratic leaders continued to quarrel over selecting Dwight Eisenhower as presidential nominee. There was a rush of enthusiasm and anxiety with Election Day five months away.

Truman came to town on 4 June just long enough for a reception with city bigwigs and a speech. However, this was not a routine presidential visit. Truman needed contact away from Washington to measure his opposition and to be seen. Since no visits were scheduled in southern states during the ten-day journey, for obvious reasons—he already knew the strength of opposition from Strom Thurmond and opponents of the civil rights proposals—Truman understood that his fate rested in the hands of big city political bosses who could turn out the vote in November.

Jack Arvey, promoter of Eisenhower as the Democratic presidential nominee, was nobody's fool. Another time, strictly by the strength of his political clout, he would be the one to assemble the guest list for a presidential reception and dinner, but not this time. Arvey publicly bowed to Mayor Martin Kennelly, who appeared neutral in national politics, for the invitations. The mayor may have asked Arvey for his ideas, but publicly the political boss moved to the background.[46] Kennelly invited newspaper publishers, churchmen, labor leaders, business executives, and just a handful of politicians, Democrats and Republicans. To keep things as neutral as possible, the mayor did not invite Democratic candidates Stevenson or Douglas. Newspapers in Chicago watched closely for signs that Arvey or Truman might snub each other or display hard feelings, but the central figures were all smiles. The president spoke briefly to the forty-five guests, stating that he intended to be running the White House in 1949.

To maintain the pretense that his tour was nonpolitical, Truman also appeared in Chicago to honor the men and women who had come from Sweden to the United States a century earlier and settled across the land.[47] Truman's presence was part of a festival in Chicago, so there was more to draw a crowd than a presidential visit. Prince Bertil of Sweden was present and joined Truman at Chicago Stadium for the president's speech.

Speaking before 20,000 people, Truman praised the immigrants and their contribution to national growth and achievement. He used the Swedish experience to make a pitch for meeting the challenge of resettlement for hundreds of thousands of displaced persons living in Germany, Austria, and Italy. "This is not solely an American problem," Truman said. "It is a world problem. But we must do our part. I have repeatedly asked the Congress to permit a substantial number of displaced persons to enter this country as immigrants."[48] Congress had not responded to his request.

Truman spent much of the speech addressing the challenges and threats of communism, pleading for a social agenda that would thwart the spread of it in the United States: "Communism succeeds only when there is weakness, or misery, or despair. It cannot succeed in a strong and healthy society." Concerning charges that his administration was weak on communism, the president stated, "I do not underestimate the challenge of communism. It is a challenge to everything we believe in."[49]

As usual with a presidential speech, reporters and columnists saw all sorts of twists and turns. The *Tribune* observed that part of Truman's domestic spending plan for dealing with communism was to challenge a bill proposed by Senator Karl Mundt and Representative Richard Nixon, both Republicans, to require registration of communists and bar them from holding public office. The U.S. House passed the bill in May, but it stalled in the Senate. A *Daily News* editorial saw the speech as a pitch for continued price controls to fight inflation. The paper opposed price controls.[50]

The Lucas-Truman relationship continued to perplex political analysts, as the senator sent and received mixed signals. During the state convention, Lucas quashed talk of being a "favorite son" who would receive votes on the first ballot. That seemed to say he did not want to be part of a tactic to deny Truman the nomination. The speculation surrounding Lucas and Truman came as the president was leaving Washington for his multi-state train journey and asked Lucas to join him on the trip to Illinois. Rumors that Lucas was on a "list" to be vice president with Truman surfaced during the president's visit to Chicago, but the *Tribune* reported he withdrew from consideration.[51]

Excitement prevailed when Republicans gathered for their national convention in Philadelphia. On the line was selection of a nominee that party officials believed would become the next president. Many eyes at the convention also focused on Illinois. The keynote speaker was Governor Green, who longed for national recognition but also faced challenges to his reelection in Illinois. Also on the line before the world were the pride and ego of the most Republican newspaper in the Midwest, the *Chicago Tribune*, with its leader front and center at the convention.

On the first day of the Republican convention, three conclusions had been reached that told the story of who controlled the party in Illinois: (1) Robert McCormick had declared that Green would not appear as a vice presidential candidate with Thomas E. Dewey; (2) Green's keynote address would reflect the *Tribune*'s editorial platform, not the national Republican Party's agenda; and (3) Robert Taft would receive most of the Illinois delegation's votes until long after Dewey had the nomination wrapped up.

Green Machine or not, no one dared challenge the *Tribune* editor and publisher. He despised Dewey, believed in Taft, and wanted Green to do his duty and run for a third term as governor. McCormick was not happy with the governor for a number of reasons. He believed Illinois conspirators who whispered that Green was disloyal for wanting to run for vice president.

McCormick's heavy editing of Green's draft keynote speech was just one indication that Green would say pretty much what the Colonel ordered. The whole business got nasty behind the scenes, which is another reason Green fell by the wayside as a vice presidential contender. The people who put the final nail in Green's coffin were Senator Brooks and others unfriendly to the governor. The senator sold McCormick on the idea that Green was going to double-cross the Colonel by joining the ticket with Dewey.[52] Brooks also claimed that Green had plotted with the *Tribune*'s Donald Maxwell against McCormick. The episode nearly cost Maxwell his job. All was not warm and fuzzy in the Tribune Tower.

Green's pursuit of the vice presidential nomination remains curious, given that everyone in the McCormick circle knew of the Colonel's contempt for Dewey and his determination to keep Green in Illinois. While Green's wish to be paired with Dewey seems illogical considering the Colonel's power, the governor may have seen it as the only road to Washington after two terms as governor. Whether it was a shot at vice president or a top cabinet post such as attorney general made little difference. He figured a break with the *Tribune*, while politically dangerous, could work by riding Dewey's coattails. Only in that context was alienating the Colonel worth the trouble.

However, Green's ambition was not enough for his leap to Washington. He needed encouragement, or at best a promise from Dewey and his associates that they would catch him after a predictable fall from the Colonel's grace. The New York governor figured he needed electoral votes from Illinois to win, and Green made that likely. Dewey wasn't going to get much of a blessing from the *Tribune* anyway. For this to work, Green had to break from McCormick well before the convention. A fiercely independent prosecutor earlier in life, Green lost his nerve in 1948. He feared the repercussions at home more than the hope of opportunities with Dewey.

McCormick pulled every trick in the book at the opening of the convention to cast aspersions on Dewey and overshadow Green's keynote speech. He "graciously consented" to an interview with a *Tribune* reporter that shared top billing on page 1 along with the report on Green's convention moment. McCormick announced his unswerving support for Robert Taft for president and Harold Stassen of Minnesota for vice president. He gave no ground to moderate Republicans such as Michigan's Arthur Vandenberg and lashed out at anyone and any group that did not agree with him. The Colonel predicted that Dewey would not carry more than twelve states if nominated, pointing to the New York governor's failed candidacy against Roosevelt in 1944.[53]

Herbert Brownell, Dewey's campaign manager, responded, "I am glad that the *Chicago Tribune* ticket is out in the open at last. I think all of the facts disprove any statement that Dewey cannot be elected if nominated. The very fact that McCormick said that means he thinks Gov. Dewey will be nominated." John S. Knight, publisher and editor of the *Daily News* and a delegate, cheered for McCormick, saying, "He makes more news here than all the candidates put together." His paper endorsed Taft. Knight, a political realist, wrote in his column before the convention, "Under certain circumstances such as the nomination of a 'mine run' [not special in any way] Republican candidate or the threat of war in the fall, President Truman will have a far better chance of re-election than the newspaper polls now indicate."[54] Knight, and his crosstown rival McCormick, both considered Dewey's candidacy a waste of time.

More than 1,000 visitors, officials, and hangers-on made their way from Illinois to Philadelphia, including 506 on two special trains. Others drove. McCormick flew. On Monday night, Green took the rostrum for his moment in the national spotlight.

Walter Trohan, *Tribune* Washington correspondent, did his best to depict Green's keynote speech as something special, but he failed. After picking and choosing a few highlights and reminding readers of applause and cheering by the true believers, Trohan had to deal with Green's demeanor. In the closing paragraph, Trohan wrote, "The conclusion of the keynote address brought a thunderous ovation for the Illinois governor, whose delivery was solemn and deliberate."[55] He could have added "uninspired" or "flat." The ovation might have been an expression of thankfulness that Green was finished.

As if taken off the *Tribune* editorial page, Green's verbiage rang bells that had made the newspaper so mighty among conservative midwesterners. To inspire the faithful, Green decried the Democratic New Deal as a coalition of "bosses, boodle, buncombe and blarney." That phrase grabbed the paper's top headline. True to form, he lambasted Roosevelt's foreign affairs performances at Yalta and Tehran and Truman's at Potsdam as giveaways. Condemned by Green were the New Deal "crackpots" who formed failed domestic programs and spent wildly. But he praised Republicans for having faith in individual Americans and the Republic.[56] Of course, the Republican-leaning newspapers applauded, because Green had done the Colonel's bidding.

As the convention opened, the presidential nomination narrowed to a contest between Dewey and Taft, with no others likely to participate. It was no secret how the Illinois delegation would perform. Once at the convention site, and after a dinner attended by 450 persons, an Illinois caucus unanimously named Green favorite son and pledged him all 56 delegate votes on the first ballot. Afterward, all but a handful voted for Taft, led by delegate-at-large McCormick.[57] Those voting for Dewey on the second ballot included Lieutenant Governor Hugh Cross, Everett Dirksen, retiring from the U.S. House because of ill health, and two labor leaders.

Illinois followed Taft to the end, in a contest that was never close after the first ballot. As momentum on the convention floor moved toward the unanimous vote for Dewey, the Colonel rose and left the Illinois section. He told a reporter: "It might have been worse. It might have been Vandenberg."[58] McCormick and the *Tribune* could not tolerate Vandenberg's willingness to cooperate with Democrats for a bipartisan foreign policy. In a two-paragraph editorial page commentary, the *Tribune* said, "The international bankers have taken the Republican party for the third successive time." The editorial concluded, "We can only hope that Mr.

Dewey will not drag down to defeat the congressional, state, and local candidates who were nominated by the Republican voters."[59]

With the Republican convention taking all the time of newspaper reporters, Democrats waited for their turn in July. Behind the scenes, however, plotting and planning continued, especially regarding the movement to replace Truman with Eisenhower on the ballot. Jack Arvey told a *Daily News* reporter before the GOP convention, "I wouldn't bet against his [Eisenhower's] running." He remained the most influential Illinois politician pursuing Eisenhower.

JULY 1948

One question remained for delegates at the Democratic national convention: Would they nominate Dwight Eisenhower for president?

With no one fully confident of the answer, a number of tactical moves were in play. Some Democrats wanted to demonstrate wide support for Eisenhower and a smooth route to the nomination. Republicans looked for ways to get the message to Eisenhower that he should sit out the 1948 election. The Republican cause and Truman's strategy were strange but understandable bedfellows, with the mutual desire of nominating the president.

Democrats and Republicans felt confident that if Eisenhower's name was placed in nomination, the game was over. He would easily be nominated and elected. Enthusiasts for the general discounted any previous statements he had made. In fact, Truman knew the outcome if Ike's name got introduced at the convention. When one of Truman's close aides stated as much, the president, according to biographer David Mc-Cullough, said, "I agree with you."[60] The aide, given license by Truman, started the presidential offensive by contacting his friend Eisenhower.

Democrats shunning Truman were high profile operatives who feared he would be a drag on state tickets, such as political heavyweights Jack Arvey, New York City mayor William O'Dwyer, and boss Frank Hague of New Jersey. Also on board were Mayor Hubert Humphrey of Minneapolis, a candidate for the U.S. Senate; Chester Bowles, former head of the Office of Price Administration; Representative Claude Pepper; Americans for Democratic Action (ADA); Walter Reuther of the United Auto Workers; Phil Murray of the CIO; southern senators John Sparkman and J. Lister Hill of Alabama; and Governor Strom Thurmond of South Carolina. Many of these represented the old Roosevelt coalition. In his diary, Truman called the conspirators "double-crossers all."[61] In those days when presidential nominations often were not won until the counting of convention votes, there was always talk of a "draft," a groundswell so overwhelming that its target could not resist. This possibility gave Eisenhower boosters hope.

The Republican National Convention had hardly ended late in June when news people turned to the anti-Truman crowd. On 1 July, Arvey told the *Tribune's* George Tagge, "If Gen. Eisenhower doesn't take himself out by a clear statement, I think there will be a stampede for him at the convention." Shortly after his comment, it was disclosed that Arvey, O'Dwyer, and James Roosevelt had sent telegrams to all delegates inviting them to a rally in Philadelphia on the eve of the convention. Arvey said O'Dwyer used his name without asking, "but it is quite all right."[62]

Reporters and party officials tried hard to discover how deep sympathy went for Truman and for Eisenhower among Illinois delegates. Many of those contacted said they were waiting for instructions from delegation leaders. Arvey said sixteen downstate delegates had announced for Eisenhower; Truman came away with more commitments. Many independent Democrats backed the president, including Benjamin S. Adamowski, who said he favored Truman "first, last, and all the time."[63]

Just as the Eisenhower push seemed to gather strength with only a few days remaining before the convention, the general issued a second "no, thank you." In yet another attempt to quash a draft or anything like it, he said, "I will not, at this time, identify myself with any political party and could not accept nomination for any public office or participate in partisan political contests."[64] While Eisenhower, who became president of Columbia University in 1948, tried to suck the wind out of the campaign, some operatives doggedly held on, finding a loophole of hope. James Roosevelt said the people want a "unity candidate" who was nonpartisan. Paul Douglas said he would not change a word of his recent speech calling for Truman to step aside. Arvey, initially stunned, responded that Eisenhower "cannot and will not refuse to serve his country."[65] He gave new meaning to "not taking 'no' for an answer."

News people did not know whether to ignore the Eisenhower boom or keep just enough life in it for future articles. Many who had jumped on the bandwagon or were close to doing it pulled back and declared that Truman would be nominated. Ringleaders went into secret sessions to plot the next moves. Breathing a sigh of relief, a *Tribune* editorial complimented the general for making Dewey's day, adding, "We see no reason to question the sincerity of his utterance. His limitations are surely no more grave than those of Mr. Truman but at least the general is aware of his."[66]

Eisenhower had left the door ever so slightly open until just before the convention began. Congressman Pepper of Florida chose to ignore the general's statement and said he would put Ike's name in nomination. That prompted "no" number three, in a telegram to Pepper. In a friendly manner, Eisenhower left no doubt as to his intentions, saying, "I will not violate my own conception of my appropriate sphere of duty. No matter in what terms, conditions, or premises a proposal might be couched, I would refuse to accept the nomination."[67] The door was shut finally, sending the remaining holdouts scurrying. The boom was a bust.

Before the convention opened, the Eisenhower episode was history. On the special train of Illinois officials, Arvey, surrounded by those who backed Truman, prepared a statement of capitulation. He said, "We have no recourse but to stand by the man who has carried our banner—President Truman. He will be nominated." In an attempt to spin the fight for Eisenhower as a "benefit" for the party, he added, "The Democratic party has been strengthened, rather than weakened, by the movement to draft Gen. Eisenhower." He didn't explain how that could be.[68]

Years later, Arvey gave his version of how the Eisenhower boom played out. He said, "Certain publishers and other people came to me saying that what this country needed was a person, either Democratic or Republican, who could unite the country and heal the wounds of the world, and reestablish the supremacy of our country in world affairs. Dwight Eisenhower was that kind of man. He was not a Democrat. He was not a Republican. He was a world war hero. At the last minute he said no."[69]

At the convention, Arvey and others implicated in the failed coup ate crow like pros. But that didn't change the convention atmosphere. Senator Alben Barkley caught the flavor with this comment: "You could cut the gloom with a corn knife."[70] Led by Arvey, the Illinois delegation voted unanimously for Truman.[71]

With Truman's nomination decided, civil rights was the main convention issue from beginning to end. Southern leaders had been looking for a fight since February, when Truman had sent his civil rights package to Congress. At the convention, they fought for a provision in the party platform that supported their version of states' rights, designed mainly to keep the federal government from being involved in integrating the South. Knowing that the southern position would fail in convention votes, Truman stayed out of the fray. Meanwhile, the platform committee, hoping to keep civil rights below the public radar, brought forward a compromise statement that Truman and his followers backed.[72] This plan failed to satisfy a segment of northern and western delegates desiring a stronger statement in support of civil rights and led by Mayor Humphrey, a candidate for the Senate from Minnesota. A member of the subcommittee who wrote the compromise plan, he rallied liberals for an amendment with stronger language.

Passions over the platform statement caused splits in the Illinois delegation. Senator Lucas, one of the platform subcommittee members who wrote the Truman-approved plank, fiercely defended the original committee report in private and in public. He brought the plan to the Illinois delegate caucus and received a unanimous vote in favor of it. When Humphrey spoke for the amendment, Lucas accused him of attempting to destroy the Democratic Party. In spite of delegation sympathies, sentiment grew for the amendment. Paul Douglas marched in the convention hall with Arvey at his side, calling for approval of the amendment. Years later, Douglas said of the platform plan, "They [supporters] proposed an innocuous plank, acceptable to the South, and felt confident they could sweep the convention."[73] Douglas said the original statement would have passed until Humphrey spoke. To the surprise of everyone, the amendment passed 651½ to 582½. Angry at that turn of events, many southerners walked out. That became the catalyst for Strom Thurmond's presidential candidacy.

Not much else went Truman's way before adjournment. Because of floor arguments, speeches, and frequent delays, the president gave his acceptance speech at 2 A.M. When the convention ended, he still had two opponents: Thurmond, soon to head the Dixiecrats, and Henry Wallace, now candidate of the Progressive Party. Fortunately for Truman, neither Wallace nor Thurmond appeared on the Illinois ballot. As far as the Illinois delegation was concerned, after the Eisenhower affair died, internal differences subsided momentarily.

Convention observers believed Truman favored Lucas for the vice presidential nomination. However, as the days passed, it became plain that the Illinoisan was out of the running, causing tension among Illinois delegates over the choice of a running mate for Truman. The president would have the final say on the nominee, of course, but delegate pressure could make a difference. At a cocktail party given by Adlai Stevenson, the subject surfaced in conversation between former mayor Kelly and former governor Stelle, between whom no love was lost.

Stelle confronted Kelly about a rumored meeting with party officials to prevent the nomination of Kentucky senator Alben Barkley. Neither confirming nor denying the meeting, Kelly said, "I think the Illinois delegation will follow the president's wishes on the vice presidency." Kelly had expressed support of Governor William Preston Lane Jr., who ran Roosevelt's 1944 campaign in Maryland. Arvey had also expressed interest in Lane. That did not soothe Stelle. "We want Barkley," he responded to Kelly. "Let's cut out the nonsense. All the people down in southern Illinois, which is close to Kentucky, say he deserves the vice presidency and would help the ticket." Stevenson and Douglas joined Stelle in support of Barkley. Mayor Kennelly noted that Illinois delegates preferred the Kentuckian. Confusing the situation was an Illinois delegation vote a day earlier to give Kennelly "favorite son" votes for vice president. Kennelly said he did not want the courtesy.[74]

The quarrel continued at a delegation caucus a day later when Stelle said it was time to give Barkley the delegation's sixty votes. Stelle's motion for Barkley carried. All delegate votes were cast for Barkley, who joined the ticket with Truman.[75]

On the heels of Truman's nomination, the party remained roiled by splits with southerners and progressives. Southerners met in Birmingham, Alabama, to form the states' rights/segregation ticket headed by Governor Thurmond with Governor Fielding Wright of Mississippi for vice president.[76] Wright had led the Mississippi-Alabama walkout over the platform statement on civil rights at the Democratic convention. Strategic discussions occurred over how far to spread the movement beyond core states of the South.

Scaring Democrats in Illinois more than Thurmond was the progressive movement, destined to nominate Henry Wallace for president. Progressives seemed strong enough to affect negatively the candidacies of Stevenson and Douglas and the party ballot all the way down to the precinct level. The most outspoken progressives hailed from Chicago and university faculties. A week after the Democratic convention, delegates from all of Chicago's fifty wards, plus supporters from downstate, were present to nominate Wallace and give a name to the movement: The United States Progressive Party.[77]

Meanwhile, the legal battle continued in Illinois over putting Progressive Party candidates on the November ballot. In April, the state supreme court had ruled the Progressive Party had a right to be on the primary election ballot. However, Democratic election officials in the county delayed action until it was too late to print ballots with progressive names on them. In July, the county appellate court overruled the April decision. Progressives said they would petition the state higher court for a hearing on the issue.[78]

With both national conventions out of the way, candidates for the top two positions on the Illinois ballot came closer to a debate than at any other time; the four appeared on back-to-back days at the sixty-sixth annual renewal of the Soldiers and Sailors Reunion in Salem, birthplace of William Jennings Bryan. Stevenson and Douglas appeared on the first day and Green and Brooks on the second. An estimated 400 persons attended, and newspaper coverage was extensive.

Notably, Salem was about twenty miles northeast of Centralia, site of the No. 5 mine explosion in March 1947. Stevenson called the performance of Republicans in affairs of coal mining "a story of neglect, buck passing and political prostitution of a public service charged with the protection of human life." Having hammered Green frequently on the disaster, Stevenson took advantage of the proximity of Centralia by laying out ideas for improved coal mine safety and elimination of politics in choosing mine inspectors:

> What am I going to do is see that Centralia never happens again under any administration, Republican or Democratic? I am going to do my best to take the mine inspectors out of politics. They must be put under civil service and removed from all possibility of political control or influence. The law must be enforced without fear or favor against mine officials and miners alike. And I am going to appoint a director of the Department of Mines and Minerals who is interested in the oil and coal industries and the men who work in them, not politics. Perhaps the present volunteer rescue team organization could be improved by establishing a few permanent full-time rescue teams. Perhaps the Mining Board should be reorganized to diminish the possibility of political interference. I do now know that politics has no place in a public service charged with the protection of life itself.[79]

On another issue of interest to southern Illinoisans, Stevenson promised a close look at the Department of Conservation and charges of politics and corruption. He said, "Wildlife refuges have become political refuges. Ask a sportsman how many game wardens there are in

Illinois who have never been closer to a quail than the devil to the truth."
He referred to accusations that the department employed a Republican
member of the legislature to purchase land for the state and to another
instance of buying land for "ten times the appraised value."[80]

Stevenson called Green "the errand boy of the *Chicago Tribune*," focusing on Robert McCormick's control of the Republican delegation to
the national convention. Quoting an editorial from the *Decatur Herald*,
he said, "The Illinois delegates and the people of Illinois, Democrats as
well as Republicans, were shamed by the spectacle of the governor of
Illinois bowing to the demands of the embittered and frustrated Chicago
publisher." He added, "Thus the citizens of Illinois finally found out who
runs the governor, who runs the Republican party in Illinois. . . . The *Tribune* has spoken." Stevenson praised Truman several times, specifically for
his "firm stand against Russian aggression."[81] He hardly had mentioned
the president in speeches before the Democratic National Convention.

In an article written by John Dreiske of the *Chicago Sun-Times*, Paul
Douglas blamed Congress for the postwar increase in the cost of living
that "drained off wartime savings." In order to "keep themselves fed,
housed and clothed[,] Americans since the peak of prosperity of 1946
have been forced to pile up personal debts double the size of the one that
helped break the back of our economy in the 1929 crash."[82]

The *Tribune's* account of Democratic speeches revealed some careful
editing and omission. No mention was made of comments about the
Centralia mine disaster or accusations of corruption and mismanagement of state affairs by the governor and others. The paper offered brief
coverage of Douglas's speech, saying it dealt primarily with the cost
of living. It stated that Douglas left the impression that he believed
price controls would have prevented erosion of wages. The *Tribune* was
a staunch opponent of price controls.

The *Tribune* story about Democratic candidates contained an example
of the paper's efforts to pin labels on Stevenson and Douglas that might be
considered negative by readers. The article's second paragraph stated: "Both
Stevenson and Douglas were advocates of World War II but neither mentioned the role of the most expensive war in history in causing inflation.
Stevenson is a former New Deal diplomat. Prof. Douglas is an economist
at the University of Chicago and a former socialist party leader."[83]

By this time in the campaign, the pattern of speeches and presentations by Green and Brooks were familiar, and presentations in Salem
were no different. Green spent his time extolling the virtues of his almost

eight years as governor. Aside from a balanced budget and the reduction of sales tax from three to two cents on the dollar, his list of achievements might have come from a Democrat. They included extension of the public aid program, increased payments to old age pensioners combined with adequate medical care, aid to dependent children without cost to local governments, providing care for 40,000 persons in state institutions, aid for construction of community hospitals, and increases in state aid to public schools.[84] His main point aimed at Stevenson, whom he did not name, was to tie the Democrat to New Deal programs.

Brooks, who had been campaigning much of the summer in Illinois while the Senate was in recess, had his own list of benefits provided by the Republican Congress. They included an income tax reduction and reducing tax rates, "progress" in reducing the cost of federal government employees, "the first real drive" against communists on federal payrolls, submitting to the states a constitutional amendment limiting a president to two terms, and protection for veterans. Brooks responded to attacks on the Republican-controlled Congress by Truman, stating, "We Republicans have raised the ire of the president because we have succeeded in fulfilling the pledges we made to the voters in 1946."[85]

In the days when the primary sources of political news were newspapers, state and presidential campaign events rarely caught much voter attention until after Labor Day. That is probably why pundits remained convinced that Republicans would retain a hold on state government and would win the presidency. Democrats such as Stevenson and Douglas had not found the issues that would end Republican rule, at least as far as political columnists thought.

On Monday, 26 July, a hot summer day in Illinois, mobster Bernie Shelton left his Golden Rule Acres Farm home near Peoria at about 10 A.M. He drove to the Parkway Club, a gambling joint on Peoria's western outskirts from which Shelton managed jukebox and slot machine operations, for a meeting with bartender Alex Ronitis. As Shelton left the club and walked to his parked car after the meeting, a single bullet from a powerful hunting rifle ripped through his chest. Ronitis had left the club with Shelton but had gone back inside to get a package of cigarettes before the shot was fired. The assassin, concealed in undergrowth at the base of a wooded hill behind the tavern, fired a .351 Winchester automatic rifle to kill Shelton and then ran from the scene. A shell from the rifle was found by police. Authorities had no leads to the assassin.

A coroner's jury the following day ruled Shelton was killed by "a person or persons unknown."[86]

Bernie, his brothers Carl and Earl, and gang associates had terrorized southern Illinois during the 1920s and 1930s, controlling illegal liquor, gambling, and other criminal activities, including murder in roadhouses, along rural roads, and in small communities of the region. Their dominance outside Chicago and Cook County rivaled the Al Capone mob, and their reputation for terrorizing the population and murdering competitors made them untouchable by rural law enforcement.

The Shelton home was in Fairfield, but the headquarters for many years was in East St. Louis and St. Clair County, where citizens lived in fear of the trio. While Carl and Earl were ruthless in taking a cut of all unlawful activities, including bootlegging and gambling, Bernie had earned the reputation as the one most likely to berate, beat, or kill those he hated. Law enforcement officials throughout the region found it safer to ignore the brothers rather than attempt to corral them.

An exception to that rule was a little-known but gutsy sheriff in St. Clair County named Jerome Munie. In the early 1930s, with help from state officials, he thwarted the brothers at every turn, shutting down their rackets and muting their arrogance. By the time Munie stepped down as sheriff in 1934, the Sheltons had retreated to the friendly confines of their home territory.[87] As their world narrowed before and after World War II, the brothers were drawn to illegal activities in Peoria County and vicinity. They inherited slot machine operations and expanded into gambling. Along the way they made enemies. The oldest brother, Carl, was shot and killed in October 1947, and Earl retreated to the Fairfield area, where he claimed to be a farmer. That left Bernie, the youngest and most violent brother, as the operative in Peoria—at least until 26 July.

Funeral services for Bernie were held in Peoria, with an assemblage of current and former associates of the Shelton gang attending. Earl led the family contingent that included their mother, Agnes Shelton, two other brothers, Roy and Dalton, who allegedly never were associated with the gang, and a sister, Lulu Pennington, wife of a Fairfield tavern keeper. Bernie's wife, Genevieve, greeted everyone at the ranch near Bernie's expensive casket, after which she led the group to services at a Peoria funeral home.

As the world—especially the Illinois political world—would soon learn, this was not just another slaying of a notorious gang leader whose story would fade from the headlines after the funeral. The campaign for governor would never be the same.

5. Beginning of the End

AUGUST 1948

St. Louis newspapers from the 1920s to 1950 developed strong reputations for aggressive investigations of crime and corruption in the city and nearby regions, including Illinois. Fueled by frequent probes, editorial pages alerted readers to ongoing illegal activities and pleaded with prosecutors to take action, especially when it came to gambling. In terms of reducing crime and punishing criminals, results were slim and, except for an occasional localized outcome, had little impact on statewide elections and public policy.

That picture changed dramatically during the latter stages of the 1948 campaign, prompted initially by the murder of Bernie Shelton and ongoing investigations by reporters at the *St. Louis Post-Dispatch* that emerged. Routine coverage of the statewide campaigns in Illinois continued in the St. Louis press but was overwhelmed by bold black headlines introducing investigations that implicated Republicans seeking reelection. The first indication of a tidal wave occurred in August.

Illinois citizens from Springfield south depended on a multitude of local daily and weekly newspapers for information about rural and small community life. For a broader picture, readers looked to large newspapers based in St. Louis. The city had two dominant publications that provided a variety of news coverage and a diversity of editorial opinions. The morning *St. Louis Globe-Democrat* appealed to conservatives, and the afternoon *Post-Dispatch* leaned to the liberal side. However, they had one news approach in common: a long history of battling crime and corruption.

Each paper had distinguished crime reporters and editors. To fuel their competition and the fight against evil, St. Louis publications set a continuing array of dastardly deeds before readers. Missouri had countless thugs as far away as Kansas City, and St. Louis was the home of brutal gangs and political shenanigans. Corruption, gang warfare, gambling of many kinds, bootlegging, and organized mobsters across the Mississippi River in Illinois provided an inviting target and opportunities to increase circulation. By 1948, the *Post-Dispatch* found many sordid tales to tell that smaller local papers often ignored.

To uncover details, editors called on reporters with experience in pursuing connections between illegal activities and political officeholders. Their names were familiar to interested readers and politicians: Roy J. Harris from Springfield, Carl Baldwin, who lived in Illinois, and St. Louis–based Selwyn Pepper, Herb Trask, and Ted Link. When required to nail a good story, they could fan out anywhere in Illinois.

Among the key reporters, Link had proven especially determined and successful. When criminals and politicians alike wanted to talk, Link got the call. Fellow crime reporter Baldwin wrote after his colleague's death in 1974, "Suave and handsome, with dark features, Link probably was the closest thing St. Louis ever had to a TV-type private eye. Gangsters like Earl Shelton and Ray Walker [a Shelton associate] had a certain romantic admiration for him, and he was chosen as the receptacle for their information." Link was a human vacuum cleaner, accumulating the little pieces of information that eventually would blossom into a major disclosure that might, say, put the heat on a public official. Baldwin said, "Link had the tools and the patience."[1]

By mid-1948, Link and his associates had gathered information about expanding gambling activities in Illinois since World War II and about the accompanying corruption of public officials. This information became critical for public consumption after the assassination of gangster Bernie Shelton in July. For months before the shooting, Link had spent time with members of the Shelton operation. Baldwin described it this way: "Link had been more than associating with gangsters. He had been living, eating and sleeping with the Sheltons" since the shooting death of Bernie's brother Carl in October 1947.[2] After Carl's death, Link received reports of plans to kill other Sheltons, namely Earl and Bernie.

Beginning on 6 August, Link's articles appeared every day through the remainder of the month, following up on the Bernie Shelton murder and introducing the implication of public officials and gangsters in protection payments across the state, payments that assured mobsters there would be no interference from county and state law enforcement officials. Although stories were written by a number of *Post-Dispatch* reporters, Link was on the front page frequently from August to November with many copyrighted articles revealing the connections of gangsters with Illinois state politics, especially the Green administration. The more often reports of scandal appeared, the greater Link became a target of those implicated. Some would say Link was the issue as much as the details he wrote about.

Threats against Link worried the reporter and his editors. To thwart any violence, Link would register at one hotel and sleep in another. He rarely took the same routes when traveling so his trail could not be traced or predicted. As Baldwin stated, "Just being around the Sheltons was dangerous enough."[3] By any measure, Link, his associates, and the *Post-Dispatch* editorial page influenced the 1948 Illinois election outcome. How much is still anyone's guess.

For much of the 1920s and 1930s, the Shelton brothers—Carl, Earl, and Bernie—ran roughshod over law enforcement throughout downstate Illinois. They, with members of their gang, committed an assortment of crimes, including murder. Their estimated annual income exceeded a million dollars. The brothers' home base was Fairfield, but eventually they moved to East St. Louis and St. Clair County, where they coerced law enforcement, terrorized citizens, and bullied small-time criminals.[4]

In East St. Louis, the brothers met their match when Jerome Munie, thirty-seven, owner of a confectionery in O'Fallon, was elected sheriff of St. Clair County in 1930. No one expected Munie to do more than show up at the office every day. Instead, he shut down illegal dog racing and began a war on the infamous "Valley" in East St. Louis, where prostitution operated without restraint. After stopping the dog races, Munie remembered being offered $100 to "lay off."[5]

Munie was fought by every special interest in the county that benefited from illegal activities. His challenge caught the interest of Governor Henry Horner, who provided funds for Munie to lead an unofficial downstate crime commission and appoint employees to clean up the mess. Their targets: the Shelton brothers. Joseph G. Schrader, a former East St. Louis detective who worked for Munie, later described the picture in the city: "I remember in the old days when the Sheltons walked around boldly with machine guns wrapped in newspapers. It was almost impossible to walk down Missouri Avenue without bumping into a Shelton red hot. Carl Shelton ran this town."[6]

Munie and his special unit of crime fighters immediately confronted the Sheltons and closed down their moneymaking operations. The Sheltons fled the county and headed back to Fairfield.[7] Later in the 1930s, the Sheltons set up headquarters in the Peoria region, where they operated without law enforcement interference.

The 1948 event that led to an August series of newspaper articles in the *Post-Dispatch* was the pistol-whipping of Richard Murphy Jr. on 30 May by Bernie Shelton and two associates near Peoria's Parkway Club. The three were indicted for assault with intent to kill; Shelton posted a $6,000 cash bond assuring his appearance for trial.[8]

Roy D. Gatewood, a former candidate for sheriff of Peoria County, gambler, and saloon owner, asked for a meeting with Bernie Shelton at the gangster's farm on 26 June. Before the meeting, with rumors of danger flying, Shelton, naturally suspicious, planned to have the conversation recorded. Jack Ashby, an employee of Shelton, purchased a wax recording device and installed a microphone in a radio located in the home's sunroom. Wires from the microphone extended to an adjoining room. When Gatewood arrived for the meeting, Ashby, his wife, and Shelton's wife, Genevieve, were in the room with the recording machine.

As the session proceeded, Gatewood, who was unaware of the recording, said his mission was to offer a deal for dismissal of the indictment by state's attorney Roy P. Hull. Gatewood said the price was $25,000 for action by the county prosecutor.[9] Gatewood said if Shelton refused the shakedown, he should hide out to avoid being jailed and interrogated by Hull.

The four recordings made of the meeting with Gatewood were Shelton's insurance. He had them placed in a bank vault and instructed Genevieve to deliver the recordings to Link at the *Post-Dispatch* "if anything happens to me." After Shelton was murdered on 26 July, his wife removed the recordings from the vault and had them delivered to Link under heavy guard by Shelton's associates. Link had a transcript made, and the newspaper published it, with details of the bribe offer. Link was not the first newspaper employee to hear the recordings. Claude U. Stone, publisher of the *Peoria Star*, heard the recordings two days before Shelton was killed, but the Shelton family did not allow the paper to report the demand for $25,000.[10]

Link also learned that Bernie Shelton had received a message warning him of an assassination plan. In a conversation with a former state highway patrol employee, Shelton was told that Peter J. Petrakos, a former Shelton associate, was the "finger man" in the murder plot. Petrakos was not in Peoria when Shelton was shot but returned the next day.

During a meeting with Link, Petrakos said he "loved Bernie" and would help find the murderer. Petrakos agreed to meet with Link, "Big Earl" Shelton, and two Shelton associates, Ray Walker and Jack Ashby, at Link's hotel room in Peoria on 30 July. According to Link, Petrakos was grilled for four hours, during which he denied having anything to do with the murder, and the session ended without harm to Petrakos.[11] Details of the event would surface again in October, with just a few days remaining in the election campaign.

The *Post-Dispatch* of 6 August hit the streets with Link's story of the bribery attempt, including names and details based on the recordings. It started a cascade of articles by Link. Until the newspaper story, Gatewood had no knowledge of the recordings. A day after the first article, state's attorney Roy Hull, in an open letter to Peoria citizens, referred to being "maliciously charged with an attempt to solicit a bribe from a group of underworld persons commonly known as the Shelton gang."[12]

As the month unfolded, Link's articles stripped away covers from illegal operations and payoffs in Peoria, nearby counties, and the state capital. Here is an abstract of a few of the reporter's findings:

- Shelton gang members told Link that Carl Shelton had paid certain state officials $2,000 a month for ten years, up to 1945, as insurance against interference by law enforcement officials in the gang's operations.
- After 1945, Bernie paid $300 a month to state officials to protect his Paradise Club in Tazewell County. He left records of the payments.
- A Peoria man served as "collector" of funds from Bernie to be distributed to officials.
- A Peoria car dealer was a partner with Carl for twelve years in slot machine operations. In the same story, Link told of $400 to $500 a month in payments from gamblers to state's attorney investigator Charles Somogyi.
- Over a period of four and a half years, slot machine operators paid $160,000 to the Peoria city treasury for protection, in spite of laws against slot machines. Payments were added to the general fund. The "unofficial tax" for the city from operators was $20 a month per machine.

- Half of the twenty Peoria city aldermen were on the slot machine "payroll" for payments of $100 to $200 a month until 1945, when a new mayor put an end to the flow of money.
- Dozens of officials or staff appeared every month at Bernie's ranch to collect payoffs. One source said the collectors "stumbled over each other" to get the loot.
- The Peoria County sheriff was accused of receiving payoffs, campaign contributions, gifts—including a pearl-handled revolver—and contributions to a "fund" to buy him a gold badge. The sheriff denied everything.

After a number of Link's disclosures, Hull said he would request a recall of the grand jury that had met months earlier to investigate charges and allegations of the May assault involving Shelton. Circuit judge Henry J. Ingram ordered the jury into session "for an investigation of all bribery charges and any crimes connected with the death of Bernie Shelton." Judge Ingram appointed Verle W. Safford, former president of the Peoria Bar Association and a respected attorney in civil affairs, as special prosecutor. He subpoenaed eight witnesses for the jury session. In his charge to the jury, Judge Ingram stated, "If any improper approaches are made to any members of this jury, I want it reported to me immediately."[13] The jury heard from the sheriff and Gatewood, who showed up under a court order compelling him to testify and granting him immunity from prosecution. Hull also appeared, having been granted immunity. The Gatewood recordings were played for the jury, and testifying were Genevieve Shelton, Jack Ashby, and Ashby's wife, who had been in an adjacent room during the conversation.[14]

A few days before the end of August, the Peoria Association of Commerce asked Governor Green and Attorney General George Barrett to begin a special investigation of political corruption in Peoria County. The request pointed out that special prosecutor Safford was limited by time and terms of his appointment to clear up bribery accusations: "It is obvious that they will not be able to complete the [necessary] job."[15] The association said volunteers would raise the money for an investigation.

As the revelations piled up, it became clear that corruption and illegal activities in Peoria did not begin with the arrival of the Sheltons. An article in the *Chicago Tribune* on 11 August offered information about Peoria as a "wide open town since the days when river traffic on the Illinois waterway was the most important transportation in a new and rough frontier country." It referred to the Shelton appearance as an "interlude" in a series of hoodlum groups that handed off operations to the next gang. One story stated that Carl Shelton had been recruited from Fairfield by Peoria gambling operatives in the late 1930s.[16] The initial activities involving the Sheltons were part of a larger illegal operation that had functioned for a number of years.

The gang first claimed rights over slot machines throughout the county's saloons, restaurants, clubs, and roadside dining locations. The *Tribune* said they also were "muscle" partners in gambling palaces, which drew customers from Peoria, Fulton, and Tazewell Counties. The paper described the Shelton gang's method of moving in on gambling joints: "The usual technique was to arrive at a gambling house in company with three or four gun toting 'boys.' Owners were told the Sheltons were taking a 30 to 40 per cent cut and a daily look at the books. The Sheltons boasted that they slapped their enemies silly instead of killing them and 'bringing down the heat.' One beating usually sufficed."[17]

Initially, Link's articles in August centered on subjects related to Bernie Shelton's death and on a history of payoffs to officials in Peoria. Nothing in these disclosures drew a direct line to current state officials. However, several articles took the payoff schemes to areas in Illinois well away from Peoria, drawing a picture of illegal activities beyond a county or two.

Reporter Carl Baldwin wrote of citizens in Ottawa being challenged to protest because eight public officials in LaSalle County indicted on nonfeasance charges had escaped prosecution. In Cairo, in the southernmost part of the state, law enforcement officers from Alexander and Pulaski Counties stood by while two crime syndicates battled for control of the gambling business, Baldwin learned. Link discovered that in the Peoria area, a "collector" of graft for state officials had been on the state payroll of Attorney General Barrett and drew about $400 a month as a sales tax investigator until 15 August. Link said the man made collections "for the state" each month from 1941 or 1942 until Bernie Shelton's murder. On the wall of the collector's office in Chicago hung two photographs of himself, one with Governor Green and another with Barrett.[18]

The connections of payoffs and state employees drew attention of a *Post-Dispatch* reporter, Roy J. Harris, who investigated gambling in Springfield. In an interview with Harris, Sangamon County sheriff Meredith J. Rhule admitted that he allowed open gambling. Rhule told the reporter, "If some night club operator wants to make me a present because he likes the color of my eyes, well, why shouldn't he?"[19] This opened up a parallel series of articles about crime in Springfield before the end of August. The Springfield Ministerial Association was considering a request for a grand jury investigation and appointment of a special prosecutor, and Governor Green had agreed to meet with the group on 13 September. Meanwhile, Mayor Harry A. Eielson and Sheriff Rhule clamped down on slot machines and dice and poker games in the city and county in the wake of newspaper accounts.

Link revealed an earlier investigation by the *Post-Dispatch* reporters alleging that four illegal funds containing returns from gambling, liquor sales, and state contracts had been sent to Springfield and Chicago. The probe determined that nearly every third Illinois county outside Cook had illegal gambling of some kind. The most notorious counties were St. Clair, Madison, Peoria, Mason, Tazewell, Alexander, and Pulaski.[20]

Link also wrote of two sources of payoffs on state contracts. One was from premiums on insurance and indemnity bonds that contractors had to furnish when working on state jobs; another was kickbacks on building and road contracts.

Commenting on the revelations in Peoria, a *Chicago Tribune* editorial added some perspective to rampant gambling in the state: "People are never going to stop gambling, but that doesn't ameliorate the evils of the practice. It is an economic burden. The gamblers are greedy. They take more out of a town than its payrolls can bear. Usually they cheat. Some years ago an enterprising reporter got into the books of a concern that makes crooked dice and found that the fanciest gambling rooms in town were its customers."[21]

People still were not paying attention to campaign politics in the heat of the summer. Consequently, Democrats and Republicans in Illinois spent most of August preparing for the final two months before Election Day, the period in which public interest in politics would increase dramatically. To keep a measure of reader awareness for one of its favored candidates, the *Tribune* produced articles from Washington about the activities of Senator C. Wayland Brooks. One featured his comments to a Senate committee on veterans' affairs. Another quoted his remarks to an American Legion boys' forum in the capital, during which he assailed liberalism and "fuzzy minded intellectuals." When a senator from Michigan praised Brooks for his inquiries about efficiencies in government, the newspaper's headline stated, "Brooks Hailed for

Support of Senate Probes." When in Illinois, as during an appearance in Litchfield, Brooks defended actions of the Republican-dominated Eightieth Congress.

Brooks mounted a personal attack on opponent Paul Douglas when the two candidates appeared late in the month at a political rally in a rural area near Rockford.[22] For the first time, both candidates appeared on the same platform on the same day. Douglas went first, extolling the Marshall Plan as a way to save farmers from low prices on crops. He also called for providing electricity for every farm in the nation. During the comments, Douglas challenged Brooks to a series of debates in the classic Lincoln-Douglas format. Brooks wasted no time rejecting the proposal: "I do not choose to debate any irresponsible person or get an audience for him. Let him get his own audiences." Brooks added, "Some people running for public office have been associated with fuzzy-minded communist and socialist outfits. I intend to make it my first order of business once more in the Senate to carry on the investigations you see reflected in present exposures."[23]

Dwight Green and Adlai Stevenson cruised through the state but added little to the disagreements between the two. Speaking at Camp Ellis to National Guardsmen and military officials, the governor said he would "fight to the last ditch" to prevent a federal takeover of National Guard units. He alluded to no specific proposal but mentioned, "There are those who would destroy the national guard as we know it."[24] Speaking in Oak Park, Stevenson criticized Green for the high cost of state government and complained that the governor was short-changing municipal governments by reducing the amount of support from the state. These comments repeated charges the Democrat made frequently.

A public statement issued in Centralia by officers and members of Local 52 of the United Mine Workers of America was a reminder of hard feelings toward Green throughout the coal mining areas of Illinois. Green had worked hard to court organized labor and was rewarded with endorsement by the Centralia Trades and Labor Assembly. When that happened, Local 52 of the UMWA withdrew from the assembly in protest and issued a statement opposing Green for reelection.[25] When Stevenson's campaign received notice of the statement and withdrawal from the organization, the candidate took advantage of another opportunity to link Green to the Centralia disaster. A *Post-Dispatch* editorial applauded the union committee's decision, saying it had "kept the faith with 111 fellow coal miners who died in the disaster."

THE EXPOSÉ DRAMA BUILDS

Ted Link and the *Post-Dispatch* had a head of steam during August, generated by disclosing widespread violations of state gambling laws, corruption, and a score of other illegal activities. Most of the newspaper's articles dealt with Peoria in the aftermath of Bernie Shelton's murder. The first signs of controversy over similar issues in Springfield surfaced late in the month. Aside from innuendo and political supposition, the scandals had not landed directly on the desks of Governor Green or Attorney General Barrett.

That picture changed on 1 September. The *Post-Dispatch* page 1 headline declared, "Gamblers Again Raising Green Campaign Funds, Gave Him $100,000 in 1944." Link wrote that the newspaper's reporters were told by those who contributed—no sources were named—that gamblers, slot machine operators, and punchboard distributors in six counties were "shaken down" for the $100,000, and likely more. The second paragraph updated the article by claiming that collectors again were on the prowl for financial aid to Green's third-term campaign. Collectors assured contributors that they would not fear interference from state or local authorities, including the state highway patrol, Link declared.[26]

Given Link's connection to remnants of the Shelton gang and their self-interest in pointing the finger at others, many observers assumed details came from that direction. About the use by reporters of unsavory informants, reporter Carl Baldwin said, "Ted Link and I had been doing a lot of associating with shady characters that summer. How else do you obtain information about ties between organized crime and public officials? The public officials certainly don't volunteer it."[27]

The six counties named and amounts allegedly given to the Green campaign were St. Clair and Madison (East St. Louis, Alton, Belleville), $40,000; Peoria and Tazewell, $35,000; and McLean and Macon (Bloomington-Normal and Decatur), $20,000. The assumption that the total amounted to more than $100,000 resulted from the omission of Sangamon (Springfield), Alexander, and Pulaski Counties, known to tolerate widespread gambling and corruption.

Link attached names to collectors for the counties. In Peoria and Tazewell, the operative was Clyde Garrison, long the area gambling czar. The article said the Sheltons had not contributed to the campaign in 1944 because they were competitors of Garrison for gambling territory. St. Clair and Madison, across the Mississippi River from St. Louis, had long histories of wide open gambling, prostitution, and corruption. Link said Dan McGlynn, lawyer and Republican kingpin in St. Clair, was the key man. George Ericksen, well-known Republican collector of protection money, had been traced to Madison joints in Venice, frequented by crowds from the St. Louis area. In Macon and McLean, the principal collector was an unnamed Decatur liquor dealer. In a later article, the Decatur man was disclosed as H. Paul Tick.[28] The *Post-Dispatch* crusade included many editorials and cartoons by D. R. Fitzpatrick that declared Green guilty of all manner of disgraceful behavior related to gambling and corruption.[29]

While Ted Link watched over unfolding stories in Peoria and Roy Harris did the same in Springfield, Carl Baldwin continued to roam distant locations in the state. A day after Link's articles about the 1944 campaign scandal, a page 1 article by Baldwin appeared from Kewanee, a small northern Illinois community. The subject was Mark A. Saunders, Governor Green's director of finance and referred to by politicians as the "invisible governor" or "Green's hatchet man." While elected officials in Illinois often had political operatives close at hand, what Baldwin found in Saunders's background made his closeness to the governor of interest in the gambling probe.[30]

Before Saunders moved to the finance job in 1945, he had been mayor of Kewanee since 1935. While serving as mayor, Saunders also had been an administrative assistant to the governor, chief clerk in the secretary of state's office, and mediator under the state Department of Labor. Baldwin wrote that soon after Saunders became mayor, slot machines appeared in Kewanee for the first time, operated by a local syndicate related to Chicago gamblers. But there had been a public uproar when the slots showed up in public locations, and Saunders had them removed. Later, slots operated on a "sneak" basis, and the local operators ran dice games in back rooms of taverns. A *Post-Dispatch* editorial compared Saunders's political activities and proximity to the governor with those of Robert Medill, former director of the Department of Mines and Minerals, who held that job until the Centralia mine disaster and disclosure of his political activities resulted in dismissal by Green.[31]

Link continued to dig into questionable past actions during the first two terms of Green's administration as a means of connecting the behavior with current state operations. In a copyrighted story on 10 September, he related how gamblers and state officials had made a noninterference pact in 1941, the first year of Green's initial term. Link stated that an assistant state treasurer, who also had served as an assistant division superintendent with the Department of Public Safety, met in East St. Louis with gamblers to discuss a method of payoffs for local and state officials in order to allow wide open activity without interference from law enforcement authorities.[32]

Link had written in August about payoffs of $2,000 a month to state officials by Carl Shelton until about 1945. The reporter said this was part of the agreement reached in 1941. Surviving Shelton gang associates described the payoff scheme this way: Carl Shelton, accompanied by a bodyguard, would drive toward Springfield from Peoria and meet a state official on the highway. Carl would hand over the money personally.

In the same *Post-Dispatch* issue, the FBI in Springfield announced an investigation into reports of kickbacks to state officials on Illinois highway contracts funded by federal money. An FBI agent said he requested authority for the probe after numerous reports that large sums were being extracted from the contracts for political reasons.[33]

For much of September, Adlai Stevenson toured southern and central Illinois communities—McLeansboro, Metropolis, Brooklyn, Shelbyville, Jacksonville, Mount Vernon—calling for Governor Green to address the charges made and suggested in the *Post-Dispatch* series. He combined this call with his all-inclusive accusation of misuse of state funds, poor budget administration, and general incompetence.[34]

Finally, during a meeting in Springfield on 13 September with twenty-five ministers and at a press conference afterward, Green said the state highway patrol's powers were limited and could not be used to deal with gambling and other illegal activities. This came after the ministers asked him to direct the patrol to close gambling establishments. "The primary job of the state police is to patrol the highways. All our laws are drafted on the basis of maintaining home rule. In the event a sheriff or state's attorney fails to perform his duty, local citizens can go into their local circuit court and request a special grand jury and a special prosecutor," the governor said. At the press conference, Green called newspaper claims that gamblers contributed $100,000 to his 1944 campaign "an outrageous falsehood, a damnable lie." When asked about comments by Stevenson, the governor said he had not read the candidate's charges.[35]

The Democrat did not let up, before or after Green's comments. Stevenson accused the governor "and his gang" of defeating bills in the legislature introduced by the state crime commission. Stevenson added, "What has happened to the Dwight Green who was once advertised as a gang buster? The Dwight Green who, so his biography says, fought the Capone mob so bravely and promised to break up the alliance between crime and politics?" Unable to avoid the growing issue of crime and corruption, the *Chicago Tribune* quoted Stevenson as saying, "Illinois has the largest, most extravagant, most wasteful, most corrupt, most cynical and most deceitful machine this state or any state has been inflicted with." In another southern Illinois speech, Stevenson declared, "My campaign won't be financed by gamblers and gangsters. I don't want a single billboard or a single poster that's paid for with dirty money."[36]

A few days later in a statewide radio program, Green again denied charges of coddling gamblers or taking their money: "I have never had any truck with hoodlums or gangsters, and I never will. I denounce as an outright lie any statement that I have ever sought or received one penny from such sources." He repeated that local law enforcement authorities were responsible for enforcing antigambling laws. Green condemned the *Post-Dispatch* articles as "a campaign of malicious vilification and innuendo."[37]

In one of its few references to the accusations during September, the *Tribune* reported Green's radio show comments as if it were the first time he had commented publicly. The paper did not report Green's earlier remarks to Springfield clergy. The report repeated essentially what the St. Louis paper said about the radio show, adding this Green quotation: "I have learned something about underworld syndicates when I was in the United States attorney's office in Chicago and we smashed the biggest syndicate by sending Al Capone to the federal penitentiary."[38]

Green's denial that he benefited from gangster connections with his administration came long after the *Post-Dispatch* articles began connecting payoffs and bribes with the administration. Green's silence and infrequent, almost perfunctory, denials left him politically vulnerable for the first time and puzzled supporters who believed he should have made a stronger defense against the accusations. Some Green supporters may have figured the charges would go away. In a strictly political sense, Adlai Stevenson finally had an issue that could stick to the incumbent, and he banged away at it every day across the state.

If the *Post-Dispatch* barrage of articles unearthed legitimate campaign issues, why didn't more papers in the state participate? Reporter Carl Baldwin gave his answer in an assessment of the paper's anticrime campaign: "Link had the Shelton gang so well sewed up during the course of the Illinois story that frustrated Chicago newspapermen could obtain information only from public officials and people like Peter Petrakos [subject of the four-hour interview with Link in August]. But Link would feed the Chicagoans scraps from time to time. It used to be a common occurrence for a *Sun-Times* reporter to run up, out of breath, and say, 'Where's Ted Link? I need a new lead for the next edition.'"[39]

Adding to the quantity of page 1 articles in the *Post-Dispatch* during September were reports related to earlier revelations in Peoria and Springfield. Link was on the scene in Peoria, and Harris contributed frequent items from Springfield. The effect was to create an impression that disclosures of criminal activities and political corruption in two major Illinois cities were under investigation after years of neglect. Major newspapers in the state sent reporters to keep track of revelations and developments, and wire services provided accounts for smaller papers and radio outlets.

The Peoria grand jury summoned in August to investigate accusations stemming from the assassination of Bernie Shelton, specifically charges of bribery, reported the outcome on 3 September.[40] In a bombshell announcement, the Peoria jury issued indictments of state's attorney Roy P. Hull, Sheriff Earl E. Spainhower, and state's attorney investigator Charles Somogyi. Hull was accused of attempted bribery and malfeasance in office through failure to suppress gambling. Spainhower was charged with perjury and malfeasance, and Somogyi with malfeasance. Hull and Spainhower were in their first elected terms, and Somogyi had been on the Peoria police force from 1935 to 1943.

The jury report commended special prosecutor Verle Safford and requested that he conduct prosecutions of the accused. The jury also noted that a more complete investigation had been hindered by the unavailability of witnesses, and the statute of limitations on the grand jury term "barred many avenues of inquiry." However, the jury concluded, "There is much evidence that too many public officials are too closely associated with racketeers and gangsters." In an editorial, the *Post-Dispatch* repeated the jury's comment, adding, "By these indictments and by this report, the people of Peoria County, through representative citizens on their grand jury, have taken the first step to reclaim their local government."[41] The report recommended that subsequent grand juries be called to continue the investigations.

If the indictments were not shocking enough, the following day Hull announced he would direct a new grand jury inquiry into Peoria gambling. Safford's appointment and the grand jury term were to end in ten days. In a statement, Hull said, "The charges against me were inspired by the Sheltons and will crumble when a full probe of gambling and its many alliances is made. . . . For three years I have fought the Shelton gambling activities and at last I am in a position to obtain convincing evidence of their crimes."[42]

Not unexpectedly, the *Post-Dispatch* editorial page erupted at the thought of Hull running the next grand jury, calling the official's statement the "weirdest turn yet" in the Peoria situation. "He should step aside and leave the investigation and prosecution of the syndicated gambling and its corruption of state and local officials to citizens with stomach for the ugly business," the editorial declared.[43]

Circuit court judge Henry J. Ingram cleared up the situation by appointing Safford as special prosecutor of Hull and Somogyi. However, he left Hull in charge of the sheriff's case. A few days later, the judge changed his order and put Safford in charge of prosecuting the sheriff also. Meanwhile, the Peoria Association of Commerce requested Attorney General Barrett to appoint a special prosecutor and special grand jury. He had kept his distance from legal matters in the city.

Continuing with revelations in Springfield, Harris of the *Post-Dispatch* wrote on 7 September that payoffs from gambling and vice to city and county officials amounted to more than $500,000 a year. He named Frank Zito, head of a liquor ring during Prohibition, as instrumental in organizing payoffs for handbooks, punchboards, poker games, slot machines, dice games, baseball pools, organized gambling, and prostitution. Harris noted that previous disclosures of illegal activities had prompted the Good Government League and Ministerial Association to press for a special grand jury session. Two weeks before the article appeared, operatives shut down most gambling operations because of increased "heat" generated by the newspaper articles. Harris attributed his information to an "intensive investigation of conditions" in Springfield and Sangamon County.[44]

An editorial in the *Post-Dispatch* reminded readers of earlier revelations that had prompted Sheriff Rhule to say he knew of widespread commercial gambling but intended to do nothing about it. The editorial claimed state's attorney John W. Curren "has shown no more interest in law enforcement against the gambling syndicates than Roy P. Hull showed in Peoria County."[45]

Harris followed that article two days later with a page 1 story identifying George Ericksen as a collector of payoffs for state officials. The paper earlier had connected Ericksen to payoffs in Madison County. The report stated that Ericksen had served as collector for seven years, nearly the entire two terms in office of the Green administration, and operated in all parts of the state.[46] Ericksen had a close association with Carl Shelton, who wrote down payoff information in a notebook obtained by Ted Link.

With pressure mounting from newspapers and good government organizations, Attorney General Barrett did an about-face from earlier pronouncements that his office would not get involved in probing illegal activities in cities and counties. He appointed investigators for Peoria and Sangamon Counties to unearth information about gambling and related crimes. Governor Green stated they would receive all assistance necessary from his office and the state patrol. In reporting Barrett's decision of 12 September, the *Chicago Tribune* provided its readers the first lengthy account of events in September.[47] Barrett's announcement appeared to confuse an already crowded agenda of grand juries, investigations, trials of public officials, and petitions to the courts.

James A. Howe, former mayor of Oak Park, was sent to oversee investigations in Peoria. The investigator assigned to Springfield was Oliver H. Bovik, a Chicago attorney and former member of the Cook County state's attorney's staff. Both were special assistants to Barrett but relinquished the positions when assigned to the investigations. Almost immediately, the two named by Barrett came under scrutiny in the *Post-Dispatch*, leading to information that questioned their qualifications for the jobs.

The St. Louis paper discovered that Bovik was under investigation by the Chicago Bar Association, which had refused to endorse him for a municipal judgeship after a committee on candidates found Bovik unqualified.[48] The bar's probe resulted from the claim that Bovik had aided in attempting to block a grand jury inquiry into the slating of Elmer Droste for state treasurer by state Republican leaders. Bovik said he had "nothing to fear" from the bar's investigation. Questions about Howe's appointment came from his legal background and reaction from "some Republicans." Howe had worked in real estate before turning to politics in Oak Park and becoming what the paper called "an errand boy" for Barrett. He had no experience in the private practice of law.[49]

The matter of a special prosecutor in Sangamon County, requested in a petition from Springfield residents, had made its way to consideration by judges of the Seventh Illinois Circuit. The petitioners, including a bank president, a superintendent of schools, and a businessman, asked the court to name an impartial prosecutor instead of the state's attorney or attorney general. The argument was based primarily on news stories in the *Post-Dispatch* of public officials taking $10,000 a week in payoffs from gamblers. State's attorney Curren said the charges were based on rumor and hearsay. Three circuit court judges on 17 September ruled that nothing prevented the state's attorney or attorney general from calling a grand jury and naming a special prosecutor. The ruling meant the court would not force the issue.[50]

One part of the ruling addressed the accusations made by the newspaper and citizens. The judges stated, "Public interest requires a grand jury investigation of public laws relating to gambling and an investigation of charges of violations by officials or other persons of other criminal laws of the state." A regular grand jury was scheduled to begin deliberations in October, and Curren said he would look into issues raised by citizens in their request to the judges but, due to a shortage of staff, probably would not be finished until November, after the election.

Continuing efforts to track Green's comments on gambling and charges of corruption during the campaign, Baldwin wrote from deep southern Illinois that the governor had called for reelection of county officials who had admitted they allowed violation of the state's gambling laws. At Mound City, Green had urged all gathered at a rally to vote for the entire Republican ticket, which included Pulaski County state's attorney Warner Wall. He told the paper earlier that the lax law enforcement was with "the consent of the people."[51] The paper's article said the FBI was investigating charges of fraud in the primary election, when Wall had won nomination. Baldwin toured Pulaski County and nearby Alexander County, taking note of gambling clubs operating openly, in spite of complaints to officials by citizens and religious organizations in Cairo and Mound City.

Post-Dispatch articles, editorials, and cartoons during September created a wave of accusations against public officials and connections to years of graft and corruption across the state, all of which remained in legal limbo by month's end. With Election Day about a month away, the newspaper barrage had created a tighter race for governor and for all state and local offices on the ballot but had not provided hardcore evidence of the governor's complicity.

SEPTEMBER 1948

For most Illinoisans, Labor Day launched the election campaign season. Establishing the list of candidates, rallying loyalists and volunteers, refining themes for stump speeches and appearances, determining favorites of the press, and raising money served as foreplay. Little said by candidates during the warm-up months would be remembered by most citizens on Election Day.

That explains why the favorites as measured by the press and its pundits in January and February remained atop the heap with two months to go. Thomas E. Dewey led Harry S. Truman by about 5 percentage points, according to polls. During September, pundits estimated that Dewey had a substantial lead in twenty states, including Illinois. Press people assumed Dwight Green had a comfortable advantage over Adlai Stevenson, and almost everyone saw Curly Brooks gliding past Paul Douglas to victory by substantial numbers. Many people believed that all Republicans had to do was not make any stupid mistakes.

On the money side, Republicans had an advantage based primarily on perceived victory and incumbency. Stevenson had sources, including some Republicans, who kept his coffers supplied. In contrast, Douglas had no money to pay staff and none for advertising. He skimped along, just barely in the hunt except for his own energy and that of his wife. The state Democratic organization provided little financial help. To say things looked grim for Democrats was an understatement on 1 September.

Gambling, crime, and corruption aside—if possible—the campaign for high state offices took off with a roar in September. On the assumption that Illinoisans had the time and inclination to listen, the parties swept from north to south and east to west, stopping at cities and hamlets, pressing the flesh and making promises.

In the race for governor, Dwight Green defended his nearly eight years in office, cruising with the confidence of an incumbent who was believed to be comfortably in the lead. As a result, he rarely referred to his competition, and never by name, in the tradition of incumbents. On several occasions he spoke in generalities rather than proposed new initiatives. When facing friendly audiences, he was congenial and aimed attacks mostly at the New Deal or its current incarnation and at the drift toward socialism, as he defined it. Appearing before audiences with Senate incumbent Brooks, they took turns lambasting the New Deal threat in Springfield and Washington. Before an audience at the Du Quoin State Fair during a GOP caravan downstate, Green said, "The New Deal inflation has brought serious problems to the cities and other local governments of Illinois. We are taking steps to help solve them. But the people of Illinois will not be fooled by New Deal proposals to rob Peter to pay Paul."[52] In the same talk, Green took credit for the decrease in the sales tax, as he did at virtually every stop, although the decision for the decrease had been made during the Horner administration.

The pace of Green's campaign picked up in the final two weeks of the month, taking him mostly to downstate locations in central and southern Illinois. He appeared at "official duties," such as dedicating a stretch of road in Rossville or crowning the "sweetheart" of the sweet corn festival in Hoopeston. The governor was proud of the expansion of airports in the state, and in Shelbyville he mentioned that $6.8 million had been appropriated for airport planning: "The result is that we have developed an expanding network of airports which now includes 170 approved fields."[53] In areas of Illinois generally friendly toward Republicans, Green expressed pleasure at the turnouts. If citizens felt good about their lives during Green's two terms as governor, his demeanor and self-confidence reinforced their comfort.

While Green was on the road, the *Tribune* covered his back in Chicago. In articles that received prominent display in the paper with the largest circulation in the state, writer Arthur Evans extolled the virtues of the governor and his administration with no apologies. There was no similar attempt to explain the program ideas of Adlai Stevenson, and articles about his speeches generally were short and carried small headlines. In the first Green article, "How Green Kept Pledge on Economy," the writer asserted, "The sound condition of the Illinois state financial system is a cardinal phase of the record on which Gov. Green seeks re-election." Evans compared budget and expenditures and tax collections with a number of other states, including New York and California, demonstrating Illinois's good standing. The strength of Evans's argument for Green rested on a balanced budget, building of surpluses, and promises of increased expenditures for education and housing.[54]

Next in line was "Housing Plan of Green Held Model for U.S." The author stated that the postwar plan of Green was to stimulate building by private enterprise and to encourage large-scale investments in privately owned housing projects. The project began in 1945, and the article claimed that it was so unique and successful that "the Illinois idea may well become the basis for an effective national housing program."[55] The next day's *Tribune* carried the headline "Illinois Vets' Aid Piloted to Peak by Green." In 1943, Green created by executive order a committee on rehabilitation and employment for World War II veterans. In 1945, the legislature made it an official agency to address the needs of veterans and their dependents, and offices were set up across the state. More than half of the article provided details of the veterans' bonus plan, which was begun during a special session called by Green in 1946. The article stated that by 1948, more than $750 million had been paid to Illinois veterans.[56]

Another article in the series praised Green for passage of a law remapping the twenty-six congressional districts, "which substantially restores the basic principle of equality of representation in Congress." The article acknowledged that Democrats supported the remapping, "but both sides give full credit to Gov. Green. His persistence brought passage of the act." The law abolished congressmen-at-large and gave more districts to Cook and Lake Counties, which had 53 percent of the 1940 population. Downstate counties lost representation under the realignment.[57]

Organized labor officials proved to be one of the governor's strongest support groups. That was reaffirmed late in the month when he appeared before the annual convention of the Illinois Federation of Labor. During his talk, Green applauded the state's record of relative peace and friendly relations between labor and management, mentioning that legislatures during his eight years in office had enacted ninety-three bills sponsored by labor and defeated sixty-seven bills opposed by labor. Reuben G. Soderstrom, federation president, introduced Green as an "outstanding friend of labor" and referred to him as the "trustworthy pilot of our ship of state." Green blamed the postwar outbreak of antilabor legislation in Washington on communists who sought to destroy labor's "reputation for patriotism and loyalty to American institutions."[58]

On the stump downstate, Green said Illinois had experienced less labor trouble than other large industrial states. He added, "Under progressive labor law, there has been created in Illinois a spirit of cooperation and understanding favorable to both labor and management. Production has been higher and employment has been steadier." However, despite Green's claims and the support of labor officials, Green could not get the full endorsement of the federation's members.[59]

Stevenson had his own newspaper support that produced promotional articles and editorials. Among those were the *St. Louis Post-Dispatch* and the *Chicago Sun-Times*. Stevenson was quick to pick up on press statements that criticized Green and accused the governor of various misdeeds. Crime articles by the St. Louis newspaper ranked highest on Stevenson's list of favored subjects. Another issue of repeated value for Stevenson was the Green administration's record of political influence in the coal mining industry, the impact of which was felt most strongly among miners in southern and central Illinois.

In an attempt to counter Green's backing by organized labor voices, Stevenson took on the subject in a speech at Mount Vernon on 6 September.[60] One of the first statements concerned Soderstrom, president of the state Federation of Labor. Stevenson said, "Evidently Mr. Soderstrom has had a curious change of heart since 1944 when he said Green was 'easily the worst Governor Illinois has ever had.' He even referred to Green's administration as 'a sort of nightmare, a bad dream.'" Finished with Soderstrom, the candidate outlined measures he would take if elected:

- Conduct the Industrial Commission for the benefit of employer and employee alike, and not for the benefit of politicians first and the people second.
- Increase benefits under the Workmen's Compensation Act, in view of the inflation and general wage increases.
- Improve aid to old age pensioners.
- Appoint a director of the Department of Labor from the ranks of labor.
- Find solutions to the conflicts between labor and management.

Stevenson added, "But I shall not be a 'labor governor,' 'an employer governor,' or a 'farmer's governor.'"

He again had strong words about the Centralia mine disaster, recalling the action and inaction by Green and mining officials. He said, "It's a sorry story of neglect, buck passing and political prostitution of a public service charged with the protection of human life." He then answered the question of what he would do: "I am going to do my best to take the mine inspectors out of politics. They must be put under civil service and removed from all possibility of political control or influence. They must enforce the law without fear or favor against mine officials and miners alike. And I am going to appoint a director to the Department of Mines and Minerals who is interested in the oil and coal industries and the men who work in them, not in politics."

Each of the party candidates at the top of the tickets believed in repetition of themes as the tactic most likely to prove victorious on 2 November.

Green relentlessly promoted achievements of his administration and the positive impacts on targeted constituencies. Stevenson pounded away at alleged corruption in state government and at how politics had eroded the effectiveness of state services.

In the race for U.S. Senate, each candidate expressed his favorite themes countless times in speeches, informal talks, individual conversations, and hand-shaking events. A Republican caravan spent almost four weeks in downstate locations before campaigning the final two weeks in Chicago and Cook County. Brooks spent most of September in towns of all sizes across the state. In those appearances, faithfully covered by the *Tribune*, he condemned communism and socialism in America and especially in the federal government, defended the Taft-Hartley labor act, and spoke disparagingly of the Marshall Plan to help war-torn countries. The term "New Deal" was cast over every subject as a blanket negative. He never let an appearance pass without raising the specter of communist infiltration in government and the need for Republicans to cleanse every department and office. A few years later, those messages resonated from congressional committees and speeches across the nation in what became the communist scare that swept many parts of the nation.

No matter where Brooks began a talk or what he said during it, the central theme was fear of communism in the United States and what could be done about its eradication. In Pana, he spoke primarily against shipping electrical supplies and machinery overseas when there were still many people in rural areas of the country that did not have electricity. At one point he asserted that the Republican Party was dedicated to eliminate from public offices and agencies "those fuzzy minded individuals who would install socialism or communism in the place of our American way of life that has made us the envy of the world." In Springfield, speaking to members of the Republican women's clubs, he asked for their support and praised the roles of women.[61] Specifically, he urged the women to elect Republicans to guarantee a successful fight against communists and subversive elements in the United States.

He carried the message to LaSalle a few days later where he said, "Our immediate danger is not so much from abroad. It is right here at home, where persons with fuzzy-headed ideas labor under the delusion that we can control our heretofore free economy with totalitarian bureaucrats and at the same time preserve the personal liberties of each individual." He added, "One of the greatest menaces to our solvency and security is the presence in strategic positions of these traitorous individuals who sought to destroy our government at home while their sons and daughters were defending it on the battlefields. They must be located and punished."[62]

Brooks carried the same comments to a meeting of the American Legion and to rallies in Murphysboro and Macomb, often combining them with defense of the Taft-Hartley law. When speaking before audiences inclined to favor the law, he emphasized the need to corral union leaders, but added when speaking to union members, "If the law turns out to be injurious to labor, I will be the first to suggest remedial measures."[63] In calling out efforts of the Eightieth Congress for its proposals, Brooks said Truman was the obstacle to progress. In Galesburg, he said, "We've run up against a snag. It is the President of the United States. He won't cooperate with us in our efforts to expose, uproot and punish the communists who are plotting against this nation. There is only one thing to do and that is to get rid of President Truman." He blamed the "New Deal-communist-Democratic coalition" for fighting Republican proposals to investigate "subversive movements."[64]

As Brooks's rhetoric heated up late in the month, he became more pointed in comments about Taft-Hartley. The *Tribune* took his comments to page 1. What apparently made that worthy of more attention was the senator's repudiation of the Illinois Federation of Labor's call for repeal. The federation also had just announced its endorsement of Paul Douglas. Brooks referred to the law as "an emancipation act for the millions of workers who carry union cards. It is a bill for the rank and file of union labor. Under the Taft-Hartley Act labor has a right to know what happens to the dues it pays. Labor now has the right to know whether communists control a union."[65]

A few days earlier, the *Tribune* paused in its daily news coverage of Brooks to summarize the senator's defense of Taft-Hartley, referring to his statements as "the outstanding development on the Illinois political scene in the last fortnight." George Tagge, the paper's primary Brooks booster, wrote, "Most Republican spokesmen have been pussy-footing on the issue, while union leaders formed battle lines." Staunchly opposed to repeal, Brooks often stated to audiences containing union members, "Show me how it should be changed." He again mentioned his willingness to consider changes in the law if union leaders would step forward with ideas. "We simply must find the way for industrial peace to help industry produce at its maximum. To that end I dedicate myself," he declared.[66] To the surprise of no one, the *Tribune* endorsed Brooks for reelection. The editorial recited the senator's long political history, stating, "In the last eight years he has become a national figure and has grown to meet the responsibilities that position imposes. The people of Illinois know him. They know him personally. . . . No other man in Illinois political history has campaigned the whole state so frequently."[67]

Paul Douglas disagreed with almost everything Brooks said, or cast the issues in different terms. Brooks was opposed to U.S. aid to Europe, while Douglas supported the Marshall Plan without exception, along with most other international initiatives of the Truman administration. Douglas said during a speech in Shelbyville that the Republican Party was controlled by men opposed to "the cooperation that has grown up between the two political parties on matters of foreign affairs."[68] He declared Brooks an enemy of bipartisan foreign policy. Douglas might agree that some parts of Taft-Hartley held promise, but he wanted the law repealed. Douglas expressed concern for communism's advances outside the United States but did not make riddance of subversives a main argument. They were two men with entirely different ideas about how to conduct the affairs of international and national business. Nevertheless, it was inevitable that communism and socialism would be used against Douglas, given the candidate's background.

Fred E. Busbey, a Republican congressman from Cook County and a World War I veteran, launched accusations before an audience in Champaign that Douglas harbored communist and socialist sympathies. Most of Busbey's information came from widely known incidents in the 1920s and early 1930s, when Douglas was admittedly interested in socialism and supported Norman Thomas, socialist candidate for president in 1932. As evidence of Douglas's leanings, Busbey quoted from *The Coming of a New Party* written by Douglas in 1932 and dedicated to Thomas. The congressman also referred to a 1927 trade mission to Russia that included Douglas, implying this underscored suspicions of agreement with communism. Busbey said, "His record brands him with Red paint and his affiliations place him in Communist front organizations. It won't help the United States to spend our money and resources shadow boxing with communism in all the countries of the world and neglect it on the Potomac."[69] His references to front organizations included the American Civil Liberties Union and a number of committees devoted to improving relations with Russia.

None of these were fresh charges against Douglas. In May, Republicans made the same arguments and references to Douglas's writings and statements from the 1920s and 1930s. At that time, Douglas brushed them aside as youthful inquiries and thoughts that had evaporated when the Roosevelt administration blossomed in 1933. However, Busbey's comments constituted the first serious broadside about Douglas's sympathies and philosophies. The *Tribune* pushed articles to the front page. Before Douglas officially addressed the accusations, his campaign manager, Donald J. Walsh, called them "flagrant distortions of facts" and "smear tactics."[70] Douglas's wife appeared at a Republican meeting in DuPage County at which Busbey spoke. She attempted to take the floor for rebuttal and to read a statement, but the chairman of the meeting said she was out of order and told her to sit down.

In response, Douglas reviewed his anticommunist credentials and explained how his philosophy had changed over the years. He said the book dedicated to Thomas was harmless, and he had charted a different direction with the advent of the Roosevelt administration. He accused the *Tribune* and Busbey of smear tactics but otherwise offered no new perspective on his beliefs or how they influenced his attitudes as expressed in the campaign.[71] The issue faded quickly from the headlines. Busbey was defeated for reelection.

While Douglas's speeches and public comments made newspaper articles periodically, he spent most of his time in grassroots campaigning, speaking to small groups of people on street corners and shaking hands with union members and employees at entrances to industrial company offices, as he had done since 1947. The campaign reflected the shortage of money for more elaborate campaigning. By September, his campaign coffers were exhausted and printers would not accept any orders for materials on credit.

The saga of whether to place candidates of the Progressive Party on Illinois ballots continued to provide an element of uncertainty to the campaign. A victory or loss by the party had broad implications for Democrats and Republicans in November's election.

The Progressive battle had begun in April when a state supreme court ruling allowed party names on the primary ballot in Chicago and Cook County because the party had received more than 5 percent of the vote in a Cook County judicial election in November 1947. However, the decision came too late to include names on the ballots. Progressives won a circuit court decision in June to be placed on the November ballot. This led to an appeal by Democrats and an appellate court decision in July that Chicago and Cook County election officials could disregard the earlier court order. Progressives appealed that decision to the state supreme court. Continuing their optimism, Progressives in August named a full slate of candidates in Illinois, beginning at the top with Henry Wallace for president and Senator Glen Taylor of Idaho for vice president. Grant Oakes, a union leader, was named for governor and Curtis MacDougall for U.S. senator.[72]

Although courts could be used as a last resort, initially the state electoral board, consisting of two Republicans and one Democrat, had the responsibility to decide whether Progressives would be on the November ballot outside Cook County. The board members were Attorney General George F. Barrett and State Auditor Arthur C. Lueder, both Republicans, and Secretary of State Edward Barrett, Democrat. Because the attorney general and secretary of state were on the November ballot, they were replaced for the electoral board ruling by two justices of the state supreme court.

This was much more than a routine ruling regarding a third party ballot request. If allowed on the ballot, Progressives, to the left philosophically, would most likely damage chances of nominated Democrats. Sources speculated that as many as 400,000 votes could be cast for Progressives, most of which otherwise would be cast for Democrats. That meant Republicans had a major stake in the outcome as well. A ruling for Progressives enhanced chances of the Republican slate being elected.

A 1935 amendment to the state election law required that petitions from at least 50 of the state's 102 counties must contain 200 valid signatures for a party to be placed on the ballot. Petitions were submitted from 64 counties. County clerks from 23 claimed they had fewer than 200 valid signatures, reducing to 41 the number of counties in which Progressives met state requirements. On 1 September, the electoral board denied the Progressive Party request to be placed on the ballot, although the total number of petition signatures far exceeded the minimum of 25,000.[73] The *Tribune*, which might have wished for a different outcome, stated in an editorial that certain rights to be on a ballot "cannot overcome clear illegalities, and the Wallace petitions, from the evidence presented, seem clearly to have failed to comply with the law."[74] The Chicago and Cook County issue remained on appeal.

The state supreme court ruled a few days later that Progressives could be placed on the ballot in Chicago and Cook County.[75] On 25 September, the state high court refused to consider an appeal of the electoral board decision against the Progressive Party. Coincidentally, Wallace appeared the same day at a party rally at Wrigley Field, where he condemned the decision, announced a further appeal, and demanded action by federal courts.[76] It appeared that action by the U.S. Supreme Court would be necessary to end the controversy.

Amid the flurry of ballot activities, Curtis MacDougall, Progressive candidate for the Senate, encountered violence while campaigning in West Frankfort. The candidate and aides were the targets of stones, fists, and verbal threats during a street meeting that ended with MacDougall and his party fleeing the community. MacDougall said, "The yelling crowd moved in and tried to tip over my car and trailer. They smashed the loud speaker on it and roughed up our luggage."[77] He reported that police in Zeigler, Murphysboro, and Herrin, where the candidate planned to campaign later, refused to guarantee protection. As a result, MacDougall canceled the meetings. On the way out of West Frankfort, several cars pursued him and passengers continued to make threats, he said. The following day, spouses and female aides accompanying the candidate were sent home, while MacDougall continued his campaign farther north, away from southern Illinois locations.[78]

As Truman and Dewey presented the nation's public with dueling campaigns, polls indicated by mid-September that the challenger appeared well on his way to victory. The Gallup polling company issued its tally early in the month showing Dewey with a four-point lead with a large number of undecided voters. The poll gave Henry Wallace five points.[79] In a survey of leading newspapers by the magazine *Editor & Publisher*, Dewey had 62 percent of the endorsements and Truman 18.[80] With those indicators as backdrop, the two presidential candidates prepared for lengthy campaign tours by train, beginning just days apart. Truman launched his swing on 17 September and Dewey on 20 September. They covered similar ground over almost the same time period, with Dewey appearing to shadow the president much of the time.

Truman's two-week trek included a number of major speeches and many so-called whistle-stops, where he spoke from the back of the presidential train.[81] He planned a brief stop in Rock Island at the beginning of the journey and a full day in southern Illinois near the conclusion. Dewey also scheduled a visit to Rock Island. Both candidates scheduled stops en route to the West Coast and back. Raymond Brandt, following Dewey for the *Post-Dispatch*, wrote that the candidate intended to take the high road, speaking about national policy and avoiding personal attacks. Brandt characterized Dewey in the role of "champ" and Truman as "challenger." The writer said the New York governor planned to talk about national unity and avoid being cocky or smug. Truman, on the other hand, hacked and slashed his way along the trail, taking on Congress, Republicans, and his opponent with high energy and his own brand of down-home chatter. He referred to Republicans as "those birds" and the Republican Congress as "mossbacks" who used the "meat ax" on his programs. He introduced Mrs. Truman as "the boss" and his daughter Margaret as "the one who bosses her." Truman had nothing to lose in being aggressive, folksy, and feisty, while Dewey maintained the appearance of comfortable president-to-be.[82]

Reporters following both tours reported large, enthusiastic crowds along the way for Dewey and smaller crowds for the president. In an effort to humanize the time-consuming work of campaign stops several times a day, writers offered readers an inside-the-private-car view. Joseph Driscoll, national correspondent for the *Post-Dispatch*, writing a generally favorable column about the president, offered this tidbit: "Even on board the train, Truman leads the regular life of a countryman except for his willingness to speak at any hour. He eats well and he sleeps well and when he's tired and thirsty he takes a little bourbon with plain water; no fancy mixtures for him. He holds with another former vice president, John Nance Garner, that tap or branch water is ambrosia from the gods when properly sterilized with corn likker. Therein they differ from their former boss, the late Franklin Roosevelt, who was a martini man."[83]

Inevitably, columnists painted their own pictures of the two touring candidates, generally more favorable to Dewey for his presidential tone in spite of offering mostly generalizations. Writing from Washington after interviewing unnamed partisan "parties," the *Tribune*'s Walter Trohan poured cold water on the performances of both candidates, although given his employer, a more frigid dose for the president. Sources told the columnist that Truman appeared to be "operating more as a ward leader touring his precincts than a president touring the nation." His sources apparently suggested to Trohan that Truman should cancel the trip and make no plans for more. Trohan said Republicans were concerned more about the content of Dewey's speeches, suggesting they were "too perfect in that it borders on the artificial." The sources complained Dewey's comments were "replete with pious platitudes."[84]

Syndicated columnist Joseph Alsop, who followed the campaigns as far as Des Moines, dismissed Truman as "somehow unable to stir people, even when he makes points which should have a real meaning to them. The plain fact is that Truman has none of the stuff of political leadership about him, whereas Dewey possesses this queer, unanalyzed human chemical in increasing measure."[85] Both Trohan and Alsop commented on the inadequacy of staff and planning for Truman's tour and the contrasting efficiency and hustle of Dewey's.

TRUMAN AT ILLINOIS CROSSROADS

The importance of Illinois and its twenty-eight electoral votes to President Truman can be illustrated by the amount of time he spent in the state during September and October. There may have been some states where he campaigned more days, but not many. On separate occasions, he made a morning stop at Rock Island, devoted almost a full day to a caravan journey in southern Illinois, barnstormed by train through central Illinois, and finished off his campaign with a rip-roaring speech in Chicago. At every Truman stop there were Illinois candidates for offices along for the ride. Even Republican Dewey felt obliged to shadow the president through the Prairie State.

In addition to those planned public appearances, Truman made an unscheduled stop near Chicago in the middle of the night on 18 September en route to an early-morning appearance in Rock Island. It may have been the shortest stop, but in political terms one of the most important.

When Democratic Party officials heard that Truman would be passing through the Chicago area, they grabbed the opportunity to proclaim their allegiance directly to the president, two months after their embarrassment at the Democratic National Convention. It is safe to assume Jack Arvey had made a measure of peace with Truman before the tour, but he wanted another chance. Just after 2:15 A.M., the president, aroused from sleep, appeared in pajamas and bathrobe to greet Arvey and party officials at a service stop in Englewood.

People in the delegation talked with Truman and aides about the political situation in Chicago and downstate Illinois. Having made the reconciliation gesture, Arvey said after he got off the train, "He looked sleepy and I felt like a heel getting him up." Truman's aides had argued against the middle-of-the-night stop, but Truman overruled them and said he wanted to see the officials.[86]

Arvey need not have worried about the president. The train car in which he slept, ate, conversed, and lived while on the road was fitted for his exclusive use and comfort and contained the trappings that made time spent there as pleasant as possible. Named the Ferdinand Magellan, it was built by the Pullman Company in 1928 and in 1942 became the

travel home of Franklin D. Roosevelt.[87] The car was eighty-three feet
long and covered with armor plate; the windows were of three-inch
bulletproof glass. It contained a galley, a pantry, servants' quarters, and
a dining room that doubled as a conference room. The interior finery
featured china cabinets and a mahogany dining table and chairs. Of the
four staterooms, the First Lady's was painted in a pale peach color. The
only exterior features that identified the car as something special were
the presidential seal fixed to the rear platform and loudspeakers mounted
on top of the platform roof.

The first whistle-stop of the Truman campaign in Illinois occurred
at Rock Island. The seventeen-car train arrived at the station at 5:45
A.M., 18 September, full of people: photographers, reporters, presidential
aides, Truman's family, an assortment of public officials and candidates,
and friends of the president. Police estimated the Rock Island crowd at
5,000.[88] Typical of the quick stops, Truman spoke without script for about
ten minutes. His staff had learned on earlier campaign trips that Truman
performed better without a prepared speech in front of him. An early riser
any day, Truman smiled and waved to the crowd. He seemed buoyant.

The president urged his audience to get out the vote and not allow a
repeat of the 1946 congressional elections, when voters chose what he
called the "Republican do-nothing Congress." This became a familiar
theme. He tossed frequent barbs at the Republicans, blaming them primarily for the Great Depression. He made a point of introducing Paul
Douglas, candidate for the U.S. Senate, who accompanied the president
on all of his trips in Illinois.

Truman enjoyed the give and take with an audience, and despite the
early hour, Rock Island guests gave him the opportunity. There were
frequent "You tell 'em, Harry" comments, and one person shouted, "Bring
out Margaret." His daughter, Margaret, and wife, Bess, were aboard but
had not made an appearance. Truman responded, "Well, I'll tell you
Margaret has had a strenuous trip and I promised I wouldn't wake her
until we get to Iowa City." The crowd was not satisfied and individuals
again asked to see her. Truman said, "You see, Margaret wasn't born on
a farm. She isn't used to getting up so early." After laughing, the people
accepted his reason as the Rock Island High School band began playing
"The Field Artillery March." Truman, a member of an artillery unit in
World War I, took notice of the choice and voiced approval.[89]

Rock Island mayor Melvin C. McKay was a guest on board the train,
and Truman asked him after the remarks, "How do things look down

here?" The mayor, a Republican, said carefully, "Well, about the best I can say is that a lot of folks are going to vote for you." Truman did not ask McKay about his party affiliation but must have been briefed by staff before the conversation. There were many such occasions with Republican officials along the train route, and for the most part the exchanges were cordial. Regardless of political affiliation, officials demonstrated their respect for a president.[90]

Truman's comments would become familiar on the long campaign tour. He said, "You know the issues in this campaign are not hard to define. The issue is the people against the special interests, and if you need any proof of that, all you need to do is to review the record of this Republican 80th Congress. The object of this 80th Congress, it seemed to me, was to take the bargaining power away from labor and give it back to the special interests."

As the Truman train departed for Iowa destinations, Rock Island officials already had been at work on the next presidential campaign appearance.[91] Two days later, Dewey spoke in downtown Rock Island. The challenger, traveling on his own special campaign train, was not loafing. However, the difference in campaign styles could not have been more striking. Truman ripped the GOP Congress, painted word pictures of the disaster that he said would befall U.S. citizens with a Dewey presidency, and pleaded for a continuation of the New Deal. In Illinois, Dewey was polite, spoke in generalities, made few promises, refused to get nasty with Truman, and campaigned mostly like a successful and beloved president. He rarely gave a talk before 10 A.M.

Accompanied by fifteen Republican candidates and officials, Dewey did more than talk from the back of a train in Rock Island. He spoke at a downtown park to an estimated 12,000 residents, calling, as he did constantly, for unity and pledging to "do the biggest, toughest, unraveling housecleaning our government ever got." He offered no specific ideas but assured listeners that he would do the right thing. Dewey said, "If we Americans have a friendly and cooperative government, there is nothing on earth we can't do."[92]

Ironically, among the Republicans on hand, and prominently so, were two who had fought for a foe of Dewey at the national convention. The Illinois convention delegation, headed by Dwight Green, had cast most of its votes for Senator Robert Taft, until it was obvious Dewey would win. Senator Brooks had also favored the more conservative Taft for the nomination and campaigned as a less-known version of the Ohioan. But it was a new day, and Dewey complimented the two candidates, saying, "I have a high and warm regard for your governor and senator."

After leaving Illinois on 18 September, the Truman train cut straight through the middle of the country to California, with Dewey not far behind. On the return, Truman's campaign continued through Arizona, Texas, and Oklahoma, where the candidate seemed to catch a second wind and drew large crowds. A day after leaving Oklahoma City, the president gave sixteen speeches from 7:35 A.M. to 11:15 P.M., the most in any single day of the train campaign. Indefatigable as usual, he was ready for the first stop of 30 September in Mount Vernon, Illinois. At 7:40 A.M., already behind schedule, the train pulled into the station. After a brief talk, Truman joined a motorcade that took him through ten southern Illinois towns where thousands of people waited to see him.[93]

Exactly why Truman decided to spend much of a day traveling 140 miles by car through towns distant from large population centers is not clear, even after all these years. A news story at the start of Truman's tour listed only train stops in Mount Vernon and Carmi as a "tentative program for Southern Illinois."[94] The decision for a motorcade was obviously made on the train. The president and his aides often changed plans at the last minute, as they seemed to operate on a flexible agenda.[95]

Reporters for Chicago papers wrote that the car tour was a direct challenge to John L. Lewis, head of the United Mine Workers of America. The UMWA represented thousands of coal miners in the region.[96] Truman and Lewis rarely had anything pleasant to say about each other, and the union leader favored Dewey. This had been Republican territory, and Truman's six-hour tour was an example of his willingness to take the fight to the opposition on its own ground.

Another factor must have been Paul Powell, the Democrat from Vienna and minority leader in the state House of Representatives. He was Truman's downstate presidential campaign coordinator, and southern Illinois was his home territory. Any decision about a motorcade undoubtedly involved Powell. As the president's convertible cruised with the top down in and out of towns—Mount Vernon, West Frankfort, Benton, Herrin, Carbondale, Carterville, Marion, Eldorado, Harrisburg, and Carmi—Powell was seated in the car.

Powell made announcements to the press about the tour, tying his name closely to the president's campaign. Powell also set the rules of conduct. A day before the tour, he told wire services, "We are eliminating the hand shaking at all stops to gain time to let the president visit the men in the [Marion] Veterans Administration Hospital."[97] He claimed for years after 1948 that he brought a sitting president to southern Illinois for the first time. The first presidential appearance also was mentioned before audiences during the tour. At Eldorado, after a twenty-one-gun salute fired by American Legion members, a voice over the loudspeaker said, "We have waited 160 years for this."

A characteristic of the whistle-stops was the appearance of local and state officials and Democratic candidates on the train and at the events. U.S. Senate candidate Paul Douglas ranked first among those to be introduced. After Douglas, Truman mentioned candidates for the U.S. House of Representatives, and last, Adlai E. Stevenson for governor. Also accompanying the caravan were other Democratic candidates for state office: Edward J. Barrett, Ora Smith, Ivan Elliott, and Sherwood Dixon.

Stevenson kept his distance from underdog Truman throughout the campaign and was not present for any of the southern Illinois stops. One member of the Truman entourage, William J. Bray, wrote, "The President was very much impressed with Paul Douglas. . . . He was not too impressed with Adlai Stevenson. . . . Stevenson gave the impression he did not want to associate himself with the national end of the ticket."[98]

Senator Scott Lucas, who accompanied Truman on a second whistle-stop tour of Illinois in October, wrote later of Stevenson's attitude toward the president as one explanation for campaign estrangement. Lucas said, "Stevenson, with his Princeton background, had little love for 'Hammering Harry,' the farm boy from Missouri. . . . Stevenson wanted little or no part of Truman, believing him to be a liability rather than an asset. He may have been partially right at that time in a crucial year, but if you are a true and loyal Democrat, you don't desert the captain in a crisis."[99]

No matter how long or how little Truman lingered in a given town—he spoke for five minutes in Mount Vernon and 90 seconds in West Frankfort—the candidate repeated the themes aimed at coaxing people to vote for Democrats. He accused Republicans of representing special interests, mostly bad. Truman recalled the gloomy days of the Depression and blamed those on Republicans. Recognizing he was in farm country, he spoke of the Farm Credit Administration and other agencies started by Democrats that provided loans for needy farmers. Truman said in Mount Vernon, "They [Republicans] tried to take the liberties away from labor. They did their level best to ruin the farm program." He rarely commented without a mention of the "do-nothing, good-for-nothing 80th Congress."[100]

The longest appearance and speech Truman gave that fall day totaled twenty minutes at Southern Illinois University in Carbondale. Truman went into detail on his campaign themes, drawing more precisely the pictures of economic disaster he attributed to "the crash of 1929 and the Hoover depression." He championed the rights of workers and decried the influence of big business with Republicans. The speech made a passing reference—barely one line—to the subject of civil rights. He said, "We also continued the fight to expand our civil liberties by new measures against discrimination."[101]

Crowds lined the streets, encircled Truman's car when it stopped, and pressed to get a closer look at the president. Estimates of their numbers varied widely. In Mount Vernon, the newspaper said 10,000 people showed up at the train; a reporter for the *Chicago Sun-Times* called the crowd 4,000 strong. (In a Dewey train stop at Mount Vernon in October, the crowd was estimated at 10,000.) The largest estimated crowd was in Herrin at 18,000, and next was Carmi at 14,000. The Associated Press quoted police estimates of 100,000 for all the people who came to see Truman. The *New York Times* said 75,000. In his memoir, Paul Douglas guessed 200,000.[102] Regardless of the numbers, one consistent point was made by photographs published in local newspapers: the crowds were quite large in proportion to the size of the communities, indicating that people from surrounding communities made a day trip to see Truman. Radio stations and local newspapers promoted the visit for several days ahead of the appearance.

Public officials, Republicans and Democrats, encouraged suspension of school classes so children could see the president. In Herrin, Mayor John H. Murray called for businesses to close during the visit. He said, "Regardless of politics, religion or station in life, it is our duty to be present and to hear, respect and accord to him a hail and farewell from the finest people in Illinois."[103] Marion mayor Harry Rodd made a similar request of his town's businesses. County Republican chairman John L. Cox asked for schools to close "because we recognize that he is the president and that it is proper to extend such an opportunity to our children to see a President of the United States."[104]

Reporters covering Truman's tour were regulars from the campaign trail, Illinois daily newspapers, and local writers. In Mount Vernon, one special reporter, Patsy Hicks, editor of the high school newspaper, had a front row seat for the president's talk. She wrote in the *Register-News*, "A gray haired gentleman—the president of the United States—descended from the last car and mounted the platform. This distinguished gentleman took note of my press card and saddle shoes as he walked toward his rostrum through the mass of people. He smiled at me and tipped his hat, as if to say, 'Good morning, little girl.'"[105]

The young reporter continued with a story about Mrs. Truman and Margaret: "The elder had on a light blue suit which brought out the highlights of her gray hair. The younger woman was dressed entirely in black. Her smile was of a somber sort, more like a mischievous grin. . . . I smiled and offered my chair to Margaret. She declined graciously at first, but upon my insistence accepted the proffered seat." Patsy knelt between Paul Douglas and another guest to hear the president's comments.

Crowds included those who had some connection to the Truman family. The *Herrin Journal* said Mrs. Henry Tudor greeted the president in Carbondale, adding, "Mrs. Tudor used to play piano duets with the president in Independence, Missouri."[106] The mother of state representative Clyde Choate of Anna appeared at the rally. The paper noted she had been with her son in Washington when Truman presented him with the Congressional Medal of Honor for bravery in World War II.[107]

Truman's motorcade stopped at community monuments where he placed wreaths and spoke briefly, including the war memorial in West Frankfort and the Doughboy monument in Herrin. Also in West Frankfort, Truman noticed the large Orient No. 2 coal mine and stated, "That's really some mine. I have known something about the mine disasters you have had in this part of the country and I have tried my best to do something about it."[108]

As scheduled, the president stopped briefly at the veterans' hospital in Marion, where he greeted patients. To one veteran he said, "I hope you are getting good care and enough to eat and have a pretty nurse." During remarks to the crowd in Marion, Secret Service men visibly struggled to shield the president from a crowd eager to see and touch Truman. The local paper reported, "It was a friendly crowd, glad of an opportunity to see their chief executive and eager to make the most of it."[109]

All across the region, local pride surfaced. The Herrin newspaper carried an article with the headline "Herrin Crowds 'Best Behaved' in Truman Tour."[110] Fred Schoonover, who drove the car in which Margaret Truman rode, made the comment for the local paper. At West Frankfort, the town band intended to play the "Missouri Waltz" on Truman's departure, but attempts to obtain the music were unsuccessful. Bands played at all the stops, however.

Candidate Douglas's summary of the tour in his memoir provides a picture of how discouraged, and yet elated, Truman partisans felt on 30 September. "There was great applause, and there were constant shouts of 'Give them hell, Harry.' The newspapers were not impressed. Stevenson did not accompany us, nor had he been with us on Truman's previous trips. . . . Throughout the campaign he [Truman] was simple, unaffected, and determined. We were proud of him."[111] In spite of Douglas's critique, local and state papers gave generally straight accounts of the visit, as might be expected for a visit by any president.

Powell, a relentless cheerleader for Truman, added his version of an episode on the tour in a later newspaper interview: "Between Herrin and Carbondale, the president and I were riding in a motorcade and passed some men working in a ditch. The men had heard the sirens as we approached and had got out of the ditch. The president took his hat off and waved to them, and said to me, 'Those are my kind of people since they know enough to know what the Democratic party has done for the working people.'"[112]

The Illinois motorcade ended in Carmi, where Truman's party boarded the train after remarks. In some of the lengthier comments of the day, Truman trotted out the themes he had emphasized from the first stop in Mount Vernon. He said Democrats were the party of the people and Republicans were the party of special interests. The example he used in Carmi was what he called "the rich man's tax bill." The president said, "The first thing they [Congress] did when they got there was to vote themselves a rich man's tax bill, which I vetoed. Then they took it back and modified it, and I vetoed it again. Then they passed it over my veto. It is a rich man's tax bill, if you analyze it."[113] He accused Republicans of ruining prices for farm goods, and he pleaded with voters not to stay away from the polls as they did in the 1946 elections, when Republicans took over Congress. Two days later, the Ferdinand Magellan pulled into Washington's Union Station.

A day later, Dewey ended a lengthy train trip at Albany, the state capital of New York. He had traveled more miles than Truman, giving sixty speeches. A poll of the forty-seven journalists who accompanied Dewey on the train revealed the unanimous belief that the New Yorker would win easily. In the early days of October, just a month before the election, Dewey's aides, encouraged by comments from the *Chicago Tribune*, predicted he was "well ahead" in Illinois.

6. The Curtain Falls

You could tell October had arrived. All candidates for state offices hit the downstate roads for the first couple of weeks and then switched to campaign in Chicago and Cook County. Plans were firm for Truman and Dewey to appear in Chicago back-to-back in the last week of the month. Most newspapers unveiled their endorsements for top offices, with a few surprises. And Jack Arvey cranked up the Democratic faithful by calling on them to vote a straight ticket. The *Chicago Tribune* responded with the same appeal to Republicans.

Historically, the final month of major elections in Illinois contained few ballot-shaking surprises. Usually all the cards were on the table by the end of September, with only the rhetoric expected to increase. The gambling and corruption scandals uncovered across the state, but concentrated in Springfield and Peoria, had caused some nervousness among Republicans, but people in politics figured the unsettling wave was momentary. The status quo, backed up by conventional wisdom, is hard to overcome at election time.

The Progressive Party's efforts to get on the ballots in Illinois came to an end in October. In a 6 to 3 ruling of the U.S. Supreme Court, the party was denied placement on the 2 November ballot.[1] This ended a period of intense curiosity among officials of the Democratic and Republican Parties, who had a vested interest in the outcome. If the request had been granted, Democrats would have expected many liberals to support Progressive candidates. Republicans hoped the Progressive request would be granted, as the outcome likely would help their candidates.

The decision ended a months-long court battle involving the Illinois version of the national party and state officials. After initial jockeying through state and Cook County courts, the state electoral board late in August ruled the party had not met requirements for new parties set forth in a 1935 amendment to the state constitution. The party appealed the board's decision to the state supreme court but lost in a decision handed down on 25 September. Progressives appealed to a federal appeals court, with the support of Attorney General George F. Barrett, whose staff argued that the state law was unconstitutional.

Three judges on the appeals court—notably all Democrats—voted unanimously to deny the party's request. Among the three, Judge Michael L. Igoe was the Chicago Democratic machine candidate who had run against Scott Lucas for the U.S. Senate in 1938.[2] Another of the judges, Otto Kerner Sr., a former Illinois attorney general, was the father of Otto Kerner Jr., who would serve as Democratic governor of Illinois from 1961 to 1968.

Attorneys for the state of Illinois and Cook County appeared before the U.S. Supreme Court on 18 October. The state argued for the Progressive Party, and the county state's attorney argued against. Progressives stated that the Illinois law violated due process and equal protection clauses of the Fourteenth and Seventeenth Amendments to the U.S. Constitution. The Cook County argument was that the time had passed when names could be included on the printed ballots.[3]

Four days later, the Supreme Court stated, "It is allowable state policy to require that candidates for statewide office should have support not limited to concentrated locality." Chief Justice Fred Vinson made the announcement, although individual justices did not sign the decision. The outcome, and the fact that the Dixiecrat Party had not asked to be put on the ballot, meant the two major parties in Illinois would fight out the election without major influences from third parties.[4]

The Centralia mine disaster never stopped giving when it came to politics. It gave Adlai Stevenson plenty to talk about all across the state during the campaign for governor. It gave Governor Green constant headaches during the same time period. The disaster that killed 111 men was back in the headlines in October.

In a letter to Green, the Centralia Trades and Labor Assembly withdrew an endorsement of the governor that had been approved in June. The assembly took the action in a unanimous vote of members on 7 October. The first public announcement appeared in newspapers on 18 October. The letter stated, "Last June the Centralia Trades and Labor Assembly endorsed you for re-election to the governorship of Illinois. This endorsement was subject to the approval of the Illinois State Federation of Labor and the Southern Illinois Wage Earners and Political Educational League with headquarters in Springfield and East St. Louis, respectively. For various reasons the organizations have not seen fit to approve the endorsement. Consequently, we find we must withdraw the endorsement of your candidacy for governor."[5]

At the same time, it was learned that widows of the men killed in the Centralia mine explosion had formed the "111 Club," designed as a nonpartisan organization to promote good government and mine safety. The initial objective of the club was to defeat Green and elect Stevenson. The club planned to issue its first membership card to Driscoll Scanlan, former mine inspector who had repeatedly warned of safety issues at the mine before the explosion but was ignored by state officials.

Stevenson quickly responded to the news by flying to Centralia for a closed-door meeting with twenty widows of miners at the home of Mrs. Adolph Gutzler, president of the club. Stevenson followed the meeting with a speech in West Frankfort, where he again pledged "a hog-tight, politician-proof mine inspection service" if elected. He added, "No longer will the Department of Mines and Minerals be a political pasture." At the 111 Club meeting, Stevenson was asked why two indicted Republican officials of the mining department had not been brought to trial. Stevenson later said, "I wasn't able to tell them." Robert Medill, former head of the Department of Mining and Minerals, and his assistant, Robert Weir, were indicted eighteen months before but had not been tried. Two days later at a public meeting of the 111 Club, Scanlan received a membership card.[6]

The *Post-Dispatch* said in an editorial after the October events, "We can't conceive of Adlai Stevenson's talking one way and acting another about mine safety. Yet that is not only conceivable of Dwight Green, it is a fact of record. That is one of the many reasons why Mr. Green should be retired to private life and a man of Mr. Stevenson's manifest integrity elected the next governor of Illinois."[7]

TRUMAN RETURNS TO ILLINOIS

As Truman prepared for his second extensive whistle-stop tour of the Midwest starting 11 October, the news was not all that uplifting. Three days later, a Gallup poll showed Dewey holding a 5 percentage point lead with three weeks to Election Day.[8] Some of the national polling companies decided to stop sampling voters in October because officials believed it was a waste of time and money to track the race any further. Periodically, a news magazine or newspaper would poll reporters covering the campaigns, and Truman never got one vote of confidence. Reporters believed Dewey was a shoo-in.

Truman's whistle-stops began again in earnest with an extensive tour of Ohio on 11 October. Supporters could not believe the president would spend that much time in a state with a long history of support for Republicans. The simple fact was that he needed Ohio, and most other midwestern states. A day later the train began another campaign in Illinois, this time through the central part of the state.

Dewey, following in Truman's campaign footsteps, made a quick swing through southern Illinois on 12 October, with train stops at Carmi, McLeansboro, Mount Vernon, nearby Beaucoup, and East St. Louis. The journey made headlines for Dewey, although he might have wished for less attention to the details.

The first episode occurred in Mount Vernon when young boys perched on the roof of a nearby freight shed threw as many as six ripe tomatoes at Dewey. They fled before anyone could stop them. One tomato hit the railing of Dewey's private train car and splattered the candidate's gray suit. Another hit Frank Miller, a *Life* magazine photographer. A third struck Walter Chesney of Mount Vernon in the face. He was standing by the platform, and his wife reported that some pieces of the tomato landed in her hair. The trousers of Mayor Harry Bishop were hit, too. Police chief Verner Pigg said the incident "could be blamed on some small boys in the crowd." Dewey said, "Apparently I'm having some trouble with some small boys."[9]

The mayor, obviously chagrined, said, "It was a great shame that it had to happen after the big effort that had been made to have Governor Dewey stop in Mount Vernon." A day later, the Mount Vernon Chamber of Commerce sent its apologies in a telegram: "We sincerely hope that your impression of Mount Vernon is not wholly marred by the shameful actions of a few."[10]

The biggest newsmaker occurred in Beaucoup, a small town west of Mount Vernon and east of Nashville, Illinois. Just as Dewey began speaking from the rear platform to a crowd estimated at 1,000, the train moved toward the crowd, stopping after a few feet. No one was hurt. This surprise caused Dewey to lose his composure and blurt into the microphone: "That's the first lunatic I have had for an engineer. He probably ought to be shot at sunrise, but I guess we can let him off for no one was hurt." The train engineer, Lee Tindle, a railroad veteran of thirty years, spoke after hearing of Dewey's comment: "I think as much of Dewey as I did before and that's not very much. I was backing so slow that anybody could have easily gotten out of the way. I gave the proper backup signals. That is all there was to it."[11]

In news stories a day later, Tindle admitted he was at fault for overshooting a water tower and backing up. But he didn't give much ground to Dewey. He said, "Governor Dewey was just upset because it disturbed his speech. I'm just as sorry as he is." He added that he did not plan to vote for the Republican.[12]

As might be expected, Truman had his joke at Dewey's expense, saying, "I was highly pleased when I found out . . . that the train crew on this train are all Democrats. . . . We have had wonderful train crews all around the country."[13] The incident shared page 1 space in Illinois newspapers with Truman's central Illinois campaign.

Dewey's fifth stop in Illinois was in East St. Louis, where an estimated 5,000 persons appeared for a talk at the train's rear platform. He said what the United States needed "is unity to make sure this country doesn't go from boom to bust. We need a government whose left hand knows what the right hand is doing. I'd like to start one of the biggest, fanciest housecleaning's [sic] the U.S. government has ever had." In all his appearances during the day, Dewey continued on his theme that "only the Republican party can convince the world that the United States is not 'faltering' in its search for peace."[14]

Truman's train made four stops in Illinois on 12 October: Danville, Tolono, Decatur, and Springfield, beginning at 1:10 P.M. and ending late that night. This was the heart of Illinois farm country, where, during October, soybean and cornfields stretched as far as the eye could see in all directions. Truman was encouraged to see farmers in the field, holding up signs in support of the president. Nevertheless, it was largely Republican territory. Of the five counties through which Truman traveled during the day—Vermillion, Champaign, Piatt, Macon, and Sangamon—only

Macon, with a large labor union membership, had turned out a Democratic majority for Roosevelt in 1944.[15]

At every stop, Truman asked farmers to recognize what the Democratic Party had done for them, especially in extending credit during hard times. He reminded city dwellers of the importance of farm goods and healthy crops to the economy of towns and cities. As he did in southern Illinois, Truman characterized Republicans as insensitive to farm problems.

The other dominant theme was Abraham Lincoln. Truman made numerous references to the state's only elected president up to that time. After about a minute into his remarks at Danville, where newspapers estimated the crowd at 5,000, Truman told the first Lincoln story: "I always think about a time, a hundred years or so ago, when a group of Abraham Lincoln's lawyer friends put him on trial before a kangaroo court down at the old McCormick House because his lawyer fees were too low. Lincoln lost the case and was fined a jug of whiskey." In the same breath that Truman mentioned Lincoln's name, he also speculated on attitudes in the current Republican Party: "I want you to think how out of place Lincoln would be with the present day Republicans. They don't think any longer about 'of the people, by the people and for the people.' The record of the 80th Congress is proof of that."[16]

Truman also mentioned Lincoln in comments at Tolono, where 2,000 people heard the president speak from the back of the Ferdinand Magellan: "I am told it was just 87 years ago that Abraham Lincoln came through Tolono on his way to Washington. This was his last stop in Illinois before he went on to become President."[17]

Decatur was the only stop at which Truman did not tell a Lincoln story, although the immediate area played a sizable role in young Lincoln's life. Claiming credit for postwar prosperity, Truman recalled Depression days in Decatur and put the blame squarely on the shoulders of Republicans: "In 1933, after 12 years of Republican misrule, Decatur was in very serious trouble. I am sure you remember what it was like in the railroad shops and the mills and plants and all the stores and shops that supply the farmers in this part of Illinois. Well, you got sort of tired of that, and in 1932 you elected Franklin D. Roosevelt president of the United States. There was a steady improvement from that time on." The *Decatur Herald* said 10,000 people greeted the train in friendly Democratic territory.[18]

In Springfield, Truman quickly wrapped himself in Lincoln lore. Shortly after arriving at 5:15 P.M.—newspapers said 5,000 people greeted the train—Truman sped by motorcade to Lincoln's Tomb and placed a wreath while 1,000 citizens watched. Truman was the draw, Lincoln was the precious memory, but Paul Powell was impresario of this day in Springfield.

Powell used his position as downstate presidential campaign coordinator to orchestrate Springfield events for the president. It was Powell who brought Truman and thirty-five officials of the Springfield, Peoria, and Decatur Federations of Labor together immediately after the wreath ceremony at Lincoln's Tomb. The group met at the St. Nicholas Hotel, where Powell lived while in Springfield. Powell played the role of supreme advocate during a newspaper interview, taking a slap at the president's critics while predicting Truman would win Illinois: "Prejudiced polls don't show it and the press of privilege won't admit it, but Harry Truman will win this state if people vote like they act and talk when they are with him and when they know the true character and lofty purposes of the man." When talking about Truman's tour of southern Illinois, Powell could hardly contain himself: "The president loves common people. He speaks their language. I saw him surrounded by coal miners in their shirt sleeves, their hands and faces showing that they had just come up out of the mine, enjoying companionship with the president of the United States as if he were one of them."[19]

At every Truman event, Powell seemed to be on stage. Four hundred of the state's leading Democrats gathered for a 7 P.M. dinner at the St. Nicholas Hotel, where Powell was master of ceremonies and introduced the president. The legislator took control at the end of the dinner, too, when Dr. Richard Graebel of the First Presbyterian Church was to pronounce the benediction. As the presidential party left the ballroom, the crowd started to follow and threatened to ruin Graebel's moment. Powell grabbed a microphone and held the remainder of the crowd until Graebel could give the benediction.[20]

After the banquet, thousands more Springfield citizens lined the city's streets for a torchlight parade from downtown to the Armory, where Democrats shared the microphone before Truman spoke to a capacity crowd. Speakers included Paul Douglas and U.S. senator Scott Lucas, both of whom had joined the Truman train in Danville. Adlai Stevenson showed up in Springfield; it was the first time he campaigned in the presence of Truman. Lucas, writing in his memoir later, said of Stevenson's hesitancy with Truman, "In October I accompanied Truman by train from Danville to Springfield, and presented him that evening in the

Armory before 5,000 shouting, rabid and inspired Democrats. Stevenson again found some excuse for not coming to Danville and riding across the state with the president. With great reluctance, he finally agreed to appear on the platform with Truman in Springfield."[21]

As the evening drew to a close, Truman got his opportunity to talk. He mentioned Lincoln one more time, saying, "I just wonder what Lincoln would say if he could see how his party has become the tool of big business and special interest. . . . What do you suppose he would say to the power lobby and the railroad lobby."[22] Truman ripped the Republican farm program as he had done throughout Illinois. Repeating his comments voiced so often on the stump in farm country, Truman highlighted four initiatives that he supported:

1. A permanent flexible price-support program.
2. Expansion of the soil conservation program to stop waste "of our agricultural resources."
3. Continued and strengthened programs to assure adequate markets for bumper crops.
4. Protection of farmers' rights to do business through cooperatives, extension of rural electrification and better housing, and better roads and better educational facilities for farmers.

At the conclusion of his remarks, the presidential party went to the train station, boarded the Ferdinand Magellan about 11 P.M., and headed toward Wisconsin and Minnesota.

POLITICAL CLASHES IN PEORIA AND SPRINGFIELD

Political forces shaped a grand jury probe of gambling and corruption in Peoria County during October, after the *St. Louis Post-Dispatch* started a fire under the issues with articles by Ted Link in August and September. The paper laid accusations at the feet of top Illinois officials. Feeling the pressure, Governor Green and Attorney General Barrett decided the quickest way to put an end to further damaging revelations and headlines was to employ a friendly investigator who would shape grand jury outcomes favorable to the Republicans.

There was rarely a dull moment in Peoria during the final weeks before Election Day. James A. Howe, an assistant to Barrett, had been on the job as an investigator for several days when a public quarrel occurred between the Peoria Association of Commerce and the attorney general.

It began when the association, which had requested the probe, issued a statement accusing Howe and Barrett of being "headed toward a whitewash." Edward F. Keefer Jr., president of the group, said all Howe had done so far was interview members of the association who did not have firsthand knowledge of gambling and corruption.

Barrett lashed out at Keefer and the association in a five-page letter, using strong language and accusing the Peorians of "babbling out of the depths of your ignorance." Barrett said the citizens could not know all the people who had been interviewed, adding, "I say to you that the colossal collective ignorance of facts on the part of you petitioners makes a mockery of your complaints and of your self-inflated demands upon me as a public official." He went on to accuse the business organization of making a contribution "to the Democratic smear campaign that Mr. Howe has been remiss in not rushing before the grand jury currently in recess." The grand jury was scheduled to convene when Howe finished the investigation.[23]

Barrett referred to an earlier agreement that the investigation would proceed without publicity, saying, "I do propose to make available to the press this appraisal of your grandstand plays and blowhard tactics." The association had little to say in response, other than to remind Barrett that he needed to make good on promises regarding the investigation.[24]

With those outbursts behind them, Howe, with Barrett's backing, began calling witnesses before the grand jury on 12 October. This was a new jury session. An earlier grand jury began meeting in May; its term expired in September. Before concluding business, the jury indicted three county officials for implication in gambling and corrupt practices. The earlier jury stated in its indictment report, "There is much evidence that too many public officials are too closely associated with racketeers and gamblers."

A day before the jury met, Howe interviewed Carl Baldwin, a *Post-Dispatch* reporter, about alleged associations by the newspaper with gamblers. Baldwin said Howe asked, "Are you an associate of gangsters?," "How well did you know Bernie Shelton?," and "Did Ted Link help get Shelton [and associates] out of jail?"[25] Howe also interviewed news people from the *Peoria Journal*.

Among the first witnesses were members of the Peoria Association of Commerce and Arnold Burnett, managing editor of the *Journal*. The star witness the following day was Clyde Garrison, often called the czar of gambling in Peoria County, followed by the operator of a dice game in a city nightclub. They acknowledged previous gambling activities but said they had not been in the business for several years. Both men claimed they had given up the gambling business because of hard times. They, and others testifying, said other more prosaic businesses paid better and were safer. Garrison admitted that city officials had received payoffs and police had provided protection.[26]

Moving into the second week, prosecutor Howe maintained silence on the identity of witnesses and their testimonies. However, reporters quizzed people as they left the jury room and learned that few had any specific information for jurors about current gambling activities. The witness lineup included a gambler and graft collector, a jukebox operator and dice game partner, and an associate of the Sheltons.

As the jury neared the end of its session, Howe called Peter J. Petrakos to the stand. Appearing without a subpoena, he told reporters he was questioned about payoffs made by the Shelton brothers to an unnamed prominent Peoria citizen.[27] Petrakos knew of the infamous "Gatewood tapes," which recorded an alleged bribery attempt involving Bernie Shelton and the state's attorney. Late in July, Petrakos had been grilled by Earl Shelton, Ted Link, and Shelton associates in a hotel room for hours about the murder of Bernie Shelton.

The jury issued its report and indictments on 23 October. The *Peoria Journal* banner headline across page 1 read "Gambling Inquiry 'Whitewashed,'" and the subhead told the story: "Jurors Return 3 Indictments against Four."[28] The big name among the indicted persons was Ted Link, who was mentioned in three indictments charging kidnapping, conspiracy, and intimidation in the questioning of Petrakos. Indicted with Link were Earl Shelton and Shelton associates Ray Walker and Jack Ashby, all of whom were in the hotel room with Petrakos. The *Post-Dispatch* headline declared "Theodore C. Link Is Charged with Kidnapping Man He Interviewed," but that seemed an understatement when compared to the outrage inside the newspaper and in its editions. In Chicago, the *Tribune* put the story on page 1 under a one-column headline, "County Aids Cleared by Grand Jury."[29] No other indictments resulted from the investigation by Howe.

The grand jury report made these key points[30]:

- We find not one iota of evidence to show that our public officials are or have been associated with or in alliance with racketeers, gangsters, gamblers, or syndicate gamblers.

- We find no evidence to sustain the allegation that Peoria County was to be opened up to gambling after this fall's election nor any evidence to support the allegation that Peoria County was to be opened to gambling at any time in the future.
- We find no evidence to sustain the allegation that the law-enforcing agencies of the city of Peoria and of the county of Peoria have broken down in their law enforcement against gambling and vice.
- We find no evidence to sustain the allegation that gamblers paid off to any public officials, nor to any agents or representatives of public officials of this state, county, or city.
- We find no evidence to sustain the charge that county and city officials in law enforcement were interfered with or hindered by any outside agency.

The jury censured the *Post-Dispatch* and Link for "publication of these charges and allegations and more particularly for his avoidance of service to appear before this grand jury. The evidence tends to show that Mr. Link relied for the information which he published upon the statements, unsupported and unworthy of belief, of self-admitted gamblers, brothel keepers, prostitutes, ex-convicts and others of like stripe." The jury did not stop there, leveling censure at leaders of the Peoria Association of Commerce for being inspired and influenced by publication of "such unreliable newspaper articles to promote public hysteria over these allegations." As if to add insult to injury, the report heaped praise on Barrett and Howe "for their outstanding public service to the community in the thorough, complete and competent investigation they have conducted into these allegations."

The contradiction in grand jury reports between September and October could not have been greater in outcome or tone, assuming they had access to similar information and testimony. Grand jury deliberations were not held in open courtrooms, and prosecutors led the discussion and questioning of witnesses in both instances. The October outcome seemed a complete repudiation of the report in September, which had indicted three county officials.

To suggest the roof blew off at newspapers circulated in Illinois hardly captures the force of eruption. As might be expected, the *Post-Dispatch* immediately went on the offense. Ben Reese, managing editor of the paper, said in a statement, "The *Post-Dispatch* will furnish cash bond for the appearance of Mr. Link for trial at Peoria, and will defend him to the last ditch."[31] In addition to following the breaking news, the paper recapped in great detail Link's investigations and revelations after the death of Bernie Shelton. The full text of the grand jury report appeared in the paper and in the *Peoria Journal*. On page 1, the St. Louis paper printed a letter from special prosecutor Verle W. Safford written on 4 September as the grand jury he directed came to a close. Safford stated, "I have only the finest expression to speak on behalf of Mr. Link. He is capable, intelligent, courteous and most diligent. Due to Mr. Link's very thorough investigation and previous delving into the matters under consideration, his suggestions and information were most valuable to the writer."[32] Safford had no role in the deliberations of the October grand jury.

Two days after word of the grand jury report, the *Post-Dispatch* published an article by Link outlining additional information he had turned up regarding the ambush shooting of Bernie Shelton.[33] The names and information cast doubt on the story of Petrakos and, according to Link, might have opened new avenues of investigation for the grand jury. He offered the information to the grand jury foreman, but it was turned down. The foreman said there was not time to consider it. However, the jury did have time remaining before an 8 November deadline. Link also offered additional information about not responding to a subpoena to testify. Link stated that Sheriff Earl Spainhower had called him at a Chicago hotel to tell him of the summons. Link said he was unable to testify at the time specified but offered to appear a few days later. The jury reported before Link could appear. Two others indicted, Ray Walker and Jack Ashby, were not called before the jury.

The *Post-Dispatch* editorial page went ballistic. The opening paragraph of the first editorial read, "If anyone in Illinois remained in doubt as to actual conditions under the administration of Gov. Dwight H. Green and Attorney General George F. Barrett, that doubt should be ripped away by the trumped-up indictment of the *Post-Dispatch*'s reporter, Theodore C. Link, at Peoria." The editorial concluded, after several paragraphs of condemnation, "Thanks to this fake indictment, votes are being made right and left for Democratic nominees for state office in Illinois, headed by Adlai E. Stevenson, Gov. Green's crusading opponent. The truth about the Green-Barrett misrule is being spread not only over Illinois but to every part of the United States."[34]

No newspaper could top the *Peoria Journal*'s lengthy editorial titled "The Expected Happens." The paper stated, "George Barrett stands indicted before the people of Illinois for his utter failure to represent the best interests of the people of this community and the people of the entire state, the very people whom he is calling upon to return him to office on November 2."[35] A day later, the paper published a page 1 editorial titled "Defeat George Barrett." The paper, traditionally favoring Republican candidates for office, began, "When a state official like Attorney General George F. Barrett has the effrontery to send an assistant into this community with the intention of holding a group of citizens and the entire community up to ridicule and shame as he has done, it is time for the citizens of Peoria to rise up in their might and let him know in no uncertain terms that they want no more of him as a state official."[36]

Newspapers and editors across Illinois and in many parts of the nation jumped on the bandwagon to pummel Green and Barrett and the grand jury's conclusions. The *Chicago Sun-Times*, in an editorial titled "Clean Them Out," stated, "The grand jury's powers were used not to supplement and develop the evidence obtained by a responsible newspaper, but to exact retribution for the charges made by that newspaper."[37] The *Daily News*, whose editorial page usually supported Republicans, said, "If the people of Illinois have the regard for decency and fair play, and the hatred of fraud and sham that we hope they have, this desperate stratagem will react not on the men indicted but on those who seem to place no limit on their will to rule or ruin." John S. Knight, editor and publisher of the paper, added, "The indictment of Reporter Theodore C. Link is obviously in retaliation for his exposures of corruption in Illinois. It is an old device favored by cynical political machines when they are hit where it hurts."[38]

Edward Lindsay, editor of the *Decatur Herald and Review*, offered this comment: "When an attorney general's grand jury turns the power of state government toward a conscientious reporter rather than the corruption he writes about, the conclusion is plain. This is a public confession by the attorney general. It says in plain words that the Illinois state administration cannot stand the spotlight of honest reporting."[39] The *Bloomington Pantagraph*, owned in part by the Stevenson family but a strong voice for Republican candidates, stated, "It [the indictment] is a direct threat to the freedom of the press. It is one of the most convincing indications that the gambling and graft situation in Illinois stinks unbearably."[40]

A few days later, the *Post-Dispatch* took full-page advertisements in newspapers across the state to reprint the paper's editorial, "The Green Machine Strikes Back," accompanied by an editorial cartoon published the same day. The ad stated, "Cowardly men in Illinois are watching the clock as the hour hand moves toward election day, Nov. 2. They think they can muzzle the Post-Dispatch. They are wrong and their effort should prove their undoing. The Post-Dispatch will not be intimidated. It will not be gagged."[41]

Ted Link posted bond of $11,000 on the charges. No action was taken for a trial before the election. On 18 February 1949, circuit judge John T. Culbertson Jr. dismissed the indictments against all four men upon recommendation of state's attorney Michael A. Shore.

While headlines generated in Springfield did not rival those of Peoria for drama during October, they followed a similar track as a grand jury met to consider accusations that local officials took payoffs from operators of gambling joints, racing handbooks, and slot machines.

Pressure for the inquiry came from Springfield citizens who read and absorbed articles about investigations by reporters of the *Post-Dispatch*. As in Peoria, citizen heat prompted Barrett to name a special investigator, Oliver H. Bovik, who also served as an assistant to Barrett. After Bovik began his probe, circuit judge Dewitt S. Crow ordered a full-scale investigation of gambling and charges that public officials acted in "criminal concert" with operators. Bovik said he would lend assistance to state's attorney John W. Curren in presenting evidence to the jury. As soon as Bovik's investigation began, gamblers put a lid on illegal operations in the county, which remained in effect through grand jury deliberations.

The jury began deliberations on 18 October and in three days heard testimony from twenty-seven witnesses, including Sangamon County sheriff Meredith Rhule and Springfield mayor Harry Eielson.[42] In a statement early in August, Rhule had admitted knowledge of gambling in the county and said he intended to let it continue. He did not say whether he had received payoffs. Also testifying for an hour was Roy J. Harris, the *Post-Dispatch* reporter who wrote most of the articles about Sangamon County crime. Several county and city law enforcement persons appeared along with a host of persons connected to illegal operations. Curren declined to discuss specific testimony with reporters.

Three days after the jury began its work, a report to Judge Crow stated that while "criminal commercialized gambling" had been prevalent for years, charges against current officials were "absolutely without foundation." The list of illegal gambling activities included coin-operated pinball machines, baseball pools, punchboards, dice games, criminal gambling, prostitution, "and other vices apparent in the county." The jury report stated, "This entire investigation was precipitated by reason of certain articles appearing in the St. Louis *Post-Dispatch*." Furthermore, the Springfield jury claimed the paper depended on unreliable sources for its articles.[43]

The report contained several references to "strictly" enforcing state laws against gambling and recommended the county board increase the sheriff's budget to allow for additional monitoring. The jury called for the state's attorney to "take prompt steps to institute appropriate criminal proceedings in the county court against those who had violated anti-gambling laws."[44] In effect, the jury did little more than wag a finger at law enforcement about its responsibilities, suggesting that known gamblers be charged with misdemeanors in county court and admonishing the public not to believe what the *Post-Dispatch* published.

Politically speaking, the Springfield grand jury and those who ran it prevented further uproar by carefully burying the issue of official corruption, unlike the Peoria example where indictments encouraged accusations of "whitewash." Victory over the *Post-Dispatch*, however comforting, may have been costly with the elections about a week away.

THE CAMPAIGN WINDS DOWN

Curly Brooks hoped voters still liked him and wanted him in the Senate. After all, they had elected him in 1940 and 1942. As recently as 1946 across the state, Republicans had unseated many Democratic members of the House and kept a strong hold on state offices. The GOP tide looked to be in place. As the 1948 campaign developed, almost all pundits and so-called political experts expected Brooks to dispatch the upstart Democrat, Paul Douglas.

Brooks used the same campaign language in 1948 that he had used with his constituents eight years earlier. He had few peers when it came to deriding the Democrats as "New Dealers" and preaching the isolationist theme that had appealed to many Illinoisans during World War II. His current foe was communism, and he linked that with Democrats in almost every speech. Nevertheless, Brooks was more than a one-note candidate; he had three negative notes in his repertoire: New Deal, communism, and internationalism. He gambled that voters were angry about the Roosevelt-Truman years.

During October, Walter Trohan, Washington correspondent for the *Chicago Tribune*, laid out what the newspaper and conservatives believed were Brooks's strong points. These were articles that masqueraded as news stories and in today's newspaper world most likely would appear as opinion page commentary. In truth, they were propaganda in its richest form. Trohan wrote four lengthy articles during the month to keep Brooks's name in print. The subjects were Brooks's service on issues of interest to Illinoisans; Brooks as a "fighter for the American Way;" Brooks as a senator who fulfilled pledges he made while campaigning for Republican candidates to the House in 1946; and Brooks as an enemy of "New Dealism."[45]

Newspapers across the state went through the election routine of feature stories about the candidates for major offices, for the most part trying to present a balanced picture. In Chicago, the *Daily News* emphasized Brooks's personal animosity toward Douglas and his unrelenting opposition to further foreign entanglements that encouraged communism. Brooks told the reporter, "I have objected, and I will always object, to the squandering of American resources in Europe to build a more powerful communistic empire. We must maintain our prestige in the world for our own security." On the personal front, Brooks said of his opponent, "Douglas is a demagogue with a lot of cockeyed theories. He'd do anything for a vote." Otherwise, most of the article was devoted to a recitation of the senator's personal and public life.[46]

The campaign had taken a toll on Douglas. Entering the final month, he was literally broke, personally and in terms of political revenue and expenses. The attacks on him by Brooks, other Republicans, and the *Tribune* and its agents had increased doubts that he could pull out a victory.[47] This was in spite of the tireless effort by him and his wife. On the final tour of southern Illinois, the campaign reached bottom, as Douglas described in his autobiography: "I went south on a final tour of that area. It rained almost constantly. The crowds were small. After contracting a heavy cold, which turned into a fever, I felt it was almost literally impossible to take another step, but somehow I forced myself through six to eight speeches a day and an incessant round of handshaking. The night at Carbondale, in a run-down and unheated old hotel, was the low point of the trip. . . . Soaked with perspiration and barely able to stand, I yet made eight meetings the next day."[48]

Douglas's approach on the stump in the final weeks leaned toward a mixture of positions on national and international issues and criticism of the Republican-dominated Eightieth Congress, along with Brooks's role. Those who characterized Douglas as a hardcore New Deal Democrat might have missed his comments on the Taft-Hartley law, which placed restrictions on union organizing. Partisans cried for repeal of the law, but Douglas departed slightly from the orthodoxy by listing six points of the law with which he disagreed, although he did not offer any solutions or ways to improve them.[49] His caution obviously was designed to hold voters outside union ranks. On a strictly personal level, Douglas preferred repeal of the law.

Through much of the campaign, Douglas attempted to draw a sharp line distinguishing his and Brooks's positions regarding internationalism. For the senator, Democrats were probably communists and were much too inclined to send money and goods to foreign nations with suspect leaders. Douglas believed the only way to craft a foreign policy that held the peace and stopped communist expansion was to eliminate partisan bickering. In one public statement, Douglas said, "Whoever is elected president I would work with administration leaders to maintain a united front in the conduct of our foreign affairs. I would do this, not merely for the sake of unity itself, but because I believe that our bipartisan foreign policy is our best guarantee that we can yet bring a just and durable peace in the world."[50]

Douglas took his arguments directly to the positions of Brooks, declaring, "Brooks is against our bipartisan foreign policy, against a strong United Nations, against a strong national defense, against an extension of social security, against low cost housing and slum clearance. I am for all these measures." He went on to say that if Brooks and Dewey were elected, the senator would oppose almost every initiative of the new president.[51] The *Tribune* answered, stating that Douglas, a man of integrity, was simply naive, or hadn't grown up yet.

Although Douglas ran an inexpensive campaign by most standards, he often did not have enough money for a modest advertising program. After the long southern Illinois campaign swing in October, Douglas returned to Chicago to learn the campaign organization was broke, staff had not been paid in a month, and contributions had stopped. In spite of the dreary outlook, Douglas said later, "Emily and I were determined not to give up. . . . As we fought on, help began to arrive, and voluntary contributions came from men and women I had never known. The crowds became larger and warmer. . . . People began to smile and wave at me. I was so much the underdog that human sympathy moved in my direction."[52]

In the final weeks, Douglas used his revived campaign bank account for newspaper advertisements that leaned heavily on his support of a bipartisan foreign policy and support of the United Nations. One ad, appearing in Chicago papers, proclaimed Douglas as a "Fighting Marine . . . Statesman and Leader, Life-long Friend of the People" and a "new, good, fighting senator for ALL the people of Illinois."

In its feature article about candidate Douglas, the *Daily News* followed the script carefully, emphasizing the Democrat's background and giving him an opportunity to comment on Brooks and to defend himself against Republican accusations. Regarding the charges about his association with socialism, he said, "I never was a member of the socialist party. I voted once for Norman Thomas. If that's bad, think of some of the candidates my critics have voted for." Responding to the accusations of communist sympathizer, Douglas stated, "I believe the Russians are faithless and treacherous." Regarding Brooks's record in the Senate, Douglas said, "He voted against lend-lease. He voted in favor of a bill that would have denuded our Army before Pearl Harbor. He opposed the draft. He fought the Marshall Plan," adding, "How does he stand on present issues? Who knows?"[53]

For all of the opposition editorials appearing in the *Tribune* throughout the campaign, the paper went out of its way during October to comment on the challenger's integrity and professional standards. In an editorial outlining what the paper said were Douglas's "contradictions" on explanations about socialism and communism, the *Tribune* declared, "As he has said in his speeches, he acted as arbitrator in many cases between management and labor in the newspaper business. The *Tribune* has been a party to some of those cases. Mr. Douglas has criticized our editorial policies, and we have opposed him politically but we are glad to testify that neither circumstance affected his fairness as an arbitrator."[54]

Although Douglas had backed an alternative presidential nominee to Truman, after the national convention he appeared at times as the only Illinois nominee to believe Truman could win. Wishful thinking or not, to some extent Douglas tied his kite to Truman, at least when the president campaigned in the state. While Douglas might have exaggerated the Truman crowds, he said newspapers and other media downgraded the figures by half. He campaigned with Truman and never feared to use his name on the campaign trail.

There were a few signs in October that Dwight Green might be worrying about chances for a third term. He continued to defend the Republican administration, condemning everything "New Deal." Adlai Stevenson battered Green, implying corruption, wasteful behavior, and padding of state departments with cronies and political pals.

The hints of concern by Green occurred on two occasions. At mid-month, he proposed that the state adopt an idea of the Illinois Municipal League to distribute a share of tax collections with cities. A *Sun-Times* editorial called Green's move an "11th Hour Conversion." This contradicted one of Green's major pledges not to give in to requests from local governments for state aid. (Stevenson had said he would share state revenues.) Green said a large portion of a state utility tax could be returned to cities, specifically adding considerable money to Chicago's coffers. According to the governor, the idea would "mean an additional revenue of several million dollars for the city of Chicago and substantial amounts for all cities." Chicago mayor Martin Kennelly endorsed the idea, to the consternation of Democrats.[55]

Many state officials, including the governor's campaign supporters, were surprised and confused by his declaration. Members of the State Revenue Commission—Democrats and Republicans appointed by the governor and deliberating proposed changes in sources of income for all levels of state governments—were stunned. While Green's message was short on details, the commission's job was not simplified by his concessions. Almost simultaneously, Richard Lyons, state revenue commissioner, publicly ridiculed the idea of additional aid to municipalities.[56]

The other indication of a slight nervousness about Green surfaced in a *Tribune* editorial on 12 October titled "Be Nice to Adlai." The paper had rarely mentioned Stevenson on the editorial page. Suggesting that the Democrat's campaign grasped at straws, the editors stated, "Adlai has tried manfully, with vivid allegations of a corrupt, wasteful Republican state machine. Following the lead of his most vociferous supporter, a Missouri newspaper, he has advanced the political theory that the governor of Illinois is also supposed to act as state's attorney and sheriff of every one of the state's 102 counties, for the purpose of suppressing gambling." The numbers from Stevenson in several budget references looked confusing, the editorial said, especially in terms of state revenues shared with cities. The opinion concluded, "Mr. Stevenson is such a charming fellow that we hope no one will get the impression from what we have said that we think he is trying to fool the voters. He isn't. Adlai just doesn't know the score."[57]

Otherwise, Green spent campaign time promoting accomplishments of his administration and accusing Democrats of wanting to create a

"Little New Deal" in Springfield. He cast the Republican net far from the campaign mainstream with appeals to organized labor and black Illinoisans. On the latter, Green claimed Democrats were latecomers to civil rights in spite of the president's proposals and accused Truman of "political demagoguery." The governor claimed, "There are three times as many Negroes in state service as under the Democratic regime eight years ago."[58]

Regarding unions, Green pledged a "fair and square deal at Springfield" if reelected. He claimed to have consulted closely with labor organizations on major issues and legislation and cited a number of social measures that passed into law. An earlier *Tribune* editorial stated, "The governor's labor program has been a model of wisdom. Legitimate needs of working men and labor unions have received every consideration."[59] However, Green was denied an outright endorsement by the state Federation of Labor, primarily due to pressures from Paul Douglas. Instead, officers of unions formed the Green for Governor Labor League of Illinois.

While the *Tribune* did all within its power to boost Green, other papers in Chicago and downstate kept a counter-conversation going with readers. Columnists for the *Sun-Times*, favoring Stevenson at almost every turn, argued that Green's campaign across downstate Illinois showed signs of failing to produce the kind of support the governor needed to offset likely Democratic margins in Chicago. *Sun-Times* managing editor Pete Akers said Green was "fighting a wholly defensive battle. He's already lost southern Illinois. . . . In Central Illinois Republican and independent newspapers such as the *Decatur Herald and Review*, *Peoria Journal*, and *Bloomington Pantagraph* have turned against the governor." Akers stated that Green seemed to be holding his own in northern parts of downstate, but that would not be enough to offset Stevenson's advantage. The columnist added, "This year, seeking third-term election, and his state house machine staggering under repeated scandals and exposures, the governor is having difficulty amassing the necessary downstate margin to save himself."[60]

Sun-Times columnist John Dreiske, a somewhat more moderate booster of Democrats, lumped Stevenson and Secretary of State Edward J. Barrett together in receiving support from Republicans who resented Green's run for a third term after saying, "There will be no third term dictatorship in Illinois." Dreiske noted that Barrett, a veteran of both world wars, was receiving support from American Legion ranks. He wrote, "This is a vocal and powerful group. They applaud his [Barrett's] constant fight against communistic influences, that being a major Legion 'plank.'" He acknowledged that Barrett had fought the Progressive movement openly, another reason for Legion backing. However, Barrett's opponent, William G. Stratton, "cannot lambast them because it is against the GOP policy." Dreiske's reference was to reports that Republicans wanted voters to associate Progressives with Democrats. He added, "Barrett has placed the Progressives right in Joe Stalin's lap."[61] What Dreiske did not mention was the influence of former governor John Stelle with veterans' groups, especially the American Legion. Stelle and Barrett had formed a longtime close political association, and Stelle worked hard for his friend.

In the news columns, the *Sun-Times* gave Green a working-over on state financial issues in a series of articles by reporter David Anderson that appeared early in October. The articles touched on these points: (1) the administration was the most expensive in the history of the state; (2) by padding payrolls, it had built up Illinois's most powerful political machine; and (3) it had destroyed the merit or civil service system in the state and was conducting a shakedown of state employees for the purpose of swelling the Republican campaign fund.[62]

The series blamed a combination of inflation and the size of Republican government on the state's rising costs. Anderson wrote, "There are two reasons for this: One is inflation which has boosted prices on everything from toothpicks to yacht anchors. The other reason is that the Green machine, in order to expand its political power, has planned it that way." Most of Anderson's comparisons contrasted 1939, when Democrats controlled state government, and the Green years. Anderson, assisted by a chart, claimed government costs increased by 143 percent. In the initial article, the reporter used costs of the Mines and Minerals Department as an example. The article stated current biennial department costs of $1,190,350 against 1939–41 expenses of $264,679. Political influence in the department had been a target of newspapers since the 1947 Centralia mine disaster. In another article, Anderson wrote about expansion of public safety and prison operations.

The *Daily News* continued its feature series about candidates for top state positions with articles about Green and Stevenson on back-to-back days. Neither of the articles probed deeper than the surface. The pattern was to give the candidate an opportunity to argue his case, in which he would sometimes slam his opponent and then devote the balance of the article reviewing education and political backgrounds. So readers learned that Green had toughened himself for football at Wabash College by driving a lumber truck and that Stevenson said he did not feel the necessity to be folksy. "I'm an Illinoisan from the heart of the corn country," he declared.

Stevenson battled to keep issues of poor governance by Green before audiences. In the Chicago area, he said the governor gave Illinois people "waste and corruption instead of the efficiency and economy he promised them. The people are entitled to an administration that places the public above politics, and that is what I intend to give them. I do not believe the Illinois public is going to buy another lemon just because it has a pretty Green wrapper."[63] Commenting on Green's alleged padding of the state payroll, Stevenson claimed, "I have good reason to believe that there are at least 20,000 more employees on the payroll of Illinois than there were in the last year of Gov. Henry Horner."[64]

A day later, the *Post-Dispatch* carried a page 1 article by Roy J. Harris with details about Republican county officials on the Illinois payroll. Harris said eighty-three county chairmen and fifty-two county secretaries drew a total of $362,256 in state pay during 1947. The article charged that the Green Machine had entrenched itself with the jobs at all levels across the state. Harris said most of the jobs were described as "field investigator," "inspector," or "messenger-clerk." He added, "Relatives of many were also on the state payroll in various capacities." He stated that fifteen of the twenty-five members of the Republican state committee had state jobs. Harris also discovered journalists on the state payroll. At the *Illinois State Register* in Springfield, whose editorials generally favored Democrats, the managing editor and a reporter also held state jobs. Of the *Springfield State Journal*, owned by the same company as the *State Register* and favorable to Republicans, Harris wrote that an editorial writer who provided commentary critical of Stevenson was also clerk of the Illinois Supreme Court.[65]

A few days later, Ted Link told of 1944 grand jury testimony that claimed kickbacks were made on Illinois state and county paving contracts. Republicans were alleged to have made the payments. Disclosure of the testimony came as a result of an FBI investigation of abuse of federal funds in highway contracts.[66]

At one point during October, Adlai Stevenson paused in his steady attack to outline approaches to governing he would take if elected. Most fell in the general category of reform ideas, but few cited precise measures of legislation:

provide adequate funds for schools

redistribute some state tax money to local communities

remove unneeded payrollers; abolish machine government

end shakedowns of business kickbacks by contractors and the sale of
favors or protection to gamblers and gangsters

cleanse civil service and the merit system of political abuses and illegalities; offer security—as nearly as that is possible—to all competent
civil servants

enforce more vigorously civil rights and an adequate fair employment

restore and improve the Illinois road system, from farm to highway to
market, by governmental consolidations, economy, and specification
changes

This list indicates Stevenson's inexperience in politics and government, although he obviously was trying to reach constituencies that
wanted change.[67]

In the days when newspapers dominated the communication of
politics, editorial endorsements weighed heavily with candidates and,
presumably, with voters. In the large cities of Chicago and St. Louis,
Stevenson fared better than Green. The governor's only major endorsement came in the *Tribune*, which counted because of its huge statewide
circulation. The other politically active papers in Chicago, the *Daily
News* and *Sun-Times*, endorsed Stevenson. The *Daily News* choice surprised observers because it routinely supported Republican candidates
for office. Predictably, the *Post-Dispatch* climbed aboard the Stevenson
bandwagon, concluding, "Dwight Green is probably the greatest dis-
appointment Illinois has ever had in the Governor's chair."[68] A number
of downstate daily newspapers supported Stevenson. He also received
endorsement by Chicago's Better Government Association. Under the
heading of better-late-than-never, Chicago mayor Kennelly finally agreed
to campaign for Stevenson.

Senator Brooks did decidedly better with endorsements than did
Green. The *Tribune* spoke enthusiastically about the senator. He also
received the nod from the *Daily News*, which stated, "We support
Brooks not only in the interests of a workable Republican majority
in the Senate, but because his position on vital issues offers the wiser
course for Illinois and the nation, and because of fundamental differences in the temperament and political philosophy of the two men." The
paper claimed Douglas was naive to get involved in support for Russia.

It stated, "We like our senators to grasp things before they become obvious to everybody."[69] Much to the disgust of Douglas, Brooks also received the endorsement of the *Bloomington Pantagraph*, which was partly owned by the Stevenson family. In its lengthy endorsement of Douglas, the *Post-Dispatch* commented on questions about the candidate's loyalty: "Disloyal persons do not volunteer in the Marines at the age of 50 and fight, as Douglas did, in the island warfare of the Pacific."[70]

Regarding endorsements for president, Dewey left Truman in his dust. The *Post-Dispatch*, given its usual editorial support of Democrats, was less than enthusiastic about Dewey but turned away from the president, implying that his programs and interests did not align with those of the newspaper. The *Post-Dispatch* never cared for Truman's association with the gangster element in Kansas City. Predictable editorial endorsements for Dewey appeared in the *Tribune*, *Peoria Journal*, and *St. Louis Star-Times*. Truman received one of his few endorsements in Illinois from the *Pantagraph*.

There may have been no more dramatic moment during the presidential race in Illinois than the two days back-to-back late in October when Truman and Dewey spoke in Chicago. Their appearances underscored the importance of Illinois and its twenty-eight electoral votes. And, of course, Chicagoans loved every minute in the spotlight.

Drama aside, most people, pundits, and journalists in Chicago considered the appearances anticlimactic. Public opinion polls had Dewey leading Truman since before the nominating conventions. Early in October, newspaper stories began speculating about a Dewey victory and who would become members of the new president's cabinet. Newspapers, regardless of how they viewed the race from the editorial pages, carried articles showing straw poll results with Dewey ahead of Truman by large numbers in many states. *Tribune* headlines in the final week of the campaign included "Truman Knows He Can't Win, Intimates Say," "Dewey Retains Huge Lead in Illinois Straws," and "Polls Indicate 430,000 G.O.P. Margin in State." The *Post-Dispatch* carried such headlines as "50–0 Prediction of Dewey Victory by News Writers" and "54 pct. Dewey Vote, or More, in 15 States," and, hours before the election, a report by pollster Archibald Crossley stated, "Final Crossley Poll: Dewey, [vice presidential candidate] Warren Sure to Win, but Truman Will Carry Missouri."

Dewey had few concerns as he toured the country, until he got to Kansas City and met with Roy Roberts, editor of the *Kansas City Star* and a power in midwestern Republican circles. Roberts said he thought Dewey was losing the farm vote and needed to promise government aid to shore up farm support. Dewey decided not to do it; straw poll results in the Midwest indicated a Dewey landslide. However, a review of Gallup polling from July to mid-October showed the president narrowing the gap. On Dewey's train excursions, crowds were smaller than those that had greeted him in 1944, reporters noted.[71]

A *Post-Dispatch* column guessed the only hope for Democrats in Washington was a slim chance to win a U.S. Senate majority. The *Tribune* proudly predicted a Republican sweep at state and federal levels, including the Illinois General Assembly.

Truman and his aides had devised one final campaign swing beginning in Washington on 24 October and concluding just before Election Day in Kansas City, with stops in Chicago, Cleveland, Boston, Providence, New York City, Brooklyn, and St. Louis.[72] The urgency was palpable. The first rally was planned for 25 October in Chicago, with Jack Arvey and the Democratic faithful prepared to produce a memorable greeting and audience for Truman's speech. This would be more than redemption for the Eisenhower candidacy fiasco. The city's Democratic leadership needed to show it could rally for the president in its finest machine tradition.

Meanwhile, Dewey felt so confident of victory that he rested much of the campaign's last week, and his final tour appeared limited. His short list of scheduled appearances included Chicago, Cleveland, Boston, and Madison Square Garden before Election Day.

Truman, after an early part of the day campaigning in Indiana, arrived in Chicago on schedule. About 5,000 people met his train, where no special event was planned. As the Truman motorcade headed to Chicago's Loop area and the Blackstone Hotel, police estimated the crowd waving and shouting along the way at 100,000.[73] This was just the beginning. Truman rode in a convertible with the top down, and by his side were Mayor Kennelly and former mayor Edward Kelly. County Commissioner Arthur X. Elrod drove the convertible, a new Cadillac, which Truman admired. Elrod reminded Truman that he had driven the party's vice presidential candidate in 1944. "But at that time I only had a Chevrolet," Elrod explained. "See how good your administration has been to me?"[74] The president was reported to have howled with approval at that remark. Mrs. Truman rode in the second car and Margaret in the third.

At the Blackstone, a women's tea for Mrs. Truman and Margaret drew about 300 guests. Margaret was a hit with reporters and seemed at ease. The president met in another part of the hotel with political delegations, and later all attended a dinner at which he spoke briefly.

The main events—a parade to Chicago Stadium and Truman's speech —awaited as the party left the hotel. Brass bands and marching ward workers led the way along a route illuminated with torchlights, fireworks, and rockets. Chicago policemen—sources said 426—were assigned to presidential events. Those favorable to Truman estimated crowds along the streets at 750,000 people. The overflow crowd at Chicago Stadium— on the West Side near the Loop—reached 26,000, according to police. As Truman prepared to speak to the crowd, down the aisle came a twelve-foot red heart from which stepped a beauty contest winner with roses for Mrs. Truman and Margaret. That ended the ceremonies, and Truman turned to his speech.

With his audience expanded greatly by national radio network coverage, Truman made perhaps the most aggressive and controversial address of the campaign.[75] Many observers at the time and historians later claimed Truman's overt attempt to appeal to Jewish and Catholic voters caused him to exceed the traditional limits of campaign oratory. Irwin Ross in his book *The Loneliest Campaign* observed, "It was a liberal version of McCarthyism, nearly two years before the term was coined, for its main theme was a strident warning that a Republican victory carried the threat of fascism."[76] Truman attempted to link actions and attitudes of people in the Republican Party to those of the Nazi Party in Germany. He listed the three main threats of fascism presented by Republican interests as unchecked inflation, concentration of economic power in a few hands, and racial prejudice.

"I know it is hard for Americans to admit this danger," he said. "American democracy has very deep roots. But if the anti-democratic forces in this country continue to work unchecked, this nation could awaken a few years from now to find that the Bill of Rights had become a scrap of paper." Regarding those who wanted to see higher inflation, Truman said, "They know that inflation—since price controls were killed just over two years ago—has sent corporation profits soaring. They are so blinded by the glitter of gold that they forget that inflation will bring on another terrible crash like the one of 1929."[77]

Truman sharpened the comparison to Hitler's Germany when he talked about the concentration of economic power. "When a few men get control of the economy of a nation, they find a 'front man' to run the country for them. Before Hitler came to power, control over the German economy had passed into the hands of a small group of rich manufacturers, bankers and landowners. They put money and influence behind Adolf Hitler. We know the rest of the story."

Finally, Truman approached the subject of racial prejudice: "We know how Hitler used anti-Semitic propaganda as a way of stupefying the German people with false ideas while he reached out for power. . . . This was not the first time such a thing has happened. The persecution of minorities goes hand in hand with the destruction of liberty." He cited the attempt by the Eightieth Congress to pass a bill limiting access to the United States by displaced persons. Truman said the proposal "cruelly discriminated against Catholics and Jews" and promised he "will never surrender" to evil forces he claimed were fomenting "racial and religious prejudice."

Almost everyone watching the Illinois political scene had an opinion of Truman's last appearance in the state, and the commentary ranged from "great" to "terrible." Paul Douglas claimed that the Truman rally in Chicago a week before Election Day topped anything Roosevelt had experienced. He wrote, "I had taken part in the great Roosevelt rallies of 1936 and 1940, which had seemed the ultimate in numbers and enthusiasm. But this one was more impressive. . . . Truman did not make a great speech, but a fighting one, and he was at home with the crowd. Throughout the campaign he was simple, unaffected, and determined. We were proud of him."[78] Douglas said he could feel an upsurge for Truman in the following days as he campaigned downstate.

As had been the case through much of the campaign, the two presidential candidates' trains almost passed in the night. A day after Truman's appearance in Chicago, Dewey appeared for a rally of his own. While it did not have quite the flare provided by the Democratic organization, the Dewey appearance also drew large crowds and buoyed hopes of the state's Republicans. Some newspapers could not resist the opportunity to compare receptions for the two candidates.

The *Tribune*'s George Tagge described the Dewey caravan from the LaSalle Street station to the Stevens Hotel as watched by 10,000 to 15,000 persons along the route. The candidate's ride to the hotel, the reporter wrote, "equaled in crowd size and surpassed in spontaneity practically the same trip made by President Truman Monday afternoon."[79] The streets were crowded as appreciative viewers applauded and cheered while tickertape fell. There were the lusty shouts of "We're for you, Dewey" and other encouragements, at which Dewey smiled, waved, and shook hands. Riding in the car behind Dewey were Governor and Mrs. Green and Senator and Mrs. Brooks. Tagge did his best to pump up the Dewey appearance, presumably fulfilling his role as Republican promoter-in-chief.

Compared to the Truman drive to Chicago Stadium for his speech, Dewey's trip paled. There were no torchlights or streets lined with policemen. Nevertheless, the stadium was packed, and thousands gathered outside to see and hear the candidate. Inside, Green and Brooks took their shots before Dewey gave the speech everyone came to hear. Brooks attacked Truman and his remarks from the night before. He belittled the president's commitment to civil rights at much the same level he had used earlier. Green defended his administration and its attack on New Deal programs. The talks were mixed with sound effects and sights that reminded a reporter of a "Hollywood prevue, a carnival, and a radio give-away show."

Dewey seemed relatively calm, and his remarks were no more combative than he had offered at almost every stop in the campaign. He called for unity to solve problems such as world peace. He lamented the feisty tone of his competitor for the job, saying, "This is the kind of campaign I refuse to wage. To me this is more than just a campaign to win an election. It is a campaign to strengthen and unite our country to meet the challenge of a troubled world."[80]

Realizing that farm issues had been thrust to the front of the battle, he said, "In all the discussions of agriculture, we hear much about the family farm, but too little about the farm family. Too many of those who work the long hours to produce our food still lack the minimum essentials for modern living. Too many farms still have no running water and no telephones." Those were not fighting words, they were Dewey's words, designed to identify an issue but not provide any ideas about what to do about it.

He offered more generalizations when talking about business and labor: "Business, labor and agriculture—all of us prosper together or fall together. No part of our country can do well for very long unless every part of our country does well. So it is equally important to you and to me—to every one of us—that we get a government that really believes in the welfare of labor—of the men and women who work for wages." Speaking more directly of labor, he added, "American labor is a cornerstone of our free society. Labor is entitled to an administration that believes wholeheartedly in the right to organize, to strike, the right to collective bargaining."

As Chicago workers cleaned the streets after Dewey's departure and others returned to their lives and jobs, and later to vote, Illinois had seen and heard all either candidate had to offer. The two men would appear for a few more days in other cities, but the race was over in Illinois.

Conclusion

President Truman ended his campaign in Kansas City on 1 November as the nation's citizens prepared to vote. Not even the closest of Truman's associates believed he would win. However, from the earliest election returns, it could be seen that Thomas Dewey was not doing well, especially in traditional Republican states. That did not convince editors at the *Chicago Tribune*, however. They ran a banner headline across the top of page 1 in an early morning edition proclaiming "Dewey Defeats Truman."[1] That headline appeared in about 150,000 copies of the paper before editors in the newsroom could see how wrong it was. Of all the images of the 1948 presidential election, the one of Harry Truman on the rear platform of the Ferdinand Magellan in St. Louis holding up a *Tribune* with its banner headline remains embedded in the minds of many Americans, even those born long after 1948.

Truman's upset victory stunned the nation, as it still does today. He received a little less than 50 percent of the popular vote to 45 percent for Dewey, 2 percent for Strom Thurmond, and 2 percent for Henry Wallace. Polls had given the minority candidates much higher numbers. Truman's plurality was 2,187,968 votes and his electoral vote total 303, with Dewey receiving 189 and Thurmond 39. In the national picture, Truman's victory rested on results in Ohio, California, and Illinois. He carried Ohio by 7,107 votes and California by 17,865 and gained Illinois's twenty-eight electoral votes by 33,612. His total plurality in the three states was 58,584 votes. The swing of a few thousand votes in three states would have put Dewey in the White House.

The president earned his paper-thin margin in Illinois by receiving just fewer than 2 million votes, 50.07 percent of the total cast. In sharp contrast, Adlai Stevenson crushed incumbent Governor Green by 572,067 votes or 57.1 percent of the total, and Paul Douglas swamped Senator Brooks by 407,728 votes, 55.07 per cent of the total.[2] Stevenson and Douglas obviously provided coattails for Truman in Illinois. All Democrats on the state ticket won. Democrats gained control of the House of Representatives, but Republicans maintained a majority in the Senate.

Illinois analysts attributed Truman's margin not so much to the votes he got—he received 84,764 fewer than Roosevelt had in 1944—but to the fact that Dewey received only 21,789 more than he did in 1944. Truman received 150,000 fewer votes in Cook County than Roosevelt had in 1944 but still had a margin of 200,836 votes. The voting power of Democrats in the Chicago region, the strong African American vote, and labor support were major advantages for Truman. Significantly, Illinoisans cast 62,975 fewer votes for president than in 1944. That trend, combined with an inability to gain appreciably more votes than in 1944, cost Dewey the Illinois electoral college votes.

How did Truman do in Illinois places where he campaigned by whistle-stop and motorcade? He won four of the six southern Illinois counties he toured. In 1944, Roosevelt had won just two of the six. Truman received 49,938 votes to 47,648 for Dewey. This signaled a considerable swing toward the Democrats. In these counties, Dewey had received 56,111 votes in 1944 and Roosevelt 49,041. At least by vote count, it could be claimed that Truman's motorcade helped him win the counties where he campaigned.

In the five central Illinois counties, Truman won only Macon, by a percentage spread of 52–49, almost exactly the same given Roosevelt in 1944. In the five-county total, Dewey received about 2,000 votes fewer than in 1944, and Truman received 5,500 fewer than Roosevelt. However, the important figure, considering statewide trends, was that Dewey received fewer votes than he had four years earlier.

In Rock Island County, Truman won by 2,350 votes, or 52 percent to 47 percent. While that looked good in Truman's column, Roosevelt did better against Dewey in 1944, where Roosevelt won by 6,122.

Truman's better showing in southern counties than in central reflects the nature of his campaign in those areas. In central Illinois, except for Springfield, Truman never left the train and spent just a few minutes at each stop. In southern Illinois, Truman spent the better part of a day campaigning at close range with citizens. A more personal touch apparently paid off for the president. Also, Dewey's brief appearances in Illinois were hardly memorable in comparison to Truman's.

Another factor helping Truman downstate was the residual ill feeling toward Republicans carrying over from the Centralia mine disaster of March 1947. State Democratic candidates, especially Adlai Stevenson, made frequent campaign trips to the area and never let audiences forget the 111 miners who died and that Republican officials shared the blame.

Voting numbers for governor from the four counties surrounding Centralia showed significant differences from 1944, when 53,116 cast ballots for governor. In 1948, only 47,054 people voted. In 1944, Green received 28,661 votes and his Democratic opponent 24,455. In 1948, Stevenson received 25,418 and Green 21,636. Although Democratic votes for governor were about the same in each year, 7,025 fewer votes were cast for Green in 1948.

During all of Truman's appearances in Illinois, he trumpeted a version of the New Deal, although as a latecomer to the position, he could have offered a more conservative program less devoted to maintaining economic redistribution and the welfare state. However, he chose to continue the New Deal pitch in spite of Republican opposition manifested in the *Tribune*'s editorial policy throughout Illinois and the Midwest.

In the opinion of the *Tribune*, none of that analysis mattered. The paper stated on its editorial page, "For the third time, a Republican convention fell under vicious influences and nominated a 'me-too' candidate who conducted a 'me-too' campaign. For the third time the strategy failed. That is why Mr. Truman was elected and with him a Democratic House and Senate."[3] It is doubtful that President Truman agreed.

Truman's opinion: "It was not my victory, but a victory of the Democratic party for the people."[4] That was easy to say, but the fact remained, as pointed out by Michael Barone in *Our Country*, the election was the best Democratic showing in congressional races between the Roosevelt victory of 1936 and the Eisenhower recession of 1958.[5] For the next two years, Truman had a party majority in both chambers of Congress, an outcome nobody expected.

All in all, election night for the *Tribune* and publisher Robert McCormick was a disaster. Embarrassed or not, the *Tribune* continued to prosper and speak its mind on the issues and people of the day. That is not to say that talk is cheap, but newspapers rarely rose or fell based on endorsement editorials. On the other hand, every Republican whose name was on the Illinois ballot lost, and McCormick could not claim a single victory. Among the losers there would be no redemption, except for William G. Stratton, who lost the race for secretary of state. After the election in 1952, he began serving the first of two terms as governor.

By any measurement, nothing in Illinois came as close to capturing the public fancy as Truman's victory. His celebrations grabbed head-lines coast to coast. Meanwhile, victory was savored at the state level by personal moments worth remembering but less reported. Just before Election Day, a pollster told Paul Douglas he would win by 400,000 votes. Surprised, the candidate later said he figured to lose by 50,000.[6] Although candidates almost always thought they could win, Douglas was a realist. After voting with his wife early on Election Day, he went home and took a nap. He awoke and could hardly believe reports that his race was close and that Truman seemed to be winning. Even then, radio reports said votes had not been counted from some Illinois Republican strongholds. En route to campaign headquarters, Douglas saw the *Tri-bune* headline declaring Dewey the winner over Truman and wondered what was happening. During the rest of the evening, Douglas either held his early lead over Brooks or expanded it. By 4 A.M., Brooks conceded defeat. The improbable had happened.

The huge victories of Adlai Stevenson and Paul Douglas to some extent resulted from voter resistance to continuation of Republican rule. A third term for the governor bothered voters. Although Senator Brooks drew more votes than Governor Green, the choice of Douglas reflected weariness with the sharp-tongued, unyielding partisanship of the in-cumbent and a solid vote by union members for the challenger. Both Democrats looked and sounded like independents, which gave them credibility against the weakened reputations of their opponents. Both Republicans sounded too much like "status quo." A dedicated liberal on domestic matters, Douglas offered a bipartisan reach on foreign affairs, which appealed to voters who split ballots, and teamed him with Truman's solid gains in overseas policy. Stevenson's victory mar-gin must be credited in large part to an effective campaign of labeling the Green administration as unethical and corrupt. Revelations by the *Post-Dispatch* over the last three months of the campaign had dimin-ished Green's standing and painted Stevenson as a decent, although inexperienced, alternative.

Scott Lucas had a somewhat different opinion of Stevenson's triumph, perhaps reflecting the strained relationship that had developed between the two. In his memoir, Lucas recalled that the huge margin for Stevenson "was the first time that the Democrats truly realized the vulnerability of Governor Dwight Green with the voters of Illinois." Lucas did not want Stevenson to think he was invincible and told the governor-elect, "Adlai, this is a remarkable victory you have achieved, but please don't take it too seriously as a personal triumph. The fact that the voters of Illinois knew you were honest, upright, and had ability was all they wanted to know in order to get Governor Green and his slick crowd out of the State House." Further in his analysis, Lucas wrote, "Stevenson probably received the greatest protest vote that had ever been cast in the annals of Illinois political history."[7]

Analysis is largely subjective, but voting figures offer further clues. Democrats up and down the ballot in Illinois benefited from party loyalty and cross-appeal to moderate Republicans, especially in the case of Stevenson and Douglas. In previous elections, Green and Brooks gained traction with Democratic voters primarily because Democratic leaders chose political hacks for top spots on the ballot from 1940 to 1948. Stevenson and Douglas offered fresh faces with appealing campaign styles.

Practically speaking, Stevenson and Douglas won their contests with huge margins in four key Democratic counties: Cook, Madison, Macon, and St. Clair. These returns, combined with strong showings in traditional Republican strongholds downstate, upset the GOP prescription for winning statewide. For example, Stevenson rolled up a huge margin in Cook County of 572,067 and gained 20,638 in Madison, 9,333 in Macon, and 30,341 in St. Clair, although Green won 56 of the state's 102 counties. Furthermore, Stevenson scored victories in two traditionally Republican counties where gambling and other criminal activities made the news daily in September and October: Peoria County by 5,170 votes and Sangamon by 2,541. Stevenson's demolition of the Republicans was complete with a downstate winning margin of 25,743, almost unheard of for a Democrat.

Douglas's margins were slightly smaller but no less spectacular, given his lack of funds and dependence on old-fashioned street corner campaigning. He came out of Cook County with a margin of 429,751 votes and kept things close downstate by drawing within 24,623 votes of Brooks. The incumbent won 58 counties while losing the Senate seat.

THE ROAD AHEAD

First among victors not on the statewide ballot were Jack Arvey and Paul Powell. In behalf of Democrats across the state, they made a successful team. Arvey's choice of Stevenson and Douglas, against the wishes of party machinery and candidate selection patterns of the past, set the stage for a Democratic comeback. He capped the triumph by turning out huge Democratic numbers in Chicago and Cook County. Boosted by downstate outcomes across the board—all Democrats on the state ticket won—and with Truman's victory, Powell's reputation spread well beyond southern Illinois, launching his career as a political titan. With victory in the air after such a long drought, Democrats had reason to believe a new dynasty was in place.

While the 1948 election buried the political careers of Dwight Green, Curly Brooks, George Barrett, and a host of others, Republicans familiar to voters led a resurrection of the party in 1950 and 1952. Everett Dirksen, a longtime servant in the U.S. House of Representatives, ended his tenure there in 1949 due to poor health. He might have survived if he had run for reelection, but Dirksen's absence from the ballot meant he prevailed without the risk of losing. Regaining his health sooner than expected, he returned in 1950 to defeat Scott Lucas for the Senate seat. Dirksen served with distinction until he died in 1969.

William G. Stratton, who lost to incumbent secretary of state Edward J. Barrett in 1948, proved his resilience and ability to separate himself from the Green debacle by winning the race for governor in 1952. He had kept alive a political career since the late 1930s by political agility and familiarity to a statewide constituency, in spite of differences with Green. Those differences left Stratton untainted by accusations of corruption. When the Democrats, led by Stevenson, lost full grip on their momentum from 1948, Stratton was there to lead a GOP rebound for governor that lasted until 1961.

Hidden in the shadows of the Republican Party was another politician who would lend strength to Republican dominance in the General Assembly during the 1960s. W. Russell Arrington of Chicago was first elected to the state House in 1944. He remained there until 1954, when he was elected to the state Senate. In that position, Arrington became one of the strongest and most successful legislative leaders in modern Illinois political history.

A Democrat on the sidelines in 1948 was Otto Kerner Jr. Arvey had convinced the Truman administration to appoint Kerner U.S. attorney for northern Illinois in 1947. Kerner watched fellow Democrats rise and fall again before seeking and winning a position in 1954 as circuit court judge in Cook County. A year later, Richard J. Daley was elected mayor of Chicago. Daley engineered Kerner's nomination and election as governor in 1960. In 1973, after becoming a judge, Kerner was convicted of accepting a bribe in the form of racetrack stock when governor. At the time of his trial, he was a federal appeals court judge.[8]

Stevenson's term as governor never provided the party leadership required for sustaining the 1948 outcome. His departure to seek the presidency in 1952 left the party desperate for a gubernatorial candidate. Many Democrats presumed leaders would turn to one of the party's most successful officeholders dating back to 1930: Edward J. Barrett had held the office of state treasurer from 1931 to 1933 and of state auditor from 1933 to 1941. In 1944, he won election as secretary of state and was reelected in 1948. Barrett was known from one end of the state to the other and had acquired an admiration society in southern and central Illinois headed by Paul Powell and John Stelle. Surprisingly, the party state central committee chose Lieutenant Governor Sherwood Dixon to run for governor in 1952, a decision promoted by Stevenson. The choice so angered Stelle and other downstate Democrats that they supported the Republican Stratton.

In 1955, Mayor Daley appointed Barrett city clerk, and he was elected to the position every four years through 1970. However, Barrett's story ended in a political tragedy. In 1972, U.S. attorney James R. Thompson, who was elected governor in 1976, charged Barrett with bribery, mail fraud, and perjury for soliciting and receiving $180,000 in bribes from a voting machine company. Found guilty in a 1973 trial, Barrett was sentenced to three years in prison and a $15,000 fine. Because of ill health, he served the sentence at home. He died in 1977.[9]

Although Stevenson effectively left Illinois in 1952 for the national and international scenes, many people who admired him and supported his 1948 campaign later made an imprint on Illinois politics. Paul Simon, who began a short but impressive career as editor and publisher of the *Troy Tribune* in 1948, became an acolyte of Stevenson, in large part because of the governor's fight against statewide gambling interests in 1950. Also, Stevenson and Simon formed something of a father-son relationship that was part of the reason Simon began a political career in

1954. Another of the 1948 winners, Paul Douglas, had a lasting influence on Simon in terms of social policy advocacy during Simon's forty years of Illinois and federal public service.

Others who worked in the Stevenson campaigns of 1948, 1952, and 1956 remained active in party affairs, often as champions of legislative reforms and battles against bossism in the party, particularly in Chicago. Notable among those was Dan Walker, who won election as governor in 1972. His political roots were deep in the Stevenson years. Other Stevenson followers tried for high office in Illinois but failed. That was the fate of Stephen A. Mitchell, an early and influential backer of Stevenson in 1948 and prominent in the Stevenson presidential campaigns. Mitchell, who sought the party nomination for governor in 1960, had the backing of Simon and other independent Democrats who wanted a candidate unaligned with the Chicago organization, but the Mitchell effort never got off the ground.[10]

Rather than living as one big happy family after the 1948 election, the Democratic Party had deep divisions—and some shallow ones, too. The rift between Stevenson and Douglas never healed, even in victory. A similar distance developed between Stevenson and Lucas, who had worked tirelessly for Stevenson during 1948. They parted company almost immediately, and Lucas believed it hurt his chances of reelection in 1950.

Of a more serious nature were differences in style, history, politics, and approach to public policy between Stevenson and members of the legislature. For the first time since the General Assembly of 1937–38, Democrats had control of the House by a margin of 79 to 74. Republicans maintained control of the Senate, 33–18. Even with the Senate margin, Democrats had an opportunity to enact much of Stevenson's agenda. A complicating factor, however, was Paul Powell.

Powell had the inside track for Speaker of the House for two reasons. First, he had served in party leadership for two sessions, including minority leader in 1947–48, which meant he had earned the support of colleagues. Second was his success as campaign coordinator for downstate Democrats. As his ascension to Speaker seemed likely, the newspaper that had been a strong supporter of Stevenson, the *St. Louis Post-Dispatch*, expressed fear that Powell would be a roadblock to the enactment of the governor's program.[11] What the paper's editors probably knew was that while Powell had worked to elect Stevenson, he did not respect the new governor. Backed by fans such as John Stelle and many in the legislature, Powell considered Stevenson an elitist, and an inexperienced elitist at that. Stevenson didn't help the situation when he refused to take a position on the Speaker selection, even after it became obvious that Powell would be chosen.

The Vienna Democrat was a strong legislative leader with his own agenda and on many issues could also corral Republican votes. He had little interest in any "reform" issues of the Stevenson administration unless they could be traded for Powell's agenda. A primary interest of Powell was passing legislation that benefited southern Illinois, and he knew how to get bipartisan help by dishing goodies to other parts of the state. This was not Stevenson's idea of cooperation. Needless to say, having control of two-thirds of state government was less of an advantage for reform-minded Democrats with two leaders who frankly did not respect or like each other. Powell's elevation to Speaker began a reign of sixteen years, during which he manipulated the General Assembly, governors, and opposing party members to create public policy that gained him friends across the state and lined his pockets and those of his pals with benefits.

THE PRESS IN RETROSPECT

There is sufficient evidence that unrelenting, no-holds-barred newspaper warfare over an Illinois election reached a climax with the 1948 contest. Newspapers in the state and on its borders had argued, disagreed, and fought prior to the first postwar presidential election. However, the intensity of the battle had no previous match for almost constant favoritism and bickering. No parts of Illinois were spared. Newspapers in Chicago and St. Louis represented some of the nation's most politically active press lords in their prime—Robert McCormick, Joseph Pulitzer II, John S. Knight, Marshall Field III—with virtually unlimited resources to put in play. By 1952, while some of the same papers and their leadership could still fling dirt at each other and at candidates, television had begun to steal their thunder, and the politics of the 1950s did not look much like 1940–48. Even the *Tribune* began to modify its rigid partisanship after McCormick's death in 1955.

As in earlier times, the *Tribune* stood atop the city's newspapers in circulation and advertising, news resources, and vitriol in 1948. Nevertheless, Chicagoland's behemoth had a fight on its hands with well-financed opposing points of view, complicated by a lineup of weakened Republican candidates. The *Tribune*'s total commitment to Republicans was no surprise, but in Chicago at least the *Sun-Times* was just as committed to Democrats, without the circulation reach of its competitor. The *Daily News*, led by John S. Knight, struck more of a middle ground with a slight leaning toward Republicans and probably was the tamest of the lot.

Further stirring the pot was the *Post-Dispatch*. Traditionally, Chicago newspapers and most in the state paid little attention to the St. Louis papers, preferring to focus on their prime territories. The *Post-Dispatch* upset that comfort zone beginning with Pulitzer-prize winning coverage of the Centralia mine disaster in 1947 and followed by investigations of statewide crime and corruption in 1948. It was one thing to cover news in southern Illinois but another when the paper carried stories almost daily in September and October about charges of criminal behavior and ineffective law enforcement in Springfield and Peoria. Those cities were within reach of Chicago newspapers, and editors did not appreciate the St. Louis intrusion. When they realized the *Post-Dispatch* had set the tone for political coverage, it was too late to do anything but play follow-the-leader or try to ignore the obvious.

There is little argument that the *Post-Dispatch* influenced the election outcome in 1948, especially the race for governor. Stevenson's downstate vote totals are evidence. Green took a pounding for more than two months, and Stevenson was held up as the light of the future. Questions remain all these years later: How much truth was there in the articles by Ted Link? Were his sources legitimate and truthful? Did the paper overplay the stories because they appeared to have political impact? In the end, did the revelations bring about results in places like Peoria and Springfield?

There was a reason for confidence in Link's articles, although he gave few if any sources for his information: he had built a strong reputation for exposing official corruption, and he had the confidence of *Post-Dispatch* editors. But public officials speculated that Shelton gang members spilled their guts to Link to shelter their complicity, and newspaper reporters admitted that gang members provided self-serving details. That raised doubts about Link's veracity.

The degree of internal newspaper checking of facts and determining reliability of sources was never discussed publicly at the time. Although newspapers today publish stories based on information from unidentified sources, internal checks and balances are generally applied. Without knowledge about specific sources in 1948, it is impossible to determine legitimacy and truthfulness. Obviously, editors thought the stories warranted prominent display, often on page 1. There typically was a tendency to believe the reporters if the information seemed sensational and exclusive, and therefore overplaying was a danger.

Although public officials professed to investigate their own operations in Springfield and Peoria and grand juries heard evidence from prosecutors, few indictments were issued, and most were dismissed or simply were never pursued further. Since the papers would trumpet any results, the lack of specific outcomes suggests that public officials successfully ducked and simply out-waited the newspapers.

The fact remains that the totality of coverage and repetition of charges unquestionably played a role in turning the Illinois tide for Democrats. The single most damaging event for Republicans was the indictment of Ted Link a week before Election Day in what appeared to be little more than a political attempt to belittle his work and intimidate the *Post-Dispatch*. It backfired in the faces of all Republicans on the ticket.

THE REARVIEW MIRROR

Sometimes the messiness of politics, the grime and grit that can leave a bad taste, gets in the way of a clear-eyed look at an election and its results. Analysis is helped if enough time has passed to identify the nuances, to put aside the unimportant happenings, and to insert historical perspective. With the passage of more than two generations, improved vision is possible when looking at the 1948 election in Illinois and assessing its importance in understanding today's political picture. The election outcome shows that underdogs can prevail by the content of their character and that voters, given a choice between corrupt behavior and honesty, between cynicism and hope, will make the wise choice. But there is more to political change than election outcomes.

The appeal of "change" as part of an election campaign is infectious. It may be the one constant element in the political rhetoric of Illinois, or in any state for that matter. It often is presented in different words—"We can do better" or "Change we can believe in"—but the meaning is the same. That was the underlying message of the 1948 elections through the voices of Democratic candidates forcing Republicans to defend the status quo. The public was ripe for the verbiage after years of wartime sacrifice. But did "change" occur?

After the election, Governor Adlai Stevenson addressed that rallying cry, and some measure of progress was made. However, it was not enough to thwart a Republican takeover in 1950 and 1952, when the cry for "change" came from different voices. Stevenson tried. For example, he made good on pledges to declare war on commercial gambling and its corruptions. Prodded by newspapers, state police in 1950 conducted a number of raids across the state outside Chicago in an attempt to change a firmly entrenched culture and slipshod law enforcement. The positive effect was momentary and fleeting. In fact, the revelations of corruption and gambling during the campaign and after did little to change habits at the local and county levels.

Stevenson also made much of Republican political shenanigans prior to the 1947 Centralia coal mine disaster that killed 111 workers. He asked audiences "to join with me in a vow that there will be no more Centralia tragedies." He pledged to strip politics from the Department of Mines and Minerals and to stop solicitations of campaign funds from coal mining companies. In the first years of his administration, Stevenson proposed reform legislation, most of which was rejected by various special interests. However, while changes were made in the Mines and Minerals Department that eliminated the more egregious behavior allowed by the Green administration, Stevenson could not claim a perfect safety record. The governor's rhetoric took a hit on 21 December 1951, when an explosion and fire in West Frankfort's New Orient No. 2 coal mine killed 119 workers, 8 more than in Centralia.

Elected reformer Dick Carter, state's attorney in St. Clair County, soon found the permissive culture in places like East St. Louis and Belleville resistant to reform. The result was a new status quo, perhaps not as bad as the 1930s and 1940s but barely a breath of fresh air.

Missing from the reform picture during these years was campaign and candidate disclosure, which might not have ended all forms of corruption but certainly would have made it riskier to continue. That did not happen until laws were passed in the 1970s and 1980s. Meanwhile, business as usual continued at the local and state levels in terms of cronyism, favors, privilege, and cash payments. As long as business could be done in the shadows, there was little incentive to change.

The most obvious benefit of the 1948 outcome was to rid the state of a bloated and corrupt political machine, in this case the Republican administration of Dwight Green. Political machines are a way of life in Illinois, most apparent in Chicago but present in smaller ways across the state. The election of 1948 did not eliminate machines, but it may have cleaned up future versions a bit, simply by making citizens more familiar with the reality of political behavior. Just as during the 1930s and 1940s, today's political organizations thrive on patronage jobs, an expensive and wasteful habit as old as politics. In that regard, nothing much has changed, although many political appointees serve well. Organized political behavior and outcomes are here to stay in some form, but disclosures that occurred during the 1948 campaign—and in all elections since—remind Illinoisans of the need to be wary and watchful.

History teaches that public mood and sentiment can affect election outcomes, occasionally in a wholesale manner, as was the case in 1948. The problem with counting too much on such an occurrence is that people's attitudes change from election to election, and with them the pressure for reform. The sweep of an election broom is momentary, and the Republican return to dominance of state affairs almost immediately after 1948 is evidence. There were changes in the state political picture from the 1940s to the 1950s and beyond, but much stayed the same.

NOTES
BIBLIOGRAPHY
INDEX

Notes

1. THE DEMOCRATS DISINTEGRATE

1. Clayton, *Illinois Fact Book*, 147–51.

2. Allen and Lacey, *Illinois Elections*, 59, 403–4.

3. Littlewood, *Horner of Illinois*, 232–36; Masters, *Governor Henry Horner*, 208–10, 214–15.

4. Schapsmeier and Schapsmeier, "Scott W. Lucas of Havana," 305.

5. Howard, *Mostly Good and Competent Men*, 267–73. See also Howard, *Illinois*, 483, 503–4, 539–45; Case and Douglas, *Midwesterner*, 149–91; and Watters, *Illinois in the Second World War*, 480.

6. Howard, *Mostly Good and Competent Men*, 269; Biles, *Big City Boss*, 70–72; Case and Douglas, *Midwesterner*, 92–201.

7. Masters, *Governor Henry Horner*, 200–5; Littlewood, *Horner of Illinois*, 219.

8. "Lieut. Governor Attacks Makers of Party Ticket," *East St. Louis Journal*, 18 February 1940, by Transradio Press, *Metro-East Journal* Collection, Louisa H. Bowen University Archives and Special Collections, Southern Illinois University–Edwardsville (hereafter Bowen Archives).

9. "Fired Nudelman as First Move; Assembly Called," *East St. Louis Journal*, 8 April 1940, by Transradio Press, Bowen Archives; Howard, *Mostly Good and Competent Men*, 262.

10. "Dwight Green, Former Illinois Governor, Dies," *St. Louis Post-Dispatch* (hereafter *SLPD*), 21 February 1958, 12A.

11. Dwight Green, "Labor Demands a Change," speech at labor luncheon in Chicago, 2 November 1940, Dwight H. Green Papers, box 5, folder 4, Speeches May 6–December 1940.

12. Allen and Lacey, *Illinois Elections*, 405–6.

13. Morgan, "The 1942 Mid-term Elections in Illinois," 117.

14. Howard, oral history memoir, 102.

15. Ibid.

16. "Dwight Green, Former Illinois Governor, Dies," *SLPD*, 21 February 1958, 12A.

17. "The Unfitness of Gov. Green," *SLPD*, 27 May 1948.

18. Howard, oral history memoir, 102.

19. "Dwight Green, Former Illinois Governor, Dies," *SLPD*, 21 February 1958, 12A.

20. Littlewood, *Horner of Illinois*, 211.

21. Kenney and Hartley, *Uncertain Tradition*, 128–29.

22. Howard, oral history memoir, 79.

23. Kenney and Hartley, *Uncertain Tradition*, 136–39; Howard, oral history memoir, 79; *Biographical Directory*, 713; Smith, *Colonel*, 401. Smith pointed out that Brooks won the senate seat after losing five previous elections. The author called Brooks "shopworn."

24. Kenney and Hartley, *Uncertain Tradition*, 136–37; Smith, *Colonel*, 442.

25. Kenney and Hartley, *Uncertain Tradition*, 137.

26. Willard Shelton, "Boss McCormick's Men," *The Nation*, 21 February 1943.

27. Morgan, "The 1942 Mid-term Elections in Illinois," 117–19.

28. Ibid., 119.

29. Kenney and Hartley, *Uncertain Tradition*, 138.

30. Qtd. in Smith, *Colonel*, 442.

31. Watters, *Illinois in the Second World War*, 481–82.

32. Ibid., 123.

33. Qtd. in ibid., 125.

34. Ibid., 484.

35. Morgan, "The 1942 Mid-term Elections in Illinois," 126.

36. Schapsmeier and Schapsmeier, "Paul H. Douglas," 317. See also Biles, *Big City Boss*, 38–39; and Watters, *Illinois in the Second World War*, 483–84.

37. Biles, *Big City Boss*, 125.

38. Roosevelt University, "History of Chicago from Trading Post to Metropolis," 1–2.

39. Theodore C. Link, "Gamblers Again Raising Green Campaign Funds, Gave Him $100,000 in 1944," *SLPD*, 1 September 1948, 1.

40. "Green's Debt to Gambling," *SLPD*, 2 September 1948.

41. Watters, *Illinois in the Second World War*, 494; Howard, *Mostly Good and Competent Men*, 271.

42. Kenney and Hartley, *Uncertain Tradition*, 132–35.

43. Schapsmeier and Schapsmeier, "Scott W. Lucas of Havana," 307.

44. Clayton, *Illinois Fact Book*, 143.

45. Hartley, "'I Worked for My Friends.'"

46. Douglas had not run for public office before 1944. Nevertheless, she was an activist in public affairs and joined her husband, Paul Douglas, in support of internationalism. Approached by Democrat leaders to run for Congress, she is reported to have said, "Gentlemen, this is so sudden." She had been a Republican before seeking the office.

47. Allen and Lacey, *Illinois Elections*, 61; Watters, *Illinois in the Second World War*, 510–11.

48. Howard, oral history memoir, 109.

49. *Bloomington Pantagraph*, 11 November 1944.

50. Biles, *Big City Boss*, 131–32; Watters, *Illinois in the Second World War*, 510–11.

51. "Bill of Particulars," *East St. Louis Journal*, 19 September 1948, Bowen Archives; Joseph Driscoll, "Dwight Green Once Denounced Third Term as 'Dictatorship,' Now Seeks One for Himself," *SLPD*, 12 December 1947. See also Milburn P. Akers, "Gov. Green Seeks 3rd Term Despite Attacks on FDR," *Chicago Sun*, 5 January 1948.

52. Clayton, *Illinois Fact Book*, 147.

53. R. W. Gisinger, "Barrett Mum on Gambling War Prospects Here," *East St. Louis Journal*, 20 May 1946, Bowen Archives.

54. Rakove, *We Don't Want Nobody Nobody Sent*, 3–4. Rakove interviewed Arvey for the chapter "Jacob Arvey," in which the subject spoke at length about his early years in Chicago. Other sources include Biles, *Big City Boss*, 145; Frankel and Alexander, "Arvey of Illinois," 9–11; and Cohen and Taylor, *American Pharaoh*, 80.

55. Qtd. in Rakove, *We Don't Want Nobody Nobody Sent*, 3.

56. Frankel and Alexander, "Arvey of Illinois," 11.

57. Biles, *Big City Boss*, 44. See also Rakove, *We Don't Want Nobody Nobody Sent*, 7.

58. Qtd. in Rakove, *We Don't Want Nobody Nobody Sent*, 7.

59. Gottfried, *Boss Cermak*, 177. The Jews of the Twenty-Fourth joined with Czechs to form an alliance to elect Cermak. See also Rakove, *We Don't Want Nobody Nobody Sent*, 8.

60. Biles, *Big City Boss*, 15–19; Rakove, *We Don't Want Nobody Nobody Sent*, 9.

61. Biles, *Big City Boss*, 51.

62. Littlewood, *Horner of Illinois*, 164; Frankel and Holmes, "Arvey of Illinois," 66; Biles, *Big City Boss*, 58.

63. Qtd. in Rakove, *We Don't Want Nobody Nobody Sent*, 10.

64. See the summary of public service in the William G. Stratton Collections, Abraham Lincoln Presidential Library; Kenney, *Political Passage*, 43–46. Kenney provides details of the campaign and strategy to unseat the incumbent, Mrs. Douglas.

65. Allen and Lacey, *Illinois Elections*, 63.

66. Ibid., 62–63.

67. Rakove, *We Don't Want Nobody Nobody Sent*, 12.

68. Ibid., 12. Arvey told John Bartlow Martin essentially the same story in an interview for *Adlai Stevenson of Illinois*, 266.

69. Biles, *Richard J. Daley*, 29.

70. Federal Bureau of Investigation File 92-2810 (Frank Wortman), November 1957. See also FBI 63-32-29, 22 October 1959, memo to Director, FBI, 2. All references to FBI documents resulted from a Freedom of Information Act request by the author dated 4 March 1989. Over several months, the FBI provided 8,000 pages of information about Wortman. The bulk of material came from FBI titles 63-2 and 92-2810, with lesser amounts from files 92-4512, 122-3751, and 66-67.

71. From 1946 to 1950, the *East St. Louis Journal* and newspapers in St. Louis wrote frequently about links between Capone agents and Wortman, often mentioning no sources. Much of the testimony and documents produced at the Kefauver Committee hearings in St. Louis in February 1951 spoke of collaborations. FBI reports through the years mentioned the connection as if it were fact but offered little fresh information.

72. FBI File 92-2810, 26 August 1959, states that Chicago FBI furnished information of Wortman's connections to "Chicago top hoodlums." "Wortman Head of Mob Forged in U.S. Prison," *Chicago Tribune*, 24 July 1957, 7.

73. Charles O. Stewart, "Signs Indicate Major Invasion," *East St. Louis Journal*, 28 September 1947.

74. John Bartlow Martin, "Al Capone's Successors," *American Mercury*, June 1949, 728–34; Wagner, "Heirs of Scarface Al," 1.

75. "Gambling Probe Official; Names Six Witnesses," *East St. Louis Journal*, 11 December 1946, Bowen Archives. See also "Signs Indicate Gaming Probe by Grand Jury," *East St. Louis Journal*, 10 December 1946, Bowen Archives.

76. "Grand Jury Hears 5 While E. Side Gaming Goes on," *SLPD*, 12 December 1946.

77. "Doyle, Bowman Named," *East St. Louis Journal*, 16 December 1946, Bowen Archives.

78. "Judge Bareis Says He Will Reject Plea," *East St. Louis Journal*, 30 December 1946, Bowen Archives.

79. "Barrett Rejects Plea for Aid in Gambling Cases," *East St. Louis Journal*, 31 December 1946, Bowen Archives.

80. "Barrett Mum on Gambling War Prospects Here," *East St. Louis Journal*, 20 May 1946.

81. Alan J. Dixon, interview with author, 24 May 2005.

82. Biographical information about Carter, then candidate for East St. Louis city commission, in *East St. Louis Journal*, 19 January 1947, Bowen Archives.

83. G. Thomas Duffy, "Richard T. Carter," *East St. Louis Journal*, 23 April 1952, Bowen Archives.

84. Harry A. Barnes, "Legal Fight for Post Took Years," *East St. Louis Journal*, 2 May 1948, Bowen Archives. Barnes recounted in detail the campaign and lengthy appeal of the election results.

85. "Text of Ruling by High Court," *East St. Louis Journal*, 2 May 1948, Bowen Archives.

86. "Carter Sounds Warning to Gang Elements," *East St. Louis Journal*, 21 February 1948, Bowen Archives.

87. Ibid.

88. Carter received 19,236 votes in the primary of April 1948, to 11,713 for Zerweck, *East St. Louis Journal*, 12 October 1952, Bowen Archives. In the general election against Republican Curt C. Lindauer, Carter polled 57,715 votes to 25,115 for his opponent.

2. 1947: A YEAR OF DECISIONS

1. Donovan, *Conflict and Crisis*, 222.

2. Ibid., 223.

3. Ibid., 259.

4. McCullough, *Truman*, 556.

5. McCoy, *Presidency of Harry S. Truman*, 115.

6. Donovan, *Conflict and Crisis*, 261.

7. U.S. Department of State, *Truman Doctrine*; McCoy, *Presidency of Harry S. Truman*, 122.

8. Barone, *Our Country*, 190–93; Donovan, *Conflict and Crisis*, 299.

9. McCoy, *Presidency of Harry S. Truman*, 123–27; Barone, *Our Country*, 207.

10. McCoy, *Presidency of Harry S. Truman*, 107. See also Roberts and Klibanoff, *Race Beat*, 38.

11. McCoy, *Presidency of Harry S. Truman*, 153.

12. "Robert M. Medill," *Illinois Blue Book, 1945–46*, 509 (see Illinois Digital Archives); "Medill Has Served as Mine Director Under 3 Governors," *SLPD*, 2 April 1947, 3; "Medill Owed Job as Mine Bureau Head to Operators," *SLPD*, 9 April 1947, 3.

13. Hartley and Kenney, *Death Underground*, 73–77.

14. U.S. Senate Special Subcommittee of the Committee on Public Lands, *Investigation of Mine Explosion at Centralia*, testimony of Robert M. Medill, p. 139.

15. Hartley and Kenney, *Death Underground*, 79–81.

16. U.S. Senate Special Subcommittee of the Committee on Public Lands, *Investigation of Mine Explosion at Centralia*, testimony of Robert M. Medill, pp. 138–42.

17. Ibid.

18. Harry Wilensky, "Mine Operators 'Shaken Down' by G.O.P. for Funds in Chicago Fight," *SLPD*, 19 March 1947. Wilensky's coverage of the mine disaster helped win a Pulitzer Prize for the *Post-Dispatch*.

19. Ibid.

20. Martin, *Adlai Stevenson of Illinois*, 266; Roosevelt University, "History of Chicago from Trading Post to Metropolis," 4.

21. Martin, *Adlai Stevenson of Illinois*, 279.

22. Watters, *Illinois in the Second World War*, 511–13.

23. Hartley and Kenney, *Death Underground*, 73–81. The strife between Medill and Scanlan is documented in notes kept by Scanlan and in correspondence.

24. Centralia United Mine Workers Local 52 to Governor Dwight Green, 3 March 1946, Driscoll Scanlan Papers; "Miners Protested 'State Negligence,'" *Centralia Sentinel*, 27 March 1947.

25. John William Chapman to Medill, 11 March 1946, Driscoll Scanlan Papers.

26. Scanlan, "Mine Inspection Report (18–19 March 1947)," 7, photostat, Illinois Department of Mines and Minerals files, Illinois Department of Natural Resources, Benton.

27. Hartley and Kenney, *Death Underground*, 58-59.

28. "Whose Guilt?" *SLPD*, 26 March 1947, reprinted in special section on 30 April 1947.

29. "Senate Votes Mine Blast Inquiry as Hope Dims for 104 in Illinois," *New York Times*, 27 March 1947, 1.

30. "Impeachment Threat to Green in Mine Disaster," *SLPD*, 27 March 1947, 1.

31. "Inspector Blames Medill, Says He 'Took Chances,'" *SLPD*, 31 March 1947, 1.

32. Ibid.

33. Qtd. in Hartley and Kenney, *Death Underground*, 91.

34. Scanlan statement to Legislative Investigating Committee, 24 April 1947, Driscoll Scanlan Papers.

35. Qtd. in Hartley and Kenney, *Death Underground*, 102.

36. "Centralia's Whitewash," *St. Louis Star-Times*, 26 April 1947.

37. Qtd. in Rakove, *We Don't Want Nobody Nobody Sent*, 11–12.

38. Ibid., 11.

39. Schapsmeier and Schapsmeier, "Paul H. Douglas," 308–18. The article provides details of Douglas's activities prior to 1947.

40. Qtd. in Martin, *Adlai Stevenson of Illinois*, 274.

41. Biles, *Crusading Liberal*, 42–43.

42. Martin, *Adlai Stevenson of Illinois*, 48–259, 211. Barone, *Our Country*, 251, gives a complete but more succinct account of Stevenson's career.

43. The majority owners of the *Pantagraph*, the Merwin family, favored Republican candidates for high office in Illinois, causing periodic anguish for the Stevensons. At one point, Stevenson suggested the Merwins should take editorial endorsements to the board of directors for approval. The reply was that the board did not interfere with endorsement decisions.

44. Martin, *Adlai Stevenson of Illinois*, 125–27.

45. Ibid., 168–77. This put Stevenson in direct opposition to isolationist thinking among Illinois citizens and to the *Chicago Tribune* editorial page.

46. Ibid., 186. Knox's service with Roosevelt did not endear him to the *Tribune*, in spite of his Republican credentials.

47. Ibid., 239–50. Martin provides details of Stevenson's U.N. service.

48. Rakove, *We Don't Want Nobody Nobody Sent*, 11.

49. Lucas, autobiographical fragment, 4–5. See also Arvey, "Gold Nugget," 50–51.

50. Martin, *Adlai Stevenson of Illinois*, 270.

51. Mitchell, "Adlai's Amateurs," 67; Arvey, "Gold Nugget," 51–52.

52. Qtd. in Rakove, *We Don't Want Nobody Nobody Sent*, 10.

53. Arvey, "Gold Nugget," 52.

54. David Camelon, "How the First GI Bill Was Written," *American Legion Magazine*, February 1969, 22–26, 48–51. See also the Education Commission of the States, "John H. Stelle," James Bryant Conant Award, 2004. The citation identifies Stelle as "Father of the GI Bill." The award recognizes individuals who have had a profound impact on American education.

55. Hartley, "'I Worked for My Friends.'"

56. Hartley, *Paul Powell*, 89.

57. Qtd. in Littlewood, *Horner of Illinois*, 244. Milburn P. Akers, "Stelle Feuds Leave Scars in Party Ranks," *Chicago Sun-Times*, 8 July 1962. Akers, who quarreled with Stelle for more than twenty years, quoted his adversary as saying on his deathbed, "I worked for my friends."

58. "Machine Politicians Sidetracked as Democrats Plan State Ticket," *Chicago Sun*, 6 October 1947, 8. The following day, Akers, the *Sun*'s managing editor, wrote "Stelle Bid to Rule State Democrats Rebuffed."

59. "Slate Group to Act Today on Stevenson," *Chicago Tribune*, 29 December 1947.

60. Lucas, autobiographical fragment, 5–7.

61. Mitchell, "Adlai's Amateurs," 70; Arvey, "Gold Nugget," 50.

62. Qtd. in Rakove, *We Don't Want Nobody Nobody Sent*, 10; Martin, *Adlai Stevenson of Illinois*, 278–79.

63. Lucas, autobiographical fragment, 10–11.

64. Ibid., 11.

65. Qtd. in Rakove, *We Don't Want Nobody Nobody Sent*, 11.

66. Milburn P. Akers, "Kennelly Could Forget Lucas, Maybe He Did!," *Chicago Sun*, 1 January 1948.

67. "Let Issues Be the Test," *Chicago Sun*, 9 October 1947.

68. Kenney, *Political Passage*, 59; "Rowe Decides He'll Run for Lt. Governor," *Chicago Tribune*, 23 December 1947; "State GOP Shocked by Rowe Switch," *Chicago Daily News*, 23 December 1947.

69. "Cross, Wright Battle Green for Nomination," *Chicago Daily News*, 20 December 1947; "Wright, Cross to Enter Race for Governor," *Chicago Tribune*, 20 December 1947.

70. "Green Announces for 3rd Term," *Chicago Daily News*, 3 January 1948; "Green to Run Again," *Chicago Sun*, 4 January 1948; "Green and Brooks to Run Again," *Chicago Tribune*, 4 January 1948.

71. Smith, *Colonel*, 410–11, 460.

72. Ibid., 411.

73. Ibid., 460. In regard to McCormick, Knight said, "I fight my own fights, but I have no desire to inherit the quarrels of others."

74. Smith, *Colonel*, 460. The two most complete sources of *Chicago Tribune* history are Wendt, *"Chicago Tribune,"* and Smith, *Colonel*. This brief history is taken from both.

A more recent discussion of the *Tribune*'s editorial policy is Lemelin, "Isolationist Newspaper in an Internationalist Era."

75. Martin, *Adlai Stevenson of Illinois*, 208–9.

76. Ibid., 273–74.

77. Milburn P. Akers, "Cross to Slash Out in Series of Attacks on Green's Regime," *Chicago Sun*, 4 January 1948.

78. Tagge, preface to oral history.

79. Howard, oral history memoir, 100–102, 122.

80. Trohan, oral history interview, biographical information, 1.

81. "A Brief History of the *Globe-Democrat*," *St. Louis Globe-Democrat*, 1 July 1977.

82. Two books about the *Post-Dispatch* have been written by Daniel Pfaff: *Joseph Pulitzer II and the "Post-Dispatch": A Newspaperman's Life*, and *No Ordinary Joe: A Life of Joseph Pulitzer III*.

83. "Theodore C. Link Dies, Investigative Reporter," *SLPD*, 14 February 1974.

3. OPENING BLOWS

1. "The State Issues Drawn," *Chicago Sun*, 3 January 1948.

2. "State Democrats May Split Over Choice of Candidates," *Chicago Sun*, 1 January 1948; "Democrats Get Hint of Rival Slate," *Chicago Tribune*, 1 January 1948; Milburn P. Akers, "Kennelly Could Forget Lucas, Maybe He Did!," *Chicago Sun*, 1 January 1948.

3. "No Deals—But—," *Chicago Daily News*, 22 January 1948.

4. "'Aid Europe' Is Stevenson Campaign Cry," *Chicago Tribune*, 7 January 1948.

5. "As We See It," *Chicago Daily News*, 31 December 1947; "Opposition to Green Must Prove Leadership," *Chicago Daily News*, 15 December 1947.

6. "Green and Brooks to Run Again," *Chicago Tribune*, 4 January 1948.

7. "Cross Now All-Out for Governor Job," *Chicago Daily News*, 21 January 1948. See also Milburn P. Akers, "Cross to Slash Out in Series of Attacks on Green's Regime," *Chicago Sun*, 4 January 1948.

8. "Wright Files for Governor and Rips Foes," *Chicago Tribune*, 27 January 1948.

9. Milburn P. Akers, "Gov. Green Seeks 3rd Term Despite Attacks on FDR," *Chicago Sun*, 5 January 1948.

10. General Assembly of the State of Illinois, *Journal of the House of Representatives*, 15–27.

11. Ibid.

12. Ibid.

13. "Brooks, Green, Campaign," *Chicago Daily News*, 21 January 1948.

14. "Cross Charges Green Wants to Perpetuate Himself as Governor," *Chicago Tribune*, 4 January 1948.

15. "Cross Opens Attack on 'Green Machine,'" *Chicago Daily News*, 23 January 1948.

16. "Wright Files for Governor and Rips Foes," *Chicago Tribune*, 27 January 1948.

17. "2 Withdraw, Clear Track for Governor," *Chicago Tribune*, 2 February 1948.

18. Howard, oral history memoir, 103–4.

19. "G.O.P. Slates E. H. Droste as Treasurer," *Chicago Tribune*, 25 January 1948. See also "Primary Petition Forged by State G.O.P. Machine," *Chicago Daily News*, 10 May 1948.

20. Douglas, *In the Fullness of Time*, 136; Biles, *Crusading Liberal*, 49; Martin, *Adlai Stevenson of Illinois*, 295.

21. Douglas, *In the Fullness of Time*, 136.

22. Lucas, autobiographical fragment, 12. Lucas had a roller-coaster relationship with Stevenson. In 1950, when Lucas ran for reelection, Stevenson gave tepid backing.

23. Martin, *Adlai Stevenson of Illinois*, 294–95.

24. Lucas, autobiographical fragment, 12.

25. "Democrats' Campaign to Begin March 1," *Chicago Tribune*, 15 February 1948.

26. "Green Hits Democrat Socialism," *Chicago Tribune*, 7 February 1948.

27. Ibid.

28. "Waukegan Rally to Launch G.O.P. Campaign Saturday," *Chicago Tribune*, 3 February 1948.

29. "Green Hits Democrat Socialism," *Chicago Tribune*, 7 February 1948.

30. Charles N. Wheeler, "Stevenson Vows to Smash 'Green Machine,'" *Chicago Daily News*, 24 February 1948. See also "Test New Deal Ideas in State, Says Stevenson," *Chicago Tribune*, 24 February 1948; and Martin, *Adlai Stevenson of Illinois*, 303–4.

31. "Aid Means Tax Boost, Brooks Says," *Chicago Tribune*, 11 February 1948.

32. "Brooks Lashes Government as No. 1 Monopoly," *Chicago Tribune*, 24 February 1948.

33. Barone, *Our Country*, 216.

34. Qtd. in Roberts and Klibanoff, *Race Beat*, 39–40.

35. Ibid., 39.

36. Qtd. in ibid., 40, 41.

37. "Anti-lynch Law Asked by Truman," *Chicago Tribune*, 2 February 1948; Roberts and Klibanoff, *Race Beat*, 40; "Truman Faces Dixie Revolt over Civil Rights," *Chicago Daily News*, 5 February 1948; McCoy, *Presidency of Harry S. Truman*, 107.

38. "Truman's Message: Civil Rights," *Chicago Daily News*, 6 February 1948.

39. Henning Heldt, "Frustrated Dixie Democrats Squirm," *Chicago Daily News*, 10 February 1948.

40. Walter Trohan, "Talk of Break in Solid South is Pooh-poohed," *Chicago Tribune*, 8 February 1948; "Dixie Chiefs Spurned; Vow to Push War," *Chicago Tribune*, 23 February 1948.

41. Ambrose, *Eisenhower*, 2:459–60.

42. Barone, *Our Country*, 217.

43. *Chicago Sun-Times*, 9 February 1948.

44. "Legal Action Threat to Green for Return of Million in 'Slush,'" *Chicago Sun-Times*, 21 March 1948.

45. "Stevenson Assails Green's Collections," *Chicago Sun-Times*, 23 March 1948.

46. David Anderson, "Green's Vow of '41 on Civil Service Rings Hollow in '48," *Chicago Sun-Times*, 11 October 1948; see also "Green Machine Puts Bite on Civil Service," *Chicago Sun-Times*, 12 October 1948.

47. Milburn P. Akers, "A Self-Indictment by Green," *Chicago Sun-Times*, 11 October 1948.

48. George Tagge, "Limit Illinois Employees to One G.O.P. Gift," *Chicago Tribune*, 17 February 1948.

49. "Truman Says He Will Run if Nominated," *Chicago Tribune*, 9 March 1948; "Remember Me?," editorial, *Chicago Tribune*, 9 March 1948.

50. Martin, "Blast in Centralia No. 5," 193–220.

51. Ibid., 211–12.

52. "Green Lax on Mines: Stevenson," *Chicago Sun-Times*, 25 March 1948.

53. "Centralia Marks 1st Blast Anniversary," *Chicago Sun-Times*, 25 March 1948.

54. "Stevenson Rips Politics in Mines," *Chicago Daily News*, 2 March 1948; Martin, *Adlai Stevenson of Illinois*, 308.

55. "Storm Plagues Democrats in Hunt for Votes," *Chicago Tribune*, 2 March 1948.

56. "Stevenson Rips Politics in Mines," *Chicago Daily News*, 2 March 1948.

57. "Green Makes Pawns of Pupils—Stevenson," *Chicago Daily News*, 3 March 1948.

58. Ibid.

59. Charles N. Wheeler, "Democrats Bypass Tax Split Issue," *Chicago Daily News*, 4 March 1948.

60. Thomas Morrow, "State Pay Roll Cut Demanded by Stevenson," *Chicago Tribune*, 4 March 1948; Martin, *Adlai Stevenson of Illinois*, 309.

61. "Douglas Assails G.O.P.," *Chicago Tribune*, 4 March 1948; Charles N. Wheeler, "Stevenson Hits '47 Legislature," *Chicago Daily News*, 5 March 1948.

62. Thomas Morrow, "Stevenson Hits Green's Regime as Scandalous," *Chicago Tribune*, 6 March 1948.

63. "G.O.P. Can End Confusion, Say Brooks, Green," *Chicago Tribune*, 6 March 1948.

64. Qtd. in Martin, *Adlai Stevenson of Illinois*, 310; "Douglas Urges New Housing," *Chicago Daily News*, 12 March 1948.

65. "Not about Pants," *Chicago Sun-Times*, 21 March 1948.

66. "Green Replies to Stevenson Assembly Rap," *Chicago Tribune*, 12 March 1948; "Striped Pants Buffoonery," editorial, *Chicago Tribune*, 15 March 1948.

67. "Truman Echoes New Deal's War Cry, Green Says," *Chicago Tribune*, 19 March 1948.

68. "Douglas Urges New Housing," *Chicago Daily News*, 12 March 1948.

69. "Women Hear Stevenson in Attack on G.O.P.," *Chicago Tribune*, 31 March 1948; Douglas, *Fullness of Time*, 130–40. See also Biles, *Crusading Liberal*, 47.

70. "Brooks Rips Europe Aid as Drain on Tax Payer," *Chicago Tribune*, 13 March 1948.

71. "Arvey Informs Leader Truman Has Weakened," *Chicago Tribune*, 25 March 1948; Rakove, *We Don't Want Nobody Nobody Sent*, 10; "Arvey Out for Eisenhower," *Chicago Sun-Times*, 26 March 1948.

72. "Former Mayor Kelly Backing Truman Again," *Chicago Tribune*, 26 March 1948.

73. Ibid.; "New Dealers Now Back Ike against Truman," *Chicago Tribune*, 28 March 1948.

74. "Disclose Ike Will Not Run as a Democrat," *Chicago Tribune*, 29 March 1948.

4. A TIME FOR CEREMONIES

1. Robert P. Howard, "5 in Each Party Are Unopposed for State Jobs," *Chicago Tribune*, 1 April 1948.

2. Robert P. Howard, "Issues Sharply Drawn for Top Primary Races," *Chicago Tribune*, 1 April 1948.

3. "Democrats Pin Faith on Vets," *Chicago Sun*, 4 January 1948.

4. "Turnout Hits New Low as 30 Pct. Vote," *Chicago Tribune*, 13 April 1948; "3 Parties Map Lines for Fall Battle Royal," *Chicago Tribune*, 14 April 1948.

5. Madison West, "Local Democrats Glum," *Chicago Daily News*, 9 April 1948.

6. "Progressives Lose Last Ballot Hope," *Chicago Daily News*, 12 April 1948. See also John Dreiske, "Third Party's Bid to Enliven Fight in State Primary," *Chicago Sun-Times*, 11 April 1948.

7. "Wallace Raps N. U. 'Pressure,'" *Chicago Daily News*, 28 April 1948; "U.S. Senate Race Poses Problem for M'Dougall," *Chicago Tribune*, 28 April 1948. See also "As We See It," editorial, *Chicago Daily News*, 29 April 1948.

8. Walter Trohan, "Ike Reiterates His Refusal to Be a Candidate," *Chicago Tribune*, 11 April 1948.

9. "Arvey Goes to Tell Kelly: Quit Truman," *Chicago Tribune*, 15 April 1948.

10. "Kelly Repeats That He's Still a Truman Man," *Chicago Tribune*, 21 April 1948. See also "Mr. Truman, Mr. Arvey, and the Southern Revolt," editorial, *Chicago Tribune*, 22 April 1948; and Martin, *Adlai Stevenson of Illinois*, 312–13.

11. Smith, *Colonel*, 478. Brownell told Smith of his plan in 1993.

12. Charles N. Wheeler, "GOP Names Green Keynoter of Convention," *Chicago Daily News*, 20 April 1948; "Keynote Role Boosts Stock of Gov. Green," *Chicago Tribune*, 20 April 1948; "Why Gov. Green Heads Convention," *Chicago Tribune*, 21 April 1948; Madison West, "Gov. Green, Keynoter," *Chicago Daily News*, 23 April 1948.

13. Hartley, "'I Worked for My Friends.'"

14. Hartley, *Paul Powell*, 28–29.

15. Adlai E. Stevenson, speech, McLeansboro, Ill., 10 April 1948, Adlai E. Stevenson Papers, Princeton University. The Stevenson quotes in the next few paragraphs are from this speech.

16. Howard, oral history memoir, 84.

17. "Paul H. Douglas Explains His Stand for High Taxes," *Chicago Daily News*, 14 April 1948.

18. "'Liberal' Republicans," editorial, *Chicago Tribune*, 1 May 1948. The quotes in the next few paragraphs are from this editorial.

19. "G.O.P. Record in State and U.S. Praised," *Chicago Tribune*, 10 May 1948.

20. "GOP Opens State Convention," *Chicago Daily News*, 10 May 1948.

21. Ibid.

22. Howard, oral history memoir, 103.

23. Smith, *Colonel*, 479.

24. "Primary Petition Forged by State G.O.P. Machine," *Chicago Daily News*, 10 May 1948.

25. "Touhy Opens Probe, Hints Strong Case," *Chicago Daily News*, 10 May 1948.

26. "Droste Quiz Nears Dead End," *Chicago Daily News*, 2 June 1948.

27. Ibid.

28. "Former Candidate Rides 2 Payrolls," *Chicago Daily News*, 7 May 1948.

29. "I'm for Truman, Up to Minute, Kelly Explains," *Chicago Tribune*, 6 May 1948; "'I Am Sticking to Truman': Kelly," *Chicago Daily News*, 7 May 1948.

30. "Arvey Idea: Mayor for President," *Chicago Daily News*, 2 May 1948; "Ike Prefers Role as an Educator," *Chicago Daily News*, 22 May 1948.

31. "Arvey Reported in Maneuver to Ditch Truman," *Chicago Tribune*, 23 May 1948.

32. Robert P. Howard, "Played Bridge, Not Politics—Arvey Retorts," *Chicago Tribune*, 24 May 1948.

33. "Arvey Hangs Up 'Quiet' Sign on Nomination," *Chicago Tribune*, 28 May 1948.

34. "Democrats Open State Campaign," *Chicago Daily News*, 27 May 1948.

35. "Lucas Boards Train to Guide Truman's Venture into Illinois," *Chicago Sun-Times*, 4 June 1948; Martin, *Adlai Stevenson of Illinois*, 325.

36. "Stevenson Blasts 'Corruption and Theft' in Green Regime," *Chicago Daily News*, 27 May 1948.

37. "McDougall Will Run for Senate as Progressive," *Chicago Tribune*, 7 May 1948.

38. Madison West, "GOP Aids MacDougall?," *Chicago Daily News*, 14 May 1948.

39. "Avers Douglas Does Flip-Flop on Red Issue," *Chicago Tribune*, 6 May 1948; Biles, *Crusading Liberal*, 13–14. Biles provides a summary of the Russian trip and Douglas's reactions. See also Schapsmeier and Schapsmeier, "Paul H. Douglas," 310.

40. Douglas, *In the Fullness of Time*, 50.

41. "Avers Douglas Does Flip-Flop on Red Issue," *Chicago Tribune*, 6 May 1948.

42. Milburn P. Akers, "Fight on Douglas by Progressives Hints Ugly Motive," *Chicago Sun-Times*, 21 January 1948.

43. "Truman Off This Week on Selling Trip," *Chicago Tribune*, 30 May 1948.

44. "Expect Truman Trip to Put Him Back in Race," *Chicago Tribune*, 10 May 1948.

45. "Truman Junket Nonpolitical, Country Told," *Chicago Tribune*, 7 May 1948.

46. "Kennelly, Not Arvey, to List Guests Asked to Truman Dinner," *Chicago Tribune*, 1 June 1948; "Busy Visit for Truman Planned Here," *Chicago Daily News*, 1 June 1948. See also "Kennelly Gives Out Listing of Dinner Guests," *Chicago Tribune*, 4 June 1948.

47. "3 Flags Sent to Sweden as City's Greeting," *Chicago Tribune*, 5 June 1948.

48. "Warns Laws Can't Check Communism," *Chicago Tribune*, 4 June 1948. See also "Text of President's Talk at Stadium/Truman Makes Plea for DPs," *Chicago Tribune*, 4 June 1948.

49. "Warns Laws Can't Check Communism, *Chicago Tribune*, 4 June 1948; "Text of President's Talk at Stadium/Truman Makes Plea for DPs," *Chicago Tribune*, 4 June 1948.

50. "Text of President's Talk at Stadium/Truman Makes Plea for DPs," *Chicago Tribune*, 4 June 1948; "As We See It," *Chicago Daily News*, 7 June 1948.

51. "Lucas Chooses Not to Run for Vice President," *Chicago Tribune*, 6 June 1948; Madison West, "Lucas Key Campaigner," *Chicago Daily News*, 11 June 1948.

52. Smith, *Colonel*, 479–80; Trohan, *Political Animals*, 232–33.

53. "Tribune Editor Backs Stassen for No. 2 Spot," interview with Robert McCormick, *Chicago Tribune*, 21 June 1948. He said, "Stassen is strong with the young people but mature people think he lacks maturity."

54. "Col. McCormick Asks for Taft, Stassen Ticket," *Chicago Tribune*, 22 June 1948; John Knight, "Green's Ambition a Factor in Appraising GOP Entries," *Chicago Daily News*, 19 June 1948. At the end of his column, Knight quoted Charles Ross, Truman's press secretary: "It's much too early to sell that little guy [Truman] short."

55. Walter Trohan, "Keynoter Rips 'Bosses, Boodle, and Buncombe' of Democrats," *Chicago Tribune*, 21 June 1948.

56. Text of Governor Green's keynote speech, *Chicago Tribune*, 21 June 1948.

57. On the second ballot, the delegation gave 50 of 56 votes to Taft. Dewey received 5; Speaker of the House Joseph W. Martin Jr. received 1. Tally from the *Chicago Tribune*, 25 June 1948.

58. "Illinois Sticks to Its Guns in Fight for Taft," *Chicago Tribune*, 24 June 1948.

59. "The Nomination," editorial, *Tribune*, 25 June 1948.

60. McCullough, *Truman*, 635.

61. Ferrell, *Off the Record*, 141. See also McCullough, *Truman*, 634.

62. George Tagge, "Arvey Predicts Eisenhower to Win Nomination," *Chicago Tribune*, 1 July 1948.

63. "Call Off State Meet as Arvey Fights Truman," *Chicago Tribune*, 2 July 1948.

64. "Nomination Intentions Clarified by General," *Chicago Tribune*, 5 July 1948. McCullough, *Truman*, 633, reiterates that followers of Eisenhower were not dissuaded by his statements. Ambrose, *Eisenhower*, 1:477, 478, lays out details of Eisenhower's indecision about politics.

65. "Shocked Arvey Sees a Maybe in 'No' by Ike," *Chicago Tribune*, 6 July 1948. See also "Ike's 'No' Puts Party in Turmoil," *Chicago Tribune*, 6 July 1948.

66. "Eisenhower's Withdrawal," editorial, *Chicago Tribune*, 8 July 1948.

67. McCullough, *Truman*, 635, states that after Eisenhower's final "no," Truman called William O. Douglas to say he was the president's choice for vice president, but Douglas later declined. "Ike's 3rd 'No' Ends Plan to Stop Truman," *Chicago Tribune*, 9 July 1948.

68. "Arvey Joins Scramble to Truman Camp," *Chicago Tribune*, 9 July 1948; "Boom Swings from Ike Back to President," *Chicago Tribune*, 8 July 1948; "Illinois Caucus Likely on Train to Convention," *Chicago Tribune*, 8 July 1948.

69. Qtd. in Rakove, *We Don't Want Nobody Nobody Sent*, 18.

70. Qtd. in McCullough, *Truman*, 636.

71. "Illinois Group Backs Truman Unanimously," *Chicago Tribune*, 11 July 1948.

72. "Democrats Square Off for Floor Fight Between North and South," *Chicago Tribune*, 10 July 1948. See also Donaldson, *Truman Defeats Dewey*, 160.

73. Douglas, *In the Fullness of Time*, 132–35; "Dixie Routed on Civil Rights; Some Walk Out," *Chicago Tribune*, 14 July 1948. In "Civil Rights," editorial, *Chicago Tribune*, 15 July 1948, the newspaper condemned all sides in the controversy, claiming provisions of the 14th Amendment to the Constitution could be used to guarantee civil rights.

74. George Tagge, "Kelly and Stelle Meet—and Harmony Takes a Walk," *Chicago Tribune*, 12 July 1948.

75. "Divided Illinois Delegation to Back Barkley," *Chicago Tribune*, 13 July 1948.

76. "Rebels Pick Wright for No. 2 Spot," *Chicago Tribune*, 17 July 1948.

77. "3rd Party Group Soon to Leave for Convention," *Chicago Tribune*, 18 July 1948.

78. "3rd Party Loses High Court Move in Ballot Fight," *Chicago Tribune*, 20 July 1948. The *Tribune* editorial page continued to pillory Henry Wallace in "Mr. Wallace's Astral Self," in which it referred to those likely to vote for the candidate as "wobblies, Communists, bumpkins, and boob[s]."

79. Adlai E. Stevenson, speech at Soldiers and Sailors Reunion, 27 July 1948, pp. 15–16, Adlai E. Stevenson Papers, Princeton University Library.

80. Ibid., 16–17.

81. Ibid.

82. John Dreiske, "Green's 'Pirates' Assailed," *Chicago Sun-Times*, 27 July 1948.

83. "Prof. Douglas, Stevenson Rip G.O.P. on Prices," *Chicago Tribune*, 27 July 1948.

84. "G.O.P. Strides Recounted by Brooks, Green," *Chicago Tribune*, 28 July 1948.

85. Ibid.

86. "Gang Remnants Gathering for Shelton Rites," *Chicago Tribune*, 28 July 1948. See also "Shelton Gang on Last Ride with the Chief," *Chicago Tribune*, 30 July 1948; and "Shelton Brother Slain from Ambush," *Chicago Sun-Times*, 27 July 1948.

87. Jim Wiggs, "Jerome J. Munie," *Metro-East Journal*, 26 April 1964.

5. BEGINNING OF THE END

1. Carl Baldwin, "Underworld, Politics Were This Reporter's Beats," *SLPD*, 28 February 1974. Baldwin worked with and observed Link up close for many years.

2. Ibid. This lengthy article raised, but did not settle, the issue of Link's relationship with the Shelton gang.

3. Ibid. See also "Theodore C. Link Dies, Investigative Reporter," *SLPD*, 14 February 1974.

4. See Pensoneau, *Brothers Notorious*. While newspapers provided extensive coverage of the Shelton gang, Pensoneau brought it all together in book form.

5. Jim Wiggs, "Jerome J. Munie," *Metro-East Journal*, 26 April 1964. Wiggs provided a complete history of Munie's battle with the Shelton brothers.

6. "Man Who Routed Sheltons Convinced of Gang War," *East St. Louis Journal*, 24 October 1947. A search of state documents from the Horner administration conducted by F. Kimball Efird, Illinois State Archives archivist, was unable to unearth any official commission begun by the governor. However, Efird concluded that funds could have been provided to Munie from various funds for which no record was required. See also "East Side's Secret Crime Commission Launches Clean-up," *St. Louis Star*, 26 January 1934.

7. Tom Duffy, "Jerry Munie: Gangbuster," *East St. Louis Journal*, 5 March 1961.

8. "Disclosure by the *Post-Dispatch* of 'Gatewood Recordings' Set Off Probe of Gambling, Protection," *SLPD*, 3 September 1948 (hereafter "Disclosure"). The article provided a summary of disclosures and newspaper articles beginning 6 August, most of which were written by Ted Link. The paper published articles by Link and other reporters on 6, 7, 9, 10, 11, 13, 15, 16, 17, 19, 27, and 29 August. Most were revelations of events prior to August, as investigated by *Post-Dispatch* reporters.

9. "The Gatewood Recording: Transcript of Bribe Parley Between Bernie Shelton and Self-Styled Intermediary," *SLPD*, 3 September 1948.

10. Theodore C. Link, "Widespreading Vice and Gambling with Heavy Payoffs to Officials Bared by *Post-Dispatch* Reporter," *SLPD*, 24 October 1948 (hereafter "Widespreading Vice").

11. The Petrakos interrogation in July became a central issue in subsequent questions about Link's involvement with the Sheltons and what happened in Link's hotel room on 30 July. Carl Baldwin, in "Underworld, Politics Were This Reporter's Beats," *SLPD*, 28 February 1974, said, "What went on in the hotel room probably has never been fully told."

12. "Widespreading Vice." The *Post-Dispatch* reported Hull's reaction on 7 August.

13. "Subpoena 8 in Shelton Bribe Probe," *Chicago Tribune*, 22 August 1948. The paper used some material from Link's disclosures as background.

14. "Widespreading Vice." The Gatewood tapes were turned over to the prosecutor by the *Post-Dispatch*.

15. "Peorians Urge State to Start Clean-up Probe," *Chicago Tribune*, 25 August 1948.

16. "Peoria Known as Open Town for Many Years," *Chicago Tribune*, 11 August 1948.

17. Ibid.

18. Pensoneau, *Brothers Notorious*, 249; "Widespreading Vice." See also "Disclosure."

19. Roy J. Harris, "Evidence of Vice, No Indictments by Grand Jury at Springfield, Ill.," *SLPD*, 21 October 1948. Also, accounts appeared in "Widespreading Vice" and "Disclosure."

20. "Disclosure."

21. "Sin in Illinois," editorial, *Chicago Tribune*, 13 August 1948.

22. "Two Senatorial Candidates to Address Picnic," *Chicago Tribune*, 24 August 1948.

23. "Sen. Brooks Rejects Bid to Debate Rival," *Chicago Tribune*, 25 August 1948.

24. "Green Vows War on U.S. Rule of National Guard," *Chicago Tribune*, 23 August 1948.

25. Resolution Committee, Local 52, United Mine Workers of America, Centralia, Ill., 7 August 1948, copy in author's files.

26. Theodore C. Link, "Gamblers Again Raising Green Campaign Funds, Gave Him $100,000 in 1944," *SLPD*, 1 September 1948.

27. Carl Baldwin, "Underworld, Politics Were This Reporter's Beats," *SLPD*, 28 February 1974.

28. Tick surfaced later in the paper's exposé: Theodore C. Link, "Favored Illinois Liquor Combine Fattens on Trade in 3 Dry States," *SLPD*, 22 September 1948. Link wrote that Tick "enjoys the profitable and exclusive privilege of exporting liquor into dry states through an arrangement with distillers who control the liquor supply."

29. Fitzpatrick's distinctive style when drawing about corruption and crime was to use heavy black or dark gray colors and pictures of Governor Green with "Gambling Campaign Funds" behind him and of a large slot machine holding "corrupt officials" and labeled "The Illinois bandit's other arm." The editorial page presented commentary during September on almost every major disclosure by the paper's reporters and on events in Springfield and Peoria.

30. Carl Baldwin, "Illinois' 'Invisible Governor' Has Big Gambler Friend," *SLPD*, 2 September 1948.

31. "A Look at 'The Invisible Governor," editorial, *SLPD*, 3 September 1948.

32. Theodore C. Link, "How Gambling Payoffs Began," *SLPD*, 10 September 1948.

33. Herbert A. Trask, "FBI Inquiry on Illinois Kickbacks Ordered," *SLPD*, 10 September 1948.

34. Articles in the *Post-Dispatch* that followed Stevenson's attempt to put pressure on Green included "Stevenson Asks for Word from Green on Peoria," 4 September 1948; "Stevenson Says Illinois Is Tired of 'Greed Gang,'" 7 September 1948; and "Stevenson Asks Green to Speak Up about Gambling," 9 September 1948.

35. Roy J. Harris, "Green Meets Ministers, Puts Law Enforcement Up to Local Officials," *SLPD*, 14 September 1948.

36. "Stevenson Lays Defeat of Crime Commission Bills to Green," *SLPD*, 24 September 1948; "Stevenson Asks Green to Speak Up about Gambling," *SLPD*, 9 September 1948. See also "Stevenson Hits Green's Stand on Crime Bills," *Chicago Tribune*, 23 September 1948.

37. "Green Answers Stevenson on Gambling Issue," *Chicago Tribune*, 28 September 1948.

38. Ibid.

39. Carl Baldwin, "Underworld, Politics Were This Reporter's Beats," *SLPD*, 28 February 1974.

40. Theodore C. Link, "Prosecutor's Aid, Somogyi, Named in True Bills on Gaming Payoffs," *SLPD*, 3 September 1948. See also "Peoria's Indicted State's Attorney Will Prosecute Indicted Sheriff," *SLPD*, 8 September 1948.

41. "The People Act," editorial, *SLPD*, 4 September 1948.

42. Theodore C. Link, "Hull Says He Will Direct New Grand Jury Inquiry in Peoria Gambling," *SLPD*, 4 September 1948.

43. "No Job for Roy Hull," editorial, *SLPD*, 5 September 1948.

44. Roy J. Harris, "Vice Payoff to Officials Uncovered at Springfield," *SLPD*, 7 September 1948.

45. "No Lawlessness in Illinois?," editorial, *SLPD*, 8 September 1948.

46. Roy J. Harris, "Second Barrett Employee Identified as Collector of Graft from Gamblers," *SLPD*, 9 September 1948.

47. "State Names 2 to War on Crime, Vice," *Chicago Tribune*, 12 September 1948.

48. "Investigator for Barrett Being Investigated Himself," *SLPD*, 15 September 1948.

49. "Barrett 'Errand Boy' in Charge of Peoria Inquiry," *SLPD*, 16 September 1948.

50. Roy J. Harris, "Denial of Special Prosecutor for Inquiry Resented at Springfield," *SLPD*, 18 September 1948. See also "Fight for Special Prosecutor to Go On at Springfield," *SLPD*, 18 September 1948. These are also the sources of the ruling and responses found in the next paragraph.

51. Carl Baldwin, "Green Urges Men Allowing Gaming Be Re-elected," *SLPD*, 17 September 1948.

52. "Green, Brooks, Blast 'Tricky' New Deal Drive," *Chicago Tribune*, 3 September 1948.

53. "Green Promises to Push Rural Road Program," *Chicago Tribune*, 25 September 1948.

54. Arthur Evans, "How Green Kept Pledge on Economy," *Chicago Tribune*, 25 September 1948.

55. "Housing Plan of Green Held Model for U.S.," *Chicago Tribune*, 29 September 1948.

56. "Illinois Vets' Aid Piloted to Peak by Green," *Chicago Tribune*, 30 September 1948.

57. "Remap Battle Is Rated Major Green Victory," *Chicago Tribune*, 30 September 1948.

58. "Governor Asks More Output, Less Inflation," *Chicago Tribune*, 29 September 1948.

59. "Hails Labor Record," *Chicago Tribune*, 17 September 1948.

60. Adlai E. Stevenson, speech delivered at Mt. Vernon, Ill., 6 September 1948, pp. 6–8, Adlai E. Stevenson Papers. The quotes in the next several paragraphs are from this speech.

61. "Brooks Assails Vast Export of Electric Goods," *Chicago Tribune*, 5 September 1948; "Brooks Asks Aid of Women in Fight on Reds," *Chicago Tribune*, 8 September 1948.

62. "Brooks Assails Fuzziness of Fake Liberals," *Chicago Tribune*, 9 September 1948.

63. "Brooks Praises G.O.P. Congress for Its Realism," *Chicago Tribune*, 17 September 1948; "G.O.P. Regime Will Make U.S. Strong: Brooks," *Chicago Tribune*, 18 September 1948. See also "Back Taft Act, Brooks Appeals to Labor Ranks," *Chicago Tribune*, 29 September 1948.

64. "Brooks Brands Truman as Snag in Red Purge," *Chicago Tribune*, 30 September 1948.

65. "Brooks Defends Labor Law at Belleville Rally," *SLPD*, 16 September 1948; "Brooks Assures Remedy If Taft Law Is Faulty," *Chicago Tribune*, 16 September 1948.

66. George Tagge, "Brooks Meets Challenge of Labor Leaders," *Chicago Tribune*, 19 September 1948.

67. "Sen. Brooks: Spokesman for Illinois," editorial, *Chicago Tribune*, 13 September 1948.

68. "Douglas Backs 'Tradition,'" *Chicago Tribune*, 5 September 1948.

69. "Busbey Rips Douglas as Red Frontier," *Chicago Tribune*, 14 September 1948. See also "Busbey Blasts Prof. Douglas as 'Deceiver,'" *Chicago Tribune*, 19 September 1948; and "Busbey Queries Douglas about Red Charges," *Chicago Tribune*, 21 September 1948.

70. "Douglas Aids Hit Red Front Charge as 'Smear Tactics,'" *Chicago Tribune*, 14 September 1948.

71. Biles, *Crusading Liberal*, 50.

72. "Progressives File National, State Tickets," *Chicago Tribune*, 17 August 1948.

73. "Wallace Party Cannot Get on Illinois Ballot," *SLPD*, 1 September 1948; "3rd Party Will Ask Review of Ballot Denial," *Chicago Tribune*, 2 September 1948.

74. "The Wallace Petitions," editorial, *Chicago Tribune*, 4 September 1948.

75. "3rd Party Gets Ballot Spot in Cook County," *Chicago Tribune*, 3 September 1948.

76. "Ballot Loss in State Hit by Wallace," *Chicago Tribune*, 15 September 1948. See also Joseph Driscoll, "Uneasy Liberals in Wallace Party in Tight Pocket," *SLPD*, 5 September 1948.

77. "Candidate Attacked at W. Frankfort," *Chicago Tribune*, 3 September 1948.

78. "MacDougall's Party to Send Women Home," *Chicago Tribune*, 5 September 1948.

79. "Slight Dewey Gain in Presidency Poll," *Chicago Tribune*, 8 September 1948.

80. "Dewey Far Ahead in Press Support, Survey Shows," *SLPD*, 10 September 1948.

81. "Villages, Cities on Truman Route for Rigorous Two-Week Tour," *SLPD*, 10 September 1948.

82. Raymond P. Brandt, "Dewey Strategy: Be the Champ, Leave Truman to Hatchet Men," *SLPD*, 20 September 1948.

83. Joseph Driscoll, "Truman Meets the People in Vigorous Vote Drive," *SLPD*, 19 September 1948.

84. Walter Trohan, "Oratory Leaves Leaders of Both Parties Cold," *Chicago Tribune*, 27 September 1948.

85. Joseph Alsop, "Truman, Dewey Show Present Sad Contrast," *SLPD*, 22 September 1948.

86. Bray, "Recollections of the 1948 Campaign"; Thomas F. Reynolds, "Truman Rolls into Illinois in Wee Hours," *Chicago Sun-Times*, 18 September 1948. Portions of the Truman campaign stops during 1948 were published by Hartley, "Whistle Campaign Stopped Here." Permission to use the information was granted by Evelyn Taylor, editor.

87. McCullough, *Truman*, 653–54. The rail car was on display at the Gold Coast Railroad Museum in Miami, Fla.

88. Thomas W. Carter, "Truman Heard by 5,000 at Dawn," *Rock Island Argus*, 18 September 1948. The paper treated the brief visit with extensive written material and photographs. In "The Fighting Truman," editorial, *Rock Island Argus*, 18 September 1948, the paper stated, "It seems too much to expect that President Truman can extend Democratic tenancy of the White House beyond 16 years, but he is making a fight and the effort may help many local candidates to victory."

89. "Rear Platform and Other Informal Remarks in Illinois, Iowa and Missouri," 18 September 1948, Public Papers of the Presidents, 1945–53, Harry S. Truman (hereafter "Rear Platform").

90. James H. Payne, "Residents Rise Early to Hear, See President," *Rock Island Argus*, 18 September 1948; Richard N. Gage, "Truman Slaps G.O.P. Early; Rises at 4:45," ibid.

91. "It's Dewey Next; Governor to Give 25-Minute Talk at Spencer Park Monday Noon," *Rock Island Argus*, 18 September 1948.

92. George Wickstrom, "Dewey Talks before 12,000 in City," *Rock Island Argus*, 20 September 1948; "Eighty-one Reporters, Cameramen Ride with Dewey; Typewriters Hot," ibid.

93. Ross, *Loneliest Campaign*, 204.

94. Associated Press dispatch, 16 September 1948, dateline Washington, D.C.; Laurence Burd, "Truman Meets Cabinet on Eve of Stump Tour," *Chicago Tribune*, 17 September 1948; "Truman Leaves on Tour, Ready 'to Fight Hard,'" *Chicago Tribune*, 17 September 1948.

95. Carol Martin to author, 10 April 2006.

96. Reynolds, "Truman Invades Lewis-land," *Chicago Sun-Times*, 30 September 1948. See also "Truman Woos Miners in 8 Illinois Talks," ibid. The feud between Truman and Lewis dated to 1946, when the federal government seized coal mines across the nation to avoid a nationwide UMWA strike. See Dubofsky and Van Tine, *John L. Lewis*, 458–61.

97. "No Hand-Shaking by Truman Here," *Mt. Vernon Register-News*, 29 September 1948. In public statements to newspapers before, during, and after the motorcade, Powell reminded people that Truman was the first president to visit southern Illinois.

98. Bray, "Recollections of the 1948 Campaign," 17.

99. Lucas, autobiographical fragment, 12–13.

100. Remarks in Mt. Vernon, West Frankfort, Marion, Eldorado, and Carmi, Ill., 30 September 1948, in "Rear Platform."

101. Address at Southern Illinois University, Carbondale, 30 September 1948, Public Papers of the Presidents, 1945–53, Harry S. Truman; McCullough, *Truman*, 680–81.

102. Douglas, *In the Fullness of Time*, 138. See Guy Henry, "10,000 Greet Truman in Mt. Vernon," *Mt. Vernon Register-News*; "Highlights of Truman's Egypt Tour," *Mt. Vernon Register-News*; "Thousands Greet Truman Campaign Caravan Party through Southern Illinois," *Herrin Daily Journal*; and "Truman Blasts 80th Congress in Carmi Talk," *Carmi Democrat-Tribune*, all dated 30 September 1948.

103. "Proclamation!," *Herrin Daily Journal*, 29 September 1948.

104. "GOP Chairman Wants Students to See Truman," *Marion Daily Republican*, 27 September 1948.

105. Patsy Hicks, "Mr. Truman Tips Hat to Girl Editor," *Mt. Vernon Register-News*, 30 September 1948.

106. "Truman Visits Highlights," *Herrin Daily Journal*, 30 September 1948.

107. Ibid.

108. Remarks at West Frankfort and Herrin, Ill., 30 September 1948, in "Rear Platform."

109. "President Truman Visits Marion," *Marion Daily Republican*, 30 September 1948.

110. "Herrin Crowds 'Best Behaved' in Truman Tour," *Herrin Daily Journal*, 1 October 1948.

111. Douglas, *In the Fullness of Time*, 138.

112. V. Y. Dallman, "City Gives Truman Great Ovation," *Illinois State Register*, 13 October 1948.

113. "Truman Hits Congress in Carmi Talk," *Carmi Democrat-Tribune*, 30 September 1948.

6. THE CURTAIN FALLS

1. "Supreme Court Bars Wallace from Ballot," *Chicago Tribune*, 22 October 1948; "Wallace Plea Rejected," *New York Times*, 26 September 1948.

2. "3rd Party Turns to High Court in Ballot Fight," *Chicago Tribune*, 12 October 1948.

3. "State Says Ballot Ban Is Illegal," *Chicago Tribune*, 18 October 1948.

4. "Supreme Court Bars Wallace from Ballot," *Chicago Tribune*, 22 October 1948.

5. "Centralia Labor Withdraws Its Indorsement of Green Candidacy," *SLPD*, 19 October 1948; "Centralia Labor Assembly Withdraws Green Endorsement," *Centralia Sentinel*, 18 October 1948.

6. "Politics Is Topic for Simultaneous Meetings at Community Center," *Centralia Sentinel*, 23 October 1948. The *Post-Dispatch* published a photograph of Stevenson with officers of the III Club on 23 October 1948, captioned "Stevenson Talks with Miners' Wives." See also "Stevenson Seeks Miners' Support," *Centralia Sentinel*, 21 October 1948; "Stevenson Tells of Plans to End Politics in Mines," *SLPD*, 21 October 1948; and "Adlai in Mine Pledge," *Chicago Sun-Times*, 21 October 1948.

7. "Stevenson *Means* Mine Safety," editorial, *SLPD*, 23 October 1948.

8. Barone, *Our Country*, 217. Gallup showed Wallace getting 4 percent of the vote and Thurmond 2 percent.

9. Ross, *Loneliest Campaign*, 219; "Dewey Has Trouble with Small Boys," *Illinois State Journal*, 13 October 1948; "Small Boys Throw Ripe Tomatoes at Dewey in Illinois, Spatter Suit," *SLPD*, 13 October 1948. See also "Dewey Invades Illinois Coal Fields," *Chicago Sun-Times*, 13 October 1948.

10. Barone, *Our Country*, 219–20; "Dewey Calls Engineer a 'Lunatic,'" *Illinois State Journal*, 13 October 1948.

11. "Engineer Called 'Lunatic' for His Mistake, Doesn't 'Think Very Much' of Dewey," *Illinois State Register*, 13 October 1948; "Dewey Engineer Resents Being Called Lunatic," *Chicago Tribune*, 14 October 1948.

12. "Dewey Engineer Resents Being Called Lunatic," *Chicago Tribune*, 14 October 1948.

13. Ross, *Loneliest Campaign*, 219.

14. "Dewey in East Side Talk Stresses Theme of Unity," *SLPD*, 13 October 1948.

15. McCullough, *Truman*, 695. In 1944, Dewey defeated Roosevelt 52 to 47 percent in Vermillion County, 59 to 42 percent in Champaign County, 53 to 46 percent in Sangamon County, and 59 to 40 percent in Piatt County. See Allen and Lacey, *Illinois Elections*, 419–21.

16. Remarks from rear platform at Danville, Ill., 1:10 P.M., 12 October 1948, in "Rear Platform"; "Truman Sidelights," *Illinois State Register*, 13 October 1948.

17. Remarks from rear platform at Tolono, Ill., 2:10 P.M., 12 October 1948, in "Rear Platform."

18. Remarks from rear platform at Decatur, Ill., 3:30 P.M., 12 October 1948, in "Rear Platform"; Ellis D. Roberts, "10,000 Hear Truman Talk in Decatur," *Decatur Herald*, 13 October 1948.

19. V. Y. Dallman, "Lighter Vein," *Illinois State Register*, 12 October 1948.

20. "Truman Sidelights" and "Sidelights on Banquet," *Illinois State Journal*, 13 October 1948.

21. John Lynaugh, "Truman Pledges Farm Aid," *Illinois State Journal*, 13 October 1948; Lucas, autobiographical fragment, 12

22. Address at the Armory, Springfield, Ill., 12 October 1948, in "Rear Platform."

23. "Barrett Accuses Peoria Business Group of 'Smear' in Gaming Inquiry," *SLPD*, 6 October 1948.

24. Ibid.

25. "Peoria Jury Probe into Corruption Opens Tomorrow," *SLPD*, 12 October 1948.

26. "Second Peoria Grand Jury Begins Corruption Inquiry," *SLPD*, 13 October 1948.

27. "Peoria Grand Jury Takes Up Killing of Bernie Shelton," *SLPD*, 21 October 1948; "Peoria Grand Jury Given Evidence on 'Wide-Open' Days," *SLPD*, 22 October 1948.

28. "Gambling Inquiry 'Whitewashed,'" *Peoria Journal and Transcript*, 23 October 1948. See also "Clean Them Out," editorial, *Chicago Sun-Times*, 27 October 1948.

29. "Peoria Grand Jury Indicts *Post-Dispatch* Reporter Who Exposed Corruption," *SLPD*, 24 October 1948; "County Aids Cleared by Grand Jury," *Chicago Tribune*, 23 October 1948. See also "3 of Shelton Gang Reported Indicted," *Chicago Sun-Times*, 24 October 1948.

30. "Text of Report by Peoria Grand Jury; 'No Evidence of Corruption,'" *SLPD*, 24 October 1948; "Complete Text of Report by Grand Jury," *Peoria Journal and Transcript*, 23 October 1948. Quotes in the paragraph following the list are also from these sources.

31. "*Post-Dispatch* to Defend Reporter 'to Last Ditch,'" *Peoria Journal and Transcript*, 23 October 1948.

32. The letter to the *Post-Dispatch* from Verle W. Safford was displayed on page 1 on 24 October 1948.

33. Theodore C. Link, "Indicted Reporter Tells Petrakos's Role in Story of Bernie Shelton Killing," *SLPD*, 27 October 1948; "New Shelton Incident Uncovered by Link," *Peoria Journal and Transcript*, 26 October 1948. See also Theodore C. Link, "Ted Link Had New Evidence on Shelton Killing Peoria Grand Jury Failed to Hear," *SLPD*, 25 October 1948.

34. "The Law Turned against Itself," editorial, *SLPD*, 25 October 1948.

35. "The Expected Happens," editorial, *Peoria Journal and Transcript*, 24 October 1948. The comment outlined the contrast between two grand jury reports. See also "Peoria Citizens Predicted a Whitewash, and Barrett Called Forecast a 'Smear,'" *SLPD*, 25 October 1948.

36. "Defeat George Barrett," editorial, *Peoria Journal and Transcript*, 25 October 1948. The paper also attacked Barrett in "The High Price of Whitewash," 28 October 1948.

37. "Clean Them Out," editorial, *Chicago Sun-Times*, 27 October 1948. The *Post-Dispatch* expressed appreciation for editorial support in "The Press Guards Its Freedom," editorial, 31 October 1948.

38. John S. Knight, editorial column, *Chicago Daily News*, 24 October 1948.

39. Edward Lindsay, editorial column, *Decatur Herald and Review*, 24 October 1948.

40. "This Whitewash Turns Brown," *Bloomington Pantagraph*, 24 October 1948.

41. "The Green Machine Strikes Back," advertisement in *Chicago Tribune*, 27 October 1948. The same headline was used on a *Post-Dispatch* editorial on 24 October 1948.

42. "Grand Jury Opens Gambling Inquiry at Springfield," *SLPD*, 18 October 1948; "Grand Jury Calls Mayor of Springfield and Sheriff," *SLPD*, 19 October 1948.

43. Roy J. Harris, "Evidence of Vice, No Indictments by Grand Jury at Springfield, Ill.," *SLPD*, 21 October 1948.

44. "Plans Gambling Charges against Those Jury Cited," *SLPD*, 22 October 1948.

45. See the following articles by Walter Trohan in the *Chicago Tribune*: "State Service the Keynote of Brooks' Career," 17 October 1948; "Brooks Known as Fighter for American Way," 18 October 1948; "Brooks Stands by Pledges He Made on Stump," 19 October 1948; "Brooks an Able, Relentless Foe of New Dealism," 21 October 1948.

46. "Brooks Glad to Know Illinoisans—All but Prof. Douglas, That Is," *Chicago Daily News*, 13 October 1948.

47. Douglas, *In the Fullness of Time*, 136–37. The campaign was out of money, his opponents used "smear" tactics, the *Tribune* opposed him at every turn, and the odds-makers made him a 10 to 1 loser.

48. Ibid., 135.

49. "Douglas Avoids Taft-Hartley Repeal Demand," *Chicago Tribune*, 3 October 1948.

50. "Douglas Pleads for G.O.P. Votes on Peace Formula," *Chicago Tribune*, 23 October 1948.

51. "Douglas Pairs Taft, Brooks as Dewey Foes," *Chicago Tribune*, 17 October 1948.

52. Douglas, *In the Fullness of Time*, 136; Biles, *Crusading Liberal*, 50.

53. "A He-Man with Ideas—That's Senate Candidate Paul Douglas," *Chicago Daily News*, 24 October 1948.

54. "Mr. Douglas' Contradictions," editorial, *Chicago Tribune*, 3 October 1948.

55. "Green Urges Cities Share in Utility Tax," *Chicago Tribune*, 12 October 1948; Martin, *Adlai Stevenson of Illinois*, 342.

56. "Green Recants," *Chicago Daily News*, 13 October l948.

57. "Be Nice to Adlai," editorial, *Chicago Tribune*, 12 October 1948.

58. "Brooks, Green Assail Truman on Civil Rights," *Chicago Tribune*, 4 October 1948.

59. "Gov. Green: Politician," editorial, *Chicago Tribune*, 7 October 1948.

60. Milburn P. Akers, "Green Losing Downstate," *Chicago Sun-Times*, 10 October 1948.

61. John Dreiske, "'Gravy Votes for 2 Democrats," *Chicago Sun-Times*, 5 October 1948.

62. David Anderson, "Green's Machine Outstrips Inflation in Piling Up Costs," *Chicago Sun-Times*, 4 October 1948; Anderson, "Green Sends Price of Safety Up, Too, for State Taxpayers," *Chicago Sun-Times*, 5 October 1948. The quotes in the next two paragraphs are from these sources.

63. "Public above Politics Vowed by Stevenson," *Chicago Tribune*, 16 October 1948.

64. "Stevenson Hits at Pay Rolls in Green's Regime," *Chicago Tribune*, 27 October 1948.

65. Roy J. Harris, "Green Machine Puts 135 County Politicians on Illinois State Payroll," *SLPD*, 28 October 1948.

66. Theodore C. Link, "Says Illinois Politician Got $600,000 Paving Job 'Kickbacks,'" *SLPD*, 29 October 1948.

67. "Program He'll Act Upon Told by Stevenson," *Chicago Tribune*, 10 October 1948.

68. "For Thompson and Stevenson," editorial, *SLPD*, 10 October 1948.

69. "Brooks Rates Re-election for Service in U.S. Senate," editorial, *Chicago Daily News*, 6 October 1948.

70. "For Douglas, Not Brooks," editorial, *SLPD*, 17 October 1948.

71. Barone, *Our Country*, 215–17.

72. Ross, *Loneliest Campaign*, 234.

73. McCullough, *Truman*, 700; Ross, *Loneliest Campaign*, 234–35; Bray, "Recollections of the 1948 Campaign," 31–32. Writers gave varying figures for people in the parade and along the route. Ross put the stadium crowd at 23,000, McCullough said 24,000, and police officials estimated 26,000. Police also estimated 750,000 along the parade route, but Ross put the number at 500,000. See also "Chicago Puts on Show for Truman; Fireworks, Parade and Big Crowd," *SLPD*, 26 October 1948.

74. *Chicago Sun-Times*, 25 October 1948, from archives of the Harry S. Truman Presidential Museum and Library, "Newspaper accounts titled 'President Truman's Campaign Trip to Chicago, Cleveland, Boston, Providence, New York, Brooklyn, St. Louis and Kansas City.'"

75. "Address in the Chicago Stadium, October 25, 1948," Public Papers of the Presidents, 1945–53, Harry S. Truman. This is a record of the speech as given by Truman. See also "Text of Truman Stadium Speech Blasting G.O.P.," *Chicago Tribune*, 26 October 1948.

76. Ross, *Loneliest Campaign*, 247. McCullough called Truman's speech "a wild attack, uncalled for, in which he said a vote for Dewey was a vote for fascism" (*Truman*, 700). Zachary Karabell wrote, "Truman lit into the Republicans with something approaching hatred" (*The Last Campaign: How Harry Truman Won the 1948 Election* [New York: Alfred A. Knopf, 2000], 247). See also "Truman Likens Dewey Strategy to that of Tojo, Hitler, Mussolini," *SLPD*, 26 October 1948.

77. "Address in the Chicago Stadium, October 25, 1948," Public Papers of the Presidents, 1945–53, Harry S. Truman. The quotes in the next few paragraphs are from this source.

78. Douglas, *In the Fullness of Time*, 138.

79. George Tagge, "Triumph Marks Dewey Parade on Arrival Here," *Chicago Tribune*, 27 October 1948.

80. "Nominee, Here, Assails Truman Policy of Fear," *Chicago Tribune*, 27 October 1948. Quotes in the next few paragraphs are from this source. See also "Dewey at Chicago Omits Appeal for Brooks, Green," *SLPD*, 27 October 1948.

CONCLUSION

1. Smith, *Colonel*, 483–84.

2. All Illinois state election results for 1944 and 1948 cited hereafter are from Allen and Lacey, *Illinois Elections*, 419–27, 433–41.

3. Wendt, *"Chicago Tribune,"* 683.

4. Qtd. in Barone, *Our Country*, 221.

5. Ibid.

6. Douglas, *In the Fullness of Time*, 138–40.

7. Lucas, autobiographical fragment, 13.

8. Barnhart and Schlickman, *Kerner*, 287–319.

9. Hartley, *Big Jim Thompson*, 60.

10. Hartley, *Paul Simon*, 125.

11. "The Danger in Paul Powell," *SLPD*, 11 December 1949.

BIBLIOGRAPHY

MANUSCRIPT SOURCES

Dwight H. Green Papers. Abraham Lincoln Presidential Library, Springfield, Ill.
Scott W. Lucas Collection. Abraham Lincoln Presidential Library, Springfield, Ill.
Metro-East Journal Collection. Louisa H. Bowen University Archives and Special
    Collections. Southern Illinois University Edwardsville.
Public Papers of the Presidents, 1945–53. Harry S. Truman Presidential Museum and
    Library, Independence, Mo.
Driscoll Scanlan Papers. Held in private by Gerald Scanlan.
Adlai E. Stevenson Papers. Princeton University Library, Department of Rare
    Books and Special Collections, Princeton, N.J.
William G. Stratton Collections. Abraham Lincoln Presidential Library, Springfield, Ill.

NEWSPAPERS AND WIRE SERVICES

Associated Press
Bloomington Pantagraph
Carmi Democrat-Tribune
Centralia Morning Sentinel
Chicago American
Chicago Daily News
Chicago Sun (Chicago Sun-Times)
Chicago Tribune
Decatur Herald
Decatur Herald and Review
East St. Louis Journal (Metro-East Journal)
Herrin Daily Journal
Illinois State Journal
Illinois State Register
International News Service

Marion Daily Republican
Mt. Vernon Register-News
New York Times
Peoria Journal and Transcript
Rock Island Argus
St. Louis Globe-Democrat
St. Louis Post-Dispatch
St. Louis Star-Times
United Press

BOOKS AND SELECTED SOURCES

Allen, Howard W., and Vincent A. Lacey, eds. *Illinois Elections, 1818–1990: Candidates and County Returns for President, Governor, Senate, and House of Representatives.* Carbondale: Southern Illinois University Press, 1992.

Ambrose, Stephen. *Eisenhower: The President.* 2 vols. New York: Simon and Schuster, 1984.

Arvey, Jacob. "A Gold Nugget in Your Backyard." In *As We Knew Adlai: The Stevenson Story by Twenty-Two Friends,* edited by Edward P. Doyle. New York: Harper and Row, 1966. 50–53.

Barnhart, Bill, and Gene Schlickman. *Kerner: The Conflict of Intangible Rights.* Urbana: University of Illinois Press, 1999.

Barone, Michael. *Our Country: The Shaping of America from Roosevelt to Reagan.* New York: Free Press, 1990.

Biles, Roger. *Big City Boss in Depression and War: Mayor Edward J. Kelly of Chicago.* DeKalb: Northern Illinois University Press, 1984.

———. *Crusading Liberal: Paul H. Douglas of Illinois.* DeKalb: Northern Illinois University Press, 2002.

———. "Jacob W. Arvey, Kingmaker: The Nomination of Adlai E. Stevenson in 1952." *Chicago History* 8.3 (Fall 1979): 130–43.

———. *Richard J. Daley: Politics, Race and the Governing of Chicago.* DeKalb: Northern Illinois University Press, 1995.

Biographical Directory of the United States Congress, 1774–2005. Washington: U.S. Government Printing Office, 2005.

Bray, William J. "Recollections of the 1948 Campaign." Truman Presidential Museum and Library, Independence, Mo.

Camelon, David. "How the First GI Bill Was Written." *American Legion Magazine,* January–February 1969.

Case, Robert J., and W. A. S. Douglas. *The Midwesterner: The Story of Dwight H. Green.* Chicago: Wilcox and Follett, 1948.

Clayton, John, comp. *The Illinois Fact Book and Historical Almanac, 1673–1968.* Carbondale: Southern Illinois University Press, 1970.

Cohen, Adam, and Elizabeth Taylor. *American Pharaoh: Mayor Richard J. Daley: His Battle for Chicago and the Nation.* Boston: Little, Brown, 2000.

Donaldson, Gary. *Truman Defeats Dewey.* Lexington: University Press of Kentucky, 1999.

Donovan, Robert J. *Conflict and Crisis: The Presidency of Harry S. Truman, 1945–1948.* Columbia: University of Missouri Press, 1966.

Douglas, Paul H. *In the Fullness of Time.* New York: Harcourt, Brace, 1971.

Doyle, Edward P. *As We Knew Adlai: The Stevenson Story by Twenty-Two Friends.* New York: Harper and Row, 1966.

Dubofsky, Melvyn, and Warren Van Tine. *John L. Lewis: A Biography.* New York: Quadrangle, 1977.

Ferrell, Robert H. *Off the Record: The Private Papers of Harry S. Truman.* New York: Harper and Row, 1980.

Feustel, William J. "A Brief History of the *Globe-Democrat.*" St. Louis *Globe-Democrat,* 1 July 1977.

Frankel, Stanley, and Holmes Alexander. "Arvey of Illinois: New-Style Political Boss." *Colliers,* 23 July 1949, 9–11, 65–67.

General Assembly of the State of Illinois. *Journal of the House of Representatives.* Springfield, Ill., 8 January 1947.

Gottfried, Alex. *Boss Cermak of Chicago.* Seattle: University of Washington Press, 1962.

Hartley, Robert E. *Big Jim Thompson of Illinois.* Chicago: Rand McNally, 1978.

———. *Charles H. Percy: A Political Perspective.* Chicago: Rand McNally, 1975.

———. History of criminal activity in St. Clair and Madison Counties, Illinois (unpublished). In author's possession.

———. "'I Worked for My Friends'—John H. Stelle's Life as a Political Operator." Paper presented for the Illinois Historic Preservation Agency's history program, Springfield, Ill., 1 October 2010.

———. *Paul Powell of Illinois: A Lifelong Democrat.* Carbondale: Southern Illinois University Press, 1999.

———. *Paul Simon: The Political Journey of an Illinois Original.* Carbondale: Southern Illinois University Press, 2009.

———. "The Whistle Campaign Stopped Here: Harry S. Truman and Illinois in 1948." *Journal of Illinois History* 10.4 (Winter 2007): 250–69.

Hartley, Robert E., and David Kenney. *Death Underground: The Centralia and West Frankfort Mine Disasters.* Carbondale: Southern Illinois University Press, 2006.

Howard, Robert P. *Illinois: A History of the Prairie State.* Grand Rapids: William B. Eerdmans, 1972.

———. *Mostly Good and Competent Men: Illinois Governors, 1818–1988.* Springfield: Illinois Issues, Sangamon State University, and Illinois State Historical Society, 1988.

———. Oral history memoir (unpublished). Sangamon State University (now University of Illinois at Springfield), 1982.

Hulsey, Byron C. *Everett Dirksen and His Presidents: How a Senate Giant Shaped American Politics.* Lawrence: University Press of Kansas, 2000.

———. "'He Is My President': Everett Dirksen, John Kennedy, and the Politics of Consensus." *Journal of Illinois History* 2.3 (Autumn 1999): 183–205.

Kenney, David. *A Political Passage: The Career of Stratton of Illinois.* Carbondale: Southern Illinois University Press, 1990.

Kenney, David, and Robert E. Hartley. *An Uncertain Tradition: U.S. Senators from Illinois, 1818–2003.* Carbondale: Southern Illinois University Press, 2003.

Johnson, Walter, ed., and Carol Evans, assistant ed. *The Papers of Adlai E. Stevenson: Washington to Springfield, 1941–1948.* Vol. 2. Boston: Little, Brown, 1973.

Jones, Gene Delon. "The Origin of the Alliance between the New Deal and the
    Chicago Machine." *Journal of the Illinois State Historical Society* 67.3 (June
    1974): 253–74.
Lemelin, Bernard. "An Isolationist Newspaper in an Internationalist Era, the *Chi-
    cago Tribune* and U.S. Foreign Policy, 1945–1960." *Journal of Illinois History*
    9.4 (Winter 2006).
Littlewood, Thomas B. *Horner of Illinois*. Evanston: Northwestern University Press,
    1969.
Lucas, Scott W. Autobiographical fragment (unpublished), 1 June 1957. Scott W.
    Lucas Collection. Abraham Lincoln Presidential Library, Springfield, Ill.
Martin, John Bartlow. *Adlai Stevenson of Illinois*. Garden City: Doubleday, 1976.
———. "Al Capone's Successors." *American Mercury*, June 1949.
———. "The Blast in Centralia No. 5: A Mine Disaster No One Stopped." *Harper's
    Magazine*, March 1948, 194–219.
Masters, Charles J. *Governor Henry Horner, Chicago Politics, and the Great Depression*.
    Carbondale: Southern Illinois University Press, 2007.
McCoy, Donald R. *The Presidency of Harry S. Truman*. American Presidency Series.
    Lawrence: University Press of Kansas, 1984.
McCullough, David. *Truman*. New York: Simon and Schuster, 1992.
Mitchell, Stephen. "Adlai's Amateurs." In *As We Knew Adlai: The Stevenson Story by
    Twenty-Two Friends*, edited by Edward P. Doyle. New York: Harper and
    Row, 1966. 66–76.
Morgan, Iwan. "The 1942 Mid-term Elections in Illinois." *Journal of the Illinois State
    Historical Society* 76 (Summer 1983): 115–30.
Pensoneau, Taylor. *Brothers Notorious: The Sheltons: Southern Illinois' Legendary Gang-
    sters*. New Berlin, Ill.: Downstate Publications, 2002.
———. *Dapper and Deadly: The True Story of Black Charlie Harris*. New Berlin, Ill.:
    Downstate Publications, 2010.
Pfaff, Daniel. *Joseph Pulitzer II and the "Post-Dispatch": A Newspaperman's Life*. State
    College: Pennsylvania State University Press, 1991.
———. *No Ordinary Joe: A Life of Joseph Pulitzer III*. Columbia: University of Mis-
    souri Press, 2006.
Quatannens, Jo Anne McCormick. *Senators of the United States: A Historical Bibliog-
    raphy*. Washington: U.S. Government Printing Office, 1995.
Rakove, Milton L. *We Don't Want Nobody Nobody Sent: An Oral History of the Daley
    Years*. Bloomington: Indiana University Press, 1979.
Roberts, Gene, and Hank Klibanoff. *The Race Beat: The Press, the Civil Rights Strug-
    gle, and the Awakening of a Nation*. New York: Knopf, 2007.
Roosevelt University. "History of Chicago from Trading Post to Metropolis: Race
    and Politics, 1940–1959." *History of Chicago*. www.roosevelt.edu/Chicago
    history'mod3-chap3.htm,1–2.
Ross, Irwin. *The Loneliest Campaign: The Truman Victory of 1948*. New York: New
    American Library, 1968.
Royko, Mike. *Boss: Richard J. Daley of Chicago*. New York: E. P. Dutton, 1970.
Schapsmeier, Edward L., and Frederick H. Schapsmeier. "Dirksen and Douglas of
    Illinois: The Pragmatist and the Professor as Contemporaries in the United
    States Senate." *Illinois Historical Journal* 83.2 (Summer 1990): 75–84.

———. *Dirksen of Illinois: Senatorial Statesman.* Urbana: University of Illinois Press, 1985.

———. "Paul H. Douglas: From Pacifist to Soldier-Statesman." *Journal of the Illinois State Historical Society* 67.3 (June 1974): 307–24.

———. "Scott W. Lucas of Havana: His Rise and Fall as Majority Leader in the United States Senate." *Journal of the Illinois State Historical Society* 67.3 (June 1974): 302–19.

———. "Serving under Seven Presidents: Les Arends and His Forty Years in Congress." *Illinois Historical Journal* 85.2 (Summer 1992): 105–18.

Smith, Richard Norton. *The Colonel: The Life and Legend of Robert R. McCormick, 1880–1955.* Boston: Houghton Mifflin, 1997.

Tagge, George. Oral history interview (unpublished). Springfield: Sangamon State University (now University of Illinois at Springfield), 1984.

Trohan, Walter. Oral history interview by Jerry N. Hess, 1970, Washington, D.C. Harry S. Truman Library and Museum, Independence, Mo.

———. *Political Animals: Memoirs of a Sentimental Cynic.* New York: Doubleday, 1975.

U.S. Department of State. *The Truman Doctrine, 1947.* Office of the Historian. http://www.state.gov/r/pa/ho/time/cwr/82210.htm.

U.S. Senate. Special Subcommittee of the Committee on Public Lands. *Investigation of Mine Explosion at Centralia, Illinois.* 80th Cong., 1st Session, 1947. Washington: U.S. Government Printing Office, 1947. Testimony of Robert M. Medill, 4 April 1947, 136–42.

Wagner, Ted P. "The Heirs of Scarface Al." *St. Louis Post-Dispatch Everyday Magazine,* 2 February 1947.

Watters, Mary. *Illinois in the Second World War: The Production Front.* Vol. 2. Springfield: Illinois State Historical Society, 1952.

Wendt, Lloyd. *"Chicago Tribune": The Rise of a Great American Newspaper.* Chicago: Rand McNally, 1979.

INDEX

Robert E. Hartley, an independent historian, has specialized in writing books about Illinois history and politics. His subjects include Charles Percy, James R. Thompson, Paul Powell, Lewis and Clark in Illinois, all U.S. senators from the state, the Centralia and West Frankfort mine disasters, and Paul Simon. Four of his books have received achievement awards from the Illinois State Historical Society.